To My Fellow Multimedia Explorers

You want to do multimedia. You know you do. But you don't have a clue where to start, do you? I don't blame you; we've been living the year of multimedia for at least five years now, yet the ability to create (rather than just use) multimedia on our Macs has eluded most of us. But, no longer—because *QuickTime: The Official Guide for Macintosh Users* changes all that.

No longer will you wonder what QuickTime is good for. No longer will you wonder how to use it. And no longer will you wonder which third party software you need to use and create multimedia on your Mac because *QuickTime: The Official Guide for Macintosh Users* tells you all this, and a lot more. Besides QuickTime will give you a CD-ROM loaded with QuickTime 2.0, MoviePlayer 2.0, QuickTime editing packages, and a pile of other QuickTime software.

I've read every QuickTime book on the market, and this is the first one that really makes QuickTime make sense. It explains the essence of the audio and video experience delivered by QuickTime. And it helps you use QuickTime in everyday communication so that it becomes as important as text is to your daily Mac life.

But don't take my word for it. Read the book and tell me what you think. *QuickTime: The Official Guide for Macintosh Users* lives in the Don Crabb Macintosh Library because it delivers the inside goods on QuickTime from top experts. Let it be your companion for finding and delivering real mixed-media solutions in your Mac environment.

It's simple. *QuickTime: The Official Guide for Macintosh Users* delivers solutions and advice that will make you wonder how you got along without it.

See you on the ether,

Don Crabb

decc@cs.uchicago.edu
December 1994
Chicago, IL

QuickTime:

The Official Guide for Macintosh Users

QuickTime:

The Official Guide for Macintosh Users

Hayden Books

Judith L. Stern
Robert A. Lettieri

The Don Crabb
Macintosh Library

QuickTime: The Official Guide for Macintosh Users

Library of Congress Catalog Card Number: 94-79847

ISBN: 1-56830-129-4

96 95 94   4 3 2 1

Interpretation of the printing code: the rightmost double-digit number is the year of the book's printing; the rightmost single-digit number is the number of the book's printing. For example, a printing code of 94-1 shows that the first printing of the book occurred in 1994.

The Hayden Books Team

Publisher
David Rogelberg

Managing Editor
Pat Gibbons

Development Editor
Brad Miser

Acquisitions Editor
Oliver von Quadt

Copy Editor
Carol Light

Technical Reviewer
Donald Olson

Publishing Coordinator
Stacy Kaplan

Cover Designer
Karen Ruggles

Production Team
Dan Caparo, Brad Chinn, Kim Cofer, Lisa Daugherty, David Dean, Cynthia Drouin, David Eason, Jennifer Eberhardt, David Garratt, Erika Millen, Beth Rago, Bobbi Satterfield, Karen Walsh, Robert Wolf

Indexers
Jeanne Clark, Brad Herriman, Kathy Venable

Composed in Apple Garamond and Helvetica

To Our Readers

Dear Friend,

Thank you on behalf of everyone at Hayden Books for choosing *QuickTime: The Official Guide for Macintosh Users* to enable you to learn about this exciting technology. QuickTime has opened a whole new world for Mac users, and we have carefully crafted this book and disc to help you make the most of everything that QuickTime offers.

What you think of this book is important to our ability to better serve you in the future. If you have any comments, no matter how great or small, we'd appreciate you taking the time to send us email or a note by snail mail. Of course, we'd love to hear your book ideas.

Sincerely yours,

David Rogelberg
Publisher, Hayden Books and Adobe Press

You can reach Hayden Books at the following address:

Hayden Books
201 West 103rd Street
Indianapolis, IN 46290
(800) 428-5331 voice
(800) 448-3804 fax

Email addresses:

America Online: Hayden Bks
AppleLink: hayden.books
CompuServe: 76350,3014
Internet: bradm@hayden.com

Dedication

Dedicated to:

Our parents—Ann & Lou and Lois & Marvin, who couldn't have imagined this technology when we were born,

and

The kids—Madeleine & Nicholas & Michael & Jennifer & Jack & Dana & Destin & Alex & Ian & Eli, as well as those not yet born, who will experience technology that we can't imagine.

About the Authors

Judith L. Stern and Robert A. Lettieri are the authors of *BMUG's Quicker QuickTime*, a chapter on QuickTime in Hayden's *Virtual Playhouse for Macintosh*, and various articles on QuickTime and digital video. They also co-produced (with Jeannene Hansen) the BMUG TV-ROM series of QuickTime CD-ROMs.

Judith is an instructional multimedia specialist. Her background includes corporate training, expert systems development, educational research, and multimedia development. She has a master's degree from the University of California at Berkeley in Math, Science, and Technology Education. When not writing about QuickTime or producing CD-ROMs, she works for the University of California at Berkeley, where she provides support and training to faculty developing instructional multimedia software; she's also a software designer, programmer, and project manager for the Computer as Learning Partner Project, an NSF-funded educational research project.

Robert is a computer consultant, specializing in graphics and multimedia technologies. At the University of California at Berkeley, he is the multimedia courseware specialist for Synthesis, a National Engineering Education Coalition. He has been experimenting and working with digital and analog video for over 10 years. He has taught many people how to use graphics and desktop publishing software, both individually and in training workshops. He has a degree in Fine Art, with a concentration in Computer Graphics, from Rutgers University.

Judith and Robert live in Oakland, California, and are currently working together on several other technological projects, as well as a biological one.

Acknowledgments

So many people to thank, so little space!

First, this book wouldn't exist if QuickTime didn't exist, so thanks are due to the QuickTime team. Extra special credit goes to Peter Hoddie and Jim Batson, not only for all the amazing work they've done to make QuickTime and MoviePlayer such great software, but also for the support they've given to us.

This book is based on our earlier book, *BMUG's Quicker QuickTime*, which in turn grew out of work we did on the BMUG TV-ROM CD. Both book and CD could only have happened within a group like BMUG—the finest computer user group in the world. We thank the BMUG staff and Steve Costa for supporting these projects.

Special gratitude goes to those who helped shape *Quicker QuickTime*, and thus this book. Stephen Howard and Tim Holmes were our primary editors for *Quicker QuickTime*, and they taught us a lot about the process of writing a book. Other folks who provided feedback, copy editing, and proofreading were Kelly Pernell, Karla Aronson, Jeannene Hansen, Evelyn Shapiro, Kandy Arnold, Patrick Kammermeyer, C. J. Wallia, Jim Ivan Davis, Joyce Davis, Philip Bell, Per Casey, Mona Giannetti, Peter Linde, Ted Kanter, and Lois and Marvin Stern.

Jeannene Hansen (AKA Junior Hansen, Jr.), our TV-ROM partner, has been another QuickTime fan from the beginning and has shown us creative and inventive ways to use QuickTime. She also created some of the QuickTime clips that are on the CD that comes with this book.

Besides Jeannene, other folks who provided media for exercises in the book are Bruce Linde, Lou Zucaro at MPI Multimedia/WPA Films, Julie Kovacks at Fabulous Footage, and Rhonda Stratton at VideoFusion/Radius.

Then there are people who provided us with information and expertise of various sorts: Tom Sicurella, David Schwartz, Bruce Linde, Michael Giannetti, Joe Whitecavage, Craig O'Donnell, Bill Wood, Brandon Muramatsu, Thomas Burns,

Ray Rimmer, and the folks at MacAdam Computers. By providing software and hardware for us to evaluate, the following folks indirectly contributed to the book: Thom Hogan at Connectix, Tad Shelby at Fractal Design, all of the people at Motion Works International, Tim Myers and Randy Ubillos at Adobe Systems, and Chris Borton at Storm Software.

At Hayden, Brad Miser and Oliver von Quadt tried our patience, yet when all is said and done, we couldn't have done it without them. Brad, in particular, has been patient and helpful, even when all sorts of external happenings were competing for his attention. Thanks also to Carol Light and all of the others at Hayden who produced this book in very little time. And, we couldn't have gotten the stuff to Hayden without Crimson Duplicating Center, which is where we copied, faxed, and FedExed manuscripts.

Finally, we'd like to thank our friends and families, who put up with our mental and physical absences while we were writing this book. We're back!

If we've missed anybody, it's because of the hour at which we're writing this acknowledgment. Our apologies and sincere thanks.

Jorma RIP.

Contents at a Glance

1 QuickTime—What is It? 1

2 Playing Movies—The Standard Controller 23

3 More Ways to Play 53

4 Basic Editing—Cut, Copy, Paste, and Beyond 75

5 Power Editing—Special Effects and More 125

6 Recording Movies—Digitizing Your Video 193

7 Making Movies without Video 233

8 Compression—The Key to QuickTime 261

9 Distributing Movies—Sharing Your Work 283

A Other QuickTime Software that's on the CD 299

B About BMUG 311

   Index 325

Contents

1 QuickTime—What is It?   **1**

   Viewing a QuickTime Movie 2

      Installing QuickTime 3

      Making a Movie Play 8

   The Current Limitations of QuickTime 10

   Why QuickTime is So Great 13

      No Additional Hardware to *Play* Movies 14

      Minimal Hardware to *Create* Movies 15

      Audio Integration 16

      System Software 17

   Potential Uses for QuickTime 18

      What Else is QuickTime? 20

2 Playing Movies—The Standard Controller   **23**

      Basic Controls 24

      Applications that Use the Standard Controller 33

      Power Tricks 36

   Tracks 42

   Playing More Movies 47

   Improving Playback Performance 48

3 More Ways to Play   **53**

   Playing without the Standard Controller 54

      Playing QT Movies Upon Startup 54

      Movie Presentation 55

   Text Track Searching 59

   Interactive Playing 61

      Including QuickTime in Interactive Presentations 62

      Scripting QuickTime 63

   So How Do You Want to Play Your Movies? 73

4 Basic Editing—Cut, Copy, Paste, and Beyond   **75**

Simple Editing with the Standard Controller 76

Selecting and Copying Part of a Movie 78

Creating a New Movie 80

Selecting with More Control 81

Saving Your Movie 83

File Dependencies 86

Movie Files with Less Data Than It Seems 86

Movie Files with More Data Than It Seems 91

Why File Dependencies? 91

Previews 93

Seeing a Preview 93

Changing the Poster 95

Creating a Dynamic Preview 96

Other Types of Previews 97

Track Editing 98

Putting Tracks Together 98

Pulling Tracks Apart 106

Enabling and Disabling Tracks 109

Alternate Tracks 111

Musical Instrument Changing 115

Custom Color Tables 117

More Info 118

5 Power Editing—Special Effects and More   **125**

The Effects 126

Transitions 126

Filters 129

Compositing 130

Motion 131

Cropping and Resizing 132

Titling 132

Audio Control 133

Time Scaling 134

The Tools 134

   Overview 134

   VideoShop 138

   Premiere 148

   VideoFusion and QuickFLIX! 156

   After Effects 162

Now It's Your Turn 167

   Using VideoShop 167

   Using QuickFLIX! 176

   Using Premiere 183

The Power to Make a Masterpiece

or a Mess 190

6   Recording Movies—Digitizing Your Video   193

What You Need 194

   Macintosh 194

   Video Source 195

   Video Digitizer 195

   Audio Digitizer 198

   Can Your Macintosh Be Used to Make Movies? 199

   Digitizing Software 203

   System Extensions 204

Setting It Up 205

Doing It 210

Digitizing Options 213

   Standard Video Settings 214

   Post-Compression 217

   Video On/Off 219

   Playthrough Video During Record 219

   Standard Sound Settings 219

   Sound On/Off 222

   Record to Disk or Memory 222

   Disk to Record On 223

Crop Region 225

Window Size 226

Hardware to Improve Digitizing 227

Hardware Compression Cards 227

Video Equipment 228

Controllable Decks 229

Storage Hardware 230

A/V Hard Disks 230

Disk Arrays 231

SCSI Cards 231

In Search of Perfection? 231

7 Making Movies without Video   **233**

Video Tracks without Video 234

Starting with an Animation 234

Starting with Still Images 241

Text Track 250

Sound Track 252

Importing AIFF Files 252

Audio CD Import 253

Music Track 257

Is This Really QuickTime? 259

8 Compression—The Key to QuickTime   **261**

Why Compression is So Important 262

QuickTime and Compression 263

Lossless versus Lossy Algorithms 265

Spatial and Temporal Compression 265

Codecs 266

Compression Choices You'll Make 267

Spatial Compression in the Standard Compression
Dialog Box 268

Temporal Compression in the Standard Compression
Dialog Box 275

Compressor Summary 277

QuickTime and Still Images 279

   Compressing Still Images 279

   Opening QuickTime Compressed Images..............................281

QuickTime Learning More about Compression 281

9 Distributing Movies—Sharing Your Work　　　**283**

Digital Distribution 284

   CD-ROM 284

   QuickTime for Windows 288

   Network Playback 291

   QuickTime Movies on the Internet 292

Nondigital Distribution 294

   Outputting to Videotape 294

   Paper Output 296

Legal Issues..297

Get Your Movies Out There! 298

A Other QuickTime Software that's on the CD　　　**299**

Unsupported Utilities from Apple 300

   ConvertToMovie 300

   ComboWalker 300

   MakeMovieColorTable 300

   Dumpster 302

   MovieShop™ 303

   MovieAnalyzer™ 303

   Text Movie Converter 303

   SoundConverter 305

   SingleForkFlattener 305

   Music Configuration 306

   AddTimeCode 306

   XCMDs 306

Shareware and Freeware 307

   Easy Play 2.0 307

   FlipBookMaker 1.1 308

   MovieInfo v2.2 308

MovieTrilogy Folder 308

Sparkle 2.2 310

Theater Maker 310

B About BMUG   **311**

Contacting BMUG 312

By Phone 312

By Mail 312

Our Office Location 313

The BMUG Philosophy 313

BMUG Memberships 313

The BMUG Newsletter 315

BMUG Online: Planet BMUG and BMUG Boston BBSes 315

Meetings 316

Main Meetings 316

BMUG West 316

BMUG South 316

Special Interest Groups (SIGs) 316

Technical Assistance 317

The Helpline 317

Emergency Data Recovery 317

BMUG Software Library 317

BMUG Publications 318

BMUG CD-ROMs 318

Other BMUG Products 320

BMUG Distributes New Products! 320

Index   **325**

License Information

What's on the QuickTime Guide CD

Foreword

When we started work on QuickTime, our goal was not to make life easier for the video professional. Our goal was to bring the power of digital video to ordinary people using a personal computer. When QuickTime 1.0 was released at the end of 1992, many people with little or no previous experience with video were able to begin exploring video on their personal computers.

Since those early days, just a few short years ago, QuickTime has progressed dramatically. Industry pundits no longer snicker about "postage stamp" sized video when referring to QuickTime. On many computers, QuickTime now provides full-screen, full-motion video play back. And with some extra hardware, QuickTime is now being used by the same video professionals who initially doubted the ability of computers to manipulate video.

Two individuals who were caught up in the original excitement of QuickTime were Judith Stern and Robert Lettieri. They struggled with the technology in the early days when there were few tools and fewer experts. As QuickTime has progressed, they have continued to explore its expanding capabilities. They have combined their experiences with their teaching skills to help others make effective use of QuickTime.

Their tremendous enthusiasm and extensive knowledge provide plenty of valuable information in this highly readable book. Its hands-on approach along with the extensive step-by-step examples make it easy for you to experiment with many different aspects of QuickTime. This, combined with the sample movies and the great software on the CD, provide you with everything you need to start immediately.

QuickTime is much more than just software for playing digital video. Extensive capabilities for editing, capturing, and compressing digital media are an integral part of the QuickTime technology. QuickTime also goes well beyond just digital video. Text, MPEG, and MIDI data can be integrated into a single QuickTime movie.

Most books on QuickTime focus only on the video capabilities of QuickTime. Judy and Rob establish a framework for understanding QuickTime and build on it to explain its multitude of capabilities. This—along with up-to-date information on topics such as movie distribution and QuickTime for Windows—make *QuickTime: The Official Guide for Macintosh Users* the first complete user guide to QuickTime.

Our hope has always been that QuickTime would empower individuals to work with video with the same ease and flexibility with which they use the Macintosh to manipulate text and graphics. In this book, Judy and Rob have brought together all the knowledge and tools you'll need to get started and to move ahead into the world of QuickTime. Go forth and digitize.

Jim Batson

Peter Hoddie

QuickTime Engineering

Apple Computer

Cupertino, CA

December 7, 1994

Introduction

This book is actually an expanded version of *BMUG's Quicker QuickTime*, a book that we first wrote in 1992 because we were so excited about QuickTime.

Well, it's a couple of years later, and we're still excited about QuickTime.

QuickTime is software that many Macintosh users can take advantage of because it's relatively easy and it's relatively inexpensive. However, many people don't know just how easy it is to get started. Others aren't aware of all of QuickTime's capabilities.

Like the rest of BMUG—the world's largest and best computer user group—we don't think things should be this way. BMUG is an organization whose goal is to get as much information as possible out to computer users on how to take full advantage of their computers. Our hope is that this book, though no longer carrying the BMUG label, is worthy of BMUG's reputation.

This book isn't going to explain how to make multimedia masterpieces. Nor is it going to dive deep into the technical background of QuickTime. It will, however, lay out the basics, make you feel comfortable with QuickTime, and show you how to use it. It will also give you hints and tips, both creative and technical. Throughout the book, we've included hands-on exercises. We feel very strongly that working with technology, and not just reading about it, is the very best way to learn.

Who's This Book For?

If you've never used QuickTime before, this book will help you figure out what QuickTime is, how difficult (or easy) it is to use, what you need to use it, and how to use it. If you've already worked with QuickTime, you'll find that this book fills in missing gaps in your QuickTime knowledge and QuickTime software collection. Even if you consider yourself an advanced user, you may learn some new things, particularly concerning QuickTime 2.0 and MoviePlayer 2.0.

What Do You Need to Know?

We assume only a minimal level of familiarity with your computer. If you've copied and moved files around on your Macintosh desktop, understand how to use a word processing program, and know how to open and save files, you should be fine. The more experienced you are, the faster you'll be able to work through the exercises.

What Equipment Do You Need?

A CD-ROM containing all of the software you'll need comes with this book. Of course, this means you'll need a CD-ROM drive.

The exercises in all of the chapters but Chapter 6 require only that you have a Macintosh that can run QuickTime: any color-capable Mac or Power Mac will do, as will a Classic II, SE/30, or any PowerBook other than the PowerBook 100; the Mac needs to be running System 6.0.7, 6.0.8, or some form of System 7.

If you have the hardware to digitize movies—a video source, such as a VCR or camcorder, and an AV Macintosh or Macintosh with a digitizing card—you'll be able to try out what you learn in Chapter 6.

However, if you're missing any or all of this equipment, you can still get a lot out of this book. We've included lots and lots of figures so that you can see exactly what happens in the exercises. We know that some of you may want to read this book before you go sit at your computer. We also want you to be able to learn about QuickTime without making any additional investment. We think that when you see just how straightforward QuickTime is, you'll make that investment.

What's in the Book?

While QuickTime itself has become a standard in the multimedia world, the products and the companies in that world are constantly changing, and QuickTime is constantly being improved. This means that we couldn't possibly cover everything there is to know about QuickTime in one book. Our goal is to teach you enough so that you can understand what you read in magazines and so that you can confidently use QuickTime hardware and software and learn more on your own. Where appropriate, we refer you to other books or activities that'll take you further along on that never-ending learning curve.

How is This Book Structured?

We start in Chapter 1 by explaining what QuickTime is. Because there are many different ways to define QuickTime, you'll want to at least skim this chapter, even if you're an experienced QuickTime user.

Chapters 2 through 7 cover the how-to's of QuickTime and are divided by the different levels at which people use QuickTime:

- Most people play and use—in presentations and other settings—movie files. You'll find information on playing and using movies in Chapters 2 and 3.

- Many of those people also take movies and combine them and cut from them and embellish them and turn them into completely new movies. This is editing, which we discuss in Chapters 4 and 5.

- Some people want to create their own QuickTime movies from videotape or other media they have. We describe the methods for making your own movies in Chapters 6 and 7.

The first chapter in each pair of chapters described above covers the basics that we think most people need or want to know to get started with QuickTime. So, if you're in a rush, you may want to read Chapters 2, 4, and 6 first, and later come back to 3, 5, and 7 to get the extras.

Chapters 8 and 9, which discuss compression and distribution, are important to anyone who edits or makes their own QuickTime movies.

Finally, Appendix A covers some of the additional software on the disc. Appendix B gives you an overview of BMUG.

What Products Do We Cover?

As you read, you will come to understand that there are many hardware and software products that you can use with QuickTime. Some of these, such as Apple's MoviePlayer, Avid's VideoShop, and VideoFusion/Radius's QuickFLIX!, are discussed extensively in the book and are provided for you on the CD.

Many other products are touched on. However, mention of a product does not mean that we endorse that product. When we mention specific hardware and software, we normally do so because it's likely that you've already heard of the product or will hear about it in the future—our goal is to help you put together a coherent picture. Unfortunately, this often means that we're discussing products that have already received lots of mention in other places. Also, we may have left out some very good products, but it's just not possible to cover everything.

Which Version of QuickTime Do We Cover?

This book covers QuickTime 2.0, which was released in June 1994 and has some powerful new features.

Much of what we have to say in this book, however, applies to all versions of QuickTime. Our goal is to provide a good, solid understanding of this exciting technology, one that you'll find valuable regardless of the version.

JLS

RAL

December 7, 1994

Oakland, California

Chapter 1

QuickTime— What is It?

*T*here are three quick answers to that question. One, it's

software. Two, it's digital video.

Three, it's easy.

QuickTime—developed by Apple

Computer—is not an application, such

as a word processing or drawing

program. Rather, it is system software

that gives the Macintosh an

additional capability. This new capability, as you may well have guessed, is video. Actually, QuickTime is much more than video, but for most of us the video is the exciting part. You can convert video (including the audio portion) into digital form so that it can be stored, edited, and shown on your computer, just as you can store, edit, and show text and images. Once video is in digital form, QuickTime also enables you to easily integrate it with other types of digital data, such as audio, text, and animations.

The capabilities provided by QuickTime can be utilized by many software applications in the same way that these applications utilize the Mac's graphics capabilities. We'll show you many of the applications that use QuickTime throughout this book.

The integration of computers and video has been available for years, but never has it been so accessible to ordinary folks like us. QuickTime is not a complicated technology requiring expertise in either computers or video. Nor does it require lots of money to use. While not necessarily offering professional-level quality, QuickTime lets you do some of the things that video professionals used to spend hundreds of thousands of dollars to do.

This is a very simplified description of QuickTime, but is nevertheless a good starting point. We'll get to more details as we go.

Viewing a QuickTime Movie

The fastest way to begin to get an understanding of QuickTime is to watch a QuickTime movie. You can do this if you have a Macintosh that runs QuickTime, a CD-ROM drive, and the CD-ROM that comes with this book. If you do not have the equipment that you need at this or any other point in the book, stay with us anyway. We'll be able to show you much of what you would see if you did have the necessary equipment.

Which Macs Run QuickTime?

QuickTime will run on all Macs with 68020, 68030, 68040, or PowerPC processors. This means it will run on everything but Mac Pluses, SEs, and PowerBook 100s (and earlier models of course).

Installing QuickTime

QuickTime™

To use QuickTime, you'll need to have QuickTime installed on your computer. QuickTime is a System *extension*. Extensions (called *INITs* or *Startup documents* in systems prior to System 7) are small files containing programs that add functionality to your Macintosh system. Unlike most other software you install on your computer, extensions are never directly accessed by you. Rather, it is your applications that utilize the added functionality provided by the extension. Throughout this book, you'll also be using some of the many applications that take advantage of QuickTime's capabilities.

Which System Should You Use?

QuickTime will work with version 6.0. or later of the Macintosh Operating System. However, we recommend using System 7 or later. There may be some QuickTime applications that require System 7.

Even better, you should use System 7.5. This system has a number of features built in and comes with additional extensions that will make your QuickTime experiences smoother and happier.

Along with QuickTime, we're also going to have you install a number of other files. Most of these are also extensions; one is a control panel. All are considered *system files*. These additional files improve QuickTime's performance in a variety of ways. A brief description of each file is provided in the following list:

QuickTime™ Musical Instruments

- **QuickTime Musical Instruments version 2.0.** This extension enables special QuickTime music files to play and sound the way they're supposed to. We'll introduce you to music files in the next chapter.

QuickTime™ PowerPlug

- **QuickTime PowerPlug version 2.0**. You should install this file if you are using a Power Macintosh; it enables parts of QuickTime to run in native mode. QuickTime will perform much better with this extension than without it. If you are not using a Power Macintosh, don't bother installing this as it won't do anything for you.

Apple Multimedia Tuner

- **The Apple Multimedia Tuner version 2.0**. This extension improves QuickTime 2.0 performance in a variety of circumstances.

Sound Manager

- **Sound Manager version 3.0**. While not really an extension to QuickTime—it's important even if you're not running QuickTime—this file improves playback of QuickTime movies that contain sound by improving the way your Macintosh handles sound.

  Not everyone will need to install this extension. You already have it if your Mac is a Macintosh AV, Power Mac, or a Quadra 630. It's also part of the System Update 3.0, so if you've installed this update, you have Sound Manager 3.0. It's built into System 7.5, so System 7.5 users don't need to install it. Also, if you're running any version of System 6, no need to install it; it won't work.

Sound

- **Sound Control Panel version 8.0.1**. This is a control panel, not an extension, and it complements the Sound Manager 3.0 extension. It's the updated version of the Sound control panel that came with your Macintosh.

This file only needs to be installed if you install Sound Manager 3.0.

You should install all of the files listed previously unless they don't apply to you (for example, if you don't have a Power Mac, there is no need to install the QuickTime PowerPlug). You should not install a particular file if you know that you already have the same, or a newer, version than the one we supply on the QuickTime Guide CD.

Which Version Do You Have?

If you're not sure if you already have an extension installed, look in your Extensions folder, which is located in the System folder on your hard drive. For the Sound control panel, look in your Control Panels folder, which is also in your System folder. System 6.0.7 or 6.0.8 users simply need to look in their System folder.

If you do see a file with the same name as one of those we're going to have you install, you need to check its version number. Select the file by clicking on it once. Now choose Get Info from the File menu. You'll see a window with information about the file (see figure 1.1). The version number is toward the bottom of the screen. Unless you have a newer version than the one we provide on the CD, you're going to want to replace it.

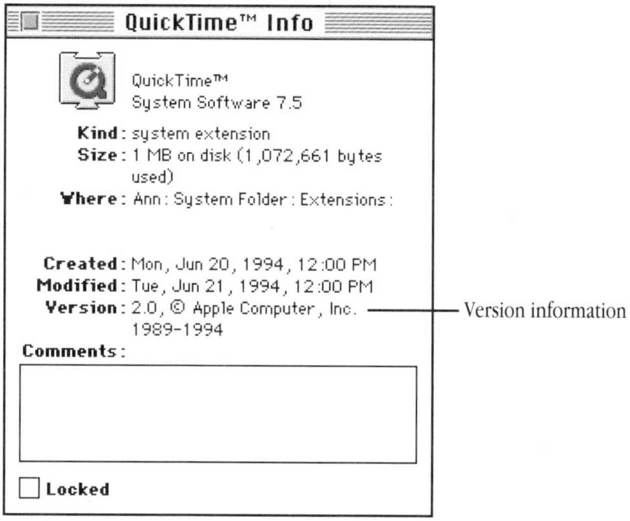

Figure 1.1　*Getting info on the QuickTime extension*

Follow these steps to install the appropriate software:

1. Determine if you have an older version of QuickTime than the one supplied on the QuickTime Guide CD. If you have an older version, remove it from your Extensions folder (within your System folder).

   Once you start your computer with QuickTime installed in the Extensions folder, QuickTime is always in use and therefore can't be replaced, so any older version needs to be moved out of the Extensions folder before you put a new one in.

2. If you haven't already done so, insert the CD that comes with this book into your computer.

3. On the CD, locate the folder called "System Files" and double-click to open it.

   You'll see the five extensions and one control panel we've described (see figure 1.2).

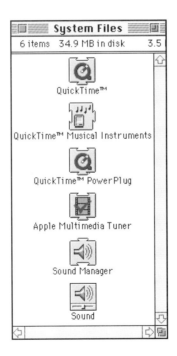

Figure 1.2   QuickTime and other system files on the CD

4. Now select the files that you want to install.

5. Drag all the selected files onto your unopened System folder.

   You will see a dialog box that asks if you want the files to be put in special places in the System folder (see figure 1.3). You won't see this dialog box if you're running System 6.

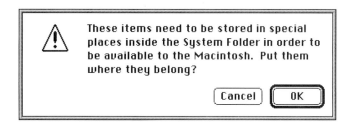

Figure 1.3   *Dialog box that appears when you drag system files onto the System folder*

6. Click on OK if you see the dialog box in figure 1.3.

   If you have copies of any of these files already installed, you will see an alert dialog box or two asking if you want to replace those files (see figure 1.4). Again, click on OK if you see a dialog box like this.

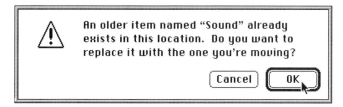

Figure 1.4   *Alert dialog box asking if you want to replace system files that are already there*

Warning!

Be sure that you're not replacing newer versions of any of these extensions with older ones!

The files will be copied, and you will see a dialog box telling you that the files have been put in the proper places (see figure 1.5).

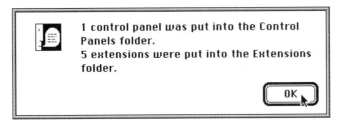

Figure 1.5   _Dialog box that appears after system files have been installed_

7. Click on OK and restart your computer.

You may notice the QuickTime, Sound Manager, and Multimedia Tuner icons on the bottom of your screen as the computer restarts.

Making a Movie Play

Now that QuickTime is completely installed, let's take advantage of the functionality that it adds to your Macintosh.

The first QuickTime application we'll use is Apple's MoviePlayer, which is on the QuickTime Guide CD that comes with this book. We'll use this application to play a QuickTime movie from the CD. To play a movie, follow these steps:

1. Insert the CD if you haven't already done so.

Warning!

If you have an old version of MoviePlayer on your hard drive, we recommend that you take it off (copy it to a floppy disk). This ensures that whenever you double-click a MoviePlayer document, the right version of MoviePlayer opens.

2. Locate the MoviePlayer folder on the QuickTime Guide CD and copy the entire folder to your hard drive.

Be sure to copy the entire folder. There are several extra files that need to be in the same folder as MoviePlayer in order for certain features to work. We'll tell you more about these features later.

3. On the CD, double-click to open the folder "Media," and then double-click to open the folder "Chapter 1." Now double-click on the file "Sunset" to open it.

Since Sunset is a MoviePlayer document, MoviePlayer will launch automatically. You'll see a window with an image of the sun setting at the beach (see figure 1.6). The window has the file name at the top, just like any other Macintosh window. At the bottom is a strip with various buttons.

Figure 1.6 *Open movie file in MoviePlayer*

4. Click once on the small triangle that's near the left side of the bottom of the window.

The movie will play.

5. After the movie is done playing, quit MoviePlayer—you can do this by choosing Quit from the File menu.

We'll discuss all of the buttons on the bottom of the window in the next chapter. For now we just wanted to make sure you've seen a QuickTime movie in action.

The Current Limitations of QuickTime

Now that you've seen a QuickTime movie, it's time to discuss the limitations of QuickTime. We'd like to jump right into talking about what's so great about QuickTime, but you may have already noticed some shortcomings in comparison to the video you normally see on TV.

One thing you surely noticed is that the image didn't fill your whole screen. Its *frame size* was not *full screen*. Can you make it bigger? Well, if you do (and we'll show you how in the next chapter), you'll get slightly worse image quality. That's because you'll simply be stretching out the information that's there. The motion also will not be as smooth if the image size is increased.

You probably also noticed that even at the small screen size, the motion isn't smooth—it's jumpy. What's happening is that you're not seeing all of the frames of the video. Normal video is 30 frames per second (fps). That is, when you watch TV for one second, you are really looking at 30 still images being shown rapidly in succession. Thirty frames per second is enough to give you the impression of smooth motion and is called *full motion*.

Real Frame Rates

Actually, normal video in the U.S. and Japan is about 30 frames per second (29.97 fps, to be exact). That's NTSC (National Television Systems Committee) video. Two other standards, PAL (Phase Alternating Line) and SECAM (Séquential Couleur à Mémoire) are 25 frames per second and are common in Europe and many other places in the world.

The movie that you just saw was recorded at 10 frames per second. Thus, it has a *frame rate* of 10 fps. What this means, in effect, is that the first of every three frames stays on the screen for one-tenth of a second, instead of three different frames being shown during that one-tenth of a second (see figure 1.7). And, if you played the movie on a slower Macintosh, the Macintosh may have played even fewer than 10 frames per second.

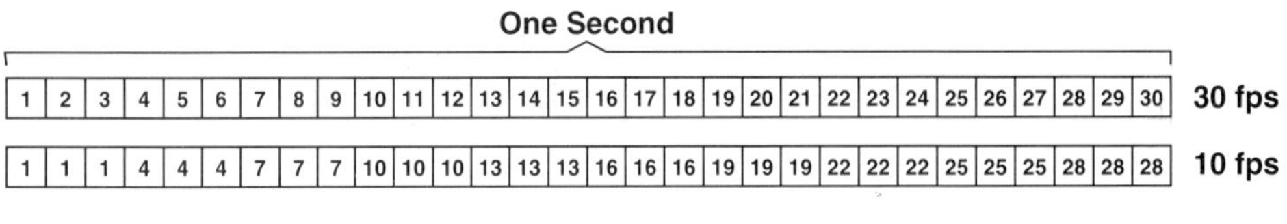

One Second

| 1 | 2 | 3 | 4 | 5 | 6 | 7 | 8 | 9 | 10 | 11 | 12 | 13 | 14 | 15 | 16 | 17 | 18 | 19 | 20 | 21 | 22 | 23 | 24 | 25 | 26 | 27 | 28 | 29 | 30 | **30 fps** |

| 1 | 1 | 1 | 4 | 4 | 4 | 7 | 7 | 7 | 10 | 10 | 10 | 13 | 13 | 13 | 16 | 16 | 16 | 19 | 19 | 19 | 22 | 22 | 22 | 25 | 25 | 25 | 28 | 28 | 28 | **10 fps** |

Figure 1.7   *30 versus 10 frames per second*

Another noticeable distinction between QuickTime movies and normal video is the quality of the image. The movie probably looked washed out and blocky, particularly if you looked closely. Details of the images that make up the movie have been removed through a process called *compression*. In figures 1.8 and 1.9, we show a slightly compressed and a highly compressed movie to illustrate the visual effects of compression.

Figure 1.8 *Slightly compressed movie*

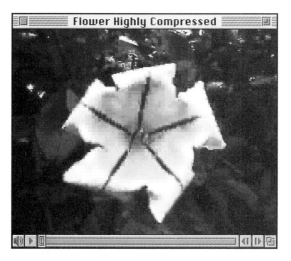

Figure 1.9 *Highly compressed movie*

Compression is necessary to keep the size of the file as small as possible. Compression also enables QuickTime movies to play at a faster frame rate because the computer doesn't have as much information to show. Indeed, without compression today's computers couldn't play digital video at all. We'll discuss compression more in Chapter 8.

Color Depth

Another factor that possibly contributes to the poor image quality is what is called *color depth*. Color depth, also called *bit depth*, refers to the number of colors that can be used to make up the images you see. Normal video uses millions of colors. Many Macintoshes have only 256 different colors available to compose an image. That means that the image is not as crisp as one might like because many of the pixels in the image are not the correct color. Instead of one of the original millions of colors, one of the 256 available colors may be substituted instead. Thus the image quality suffers.

You can determine the maximum color depth of your Macintosh by checking your Monitors control panel. The maximum number that you see in the window—next to the Colors and Grays radio buttons—is the maximum that your machine can display.

You may be interested to know that a system with the ability to show 256 colors at a time is called 8-bit because 2 raised to the power of 8 is 256. Similarly, 24-bit systems show millions of colors: 2 to the power of 24 is 16,777,216. The reason we use base two is that computers store information in binary form (the value is either 1 or 0); in fact, the term *bit* is short for *bi*nary dig*it*.

If the small window, jumpy motion, and blocky images really disturb you, you should know that they are not permanent limitations of QuickTime. Faster Macintoshes will help. Future releases of QuickTime will perform better in these areas and will also allow for the creation of movies that take up less disk space, which means longer movies. QuickTime has improved greatly since it was first released: QuickTime movies can now be twice the frame size and play twice the frame rate as movies made with the first version of QuickTime (see figure 1.10). Also, files can now be almost half the size they were with the original version. Expect improvements such as these to continue.

Now let's move on to what makes QuickTime great.

Figure 1.10 *The relative size of a standard movie with QuickTime 1.0 (160 x 120 pixels) and QuickTime 2.0 (320 x 240 pixels)*

Why QuickTime is So Great

The proponents of QuickTime (ourselves included) say that QuickTime is a revolutionary technology that helps to bring what used to be high-end professional video technology to the masses. Sounds like a bunch of hooey, eh? Well, consider the massive changes that have occurred over the last 20 years.

Twenty years ago, video cameras and recorders weren't household items—they were tools strictly for professionals—very expensive ones at that.

Ten years ago, many Americans had some video equipment. VCRs were commonplace, and video cameras weren't all that uncommon. Almost every U.S. household had a color TV.

Today, it's hard to go out in public without seeing a video camcorder. More U.S. households have VCRs than don't. Many households now have multiple color TVs and VCRs.

What happened? The cost of the technology has come down enough so that "regular" people can use it for leisure activities. That is, we no longer have to be making money with this equipment to engage in the creative activities of producing something to be shown to others. It has become reasonable to shoot video of your baby on the West Coast to send to your parents on the East Coast. Even if they don't have a camera, they probably have a VCR, which provides a way to play that video.

The next step is digital video. Digital video provides even more power to create what you want because it is much easier to edit than analog video (analog video is the video stored on tapes or film). For example, moving pieces of video around when they are in digital form is as simple as switching words around in a word processing document.

And, in the same way that analog video became inexpensive enough for many consumers, digital video has also become commonplace. To get started with digital video, you need to make an investment today of about the same magnitude as it cost to get started doing video in the early '80s; that being somewhere in the range of a few hundred dollars to a few thousand dollars. The low-end figure is for those who already have a color Macintosh and a video source, such as a VCR or a camcorder. Drop that low-end figure to zero if the color Macintosh is an AV Macintosh. The high-end figure is for those who have neither a color Mac nor a video source.

In addition to being relatively inexpensive, QuickTime is well designed. What's really great about QuickTime is this: it's easy! Like all *good* technology, it works with very little effort on your part, even though it's performing some very complicated tasks. Think about the telephone system. The telephone system is an amazingly complex computer network, but you don't notice that. You pick up the receiver, you punch in 11 digits, and suddenly you're talking to someone 3,000 miles away. Working with QuickTime is almost as easy.

Let's talk about some of the specifics.

No Additional Hardware to *Play* Movies

The most significant thing about QuickTime, from a cost standpoint, is that QuickTime movies can be played on all existing color Macintoshes (and a few noncolor Macs) without any additional hardware.

Anyone wanting to view a QuickTime movie doesn't have to install any extra boards or plug in any extra devices. Just as we know that anyone with a color Macintosh will be able to play the movies that we provide with this book, we can assure you that anyone with a color Mac can play a movie that *you* create. QuickTime movies don't have to be distributed on CD-ROM, either. You can give them to someone else on almost any kind of disk—removable media cartridge, hard disk, or even floppy disk if the file is small enough—or send them over a network.

Before QuickTime existed, if you wanted to provide someone with a system in which video was integrated with a computer, you had to supply more than just a Macintosh. The additional hardware needed, such as a laserdisc player and video monitor, could cost close to $1,000. That's not a huge investment if you're talking about setting up one workstation, but if you're thinking of getting the video out to many people, it certainly would add up.

Now QuickTime movies also can be played on Windows-compatible computers, which enables you to distribute your movies to even more people.

Minimal Hardware to *Create* Movies

Now what about creating these easy-to-play movies? Well, for *that* you probably do need additional hardware. In addition to having a Macintosh and a video source (such as a VCR or a camcorder), you'll need a device that will digitize video, a device that will digitize audio, and a few extra cables. But it's still relatively inexpensive and very easy to make movies. Most Macintoshes come with audio digitizing capabilities. You can purchase a new Macintosh that has both audio and video digitizing capabilities for under $2,000. Older Macs can be outfitted with these capabilities for under $1,000.

Macintosh   Camcorder   Video digitizer   Audio digitizer

Figure 1.11 *Components for making QuickTime digital video movies: Macintosh, camcorder, video digitizer, and audio digitizer*

There are also ways to create QuickTime movies that aren't video based, such as putting together a series of existing still images. These methods often require no hardware other than a computer.

Once you have created a QuickTime movie, you can edit it using only software. You might not think of it right away, but to make a movie that anyone but a close relative will enjoy, you'll need editing software. You can find software that enables you to do simple editing tasks; we provide one such piece of software, Apple's MoviePlayer, with this book. For more sophisticated editing tasks—including adding special effects—QuickTime editing packages are available for under $400; they are sometimes bundled with digitizing hardware. However, *you* won't need to purchase anything to get these editing capabilities—on the CD that comes with this book we include two editing programs: VideoShop from Avid and QuickFLIX! from VideoFusion/Radius.

If you were putting together a laserdisc or videotape and you needed to do some video editing, you'd pay thousands of dollars. You'd also end up with a final product that couldn't be further edited later. Not so with QuickTime.

Audio Integration

QuickTime takes care of both video and audio. When you record video into a QuickTime file, both audio and video data can be recorded and *synchronized*—this means that the right sounds are playing for the images that are currently being displayed. When QuickTime plays your movie, it does something very clever. If your computer doesn't have enough processing power to play all the video and all the audio, it will drop out frames of video in order to keep up with the audio. Under most circumstances, it won't drop out audio. Why is this so clever? In most cases, the human visual system is much better at filling in missing information than the human auditory system. Think about trying to carry on a phone conversation when you have a bad connection. It's quite difficult. Then try watching some action on TV while rapidly blinking your eyes. It works, doesn't it? Or, watch TV and notice all the "fast cuts" between scenes. You only have to see a little to pick up on what's going on.

Prior to QuickTime's introduction, keeping video and audio synchronized on a computer was a much more difficult task. Presentation programs that played both animations and audio used separate mechanisms for each. This meant that they weren't necessarily synchronized. QuickTime provides a single mechanism for presenting pictures and sound.

However, while QuickTime does a good job of integrating video and audio, it stores them in such a way that you can edit them separately.

Integrating Computers and Video without QuickTime

Other ways to integrate video with a computer exist, but they are expensive. You can give people a laserdisc, but then you must make sure they have a laserdisc player (at least $600) and an additional monitor to show the video (around $300) or a card to put into their computer that lets them show the video on their computer screen (at least $800). Alternatives to laserdisc players are frame-accurate, computer controllable VCRs, but they're even more expensive.

Frame-grabbing boards are available that enable you to capture individual frames of video and store them in a *PICS* file—PICS is a standard Mac file format for storing a series of images. These images can be played back without any additional hardware. However, the PICS format does nothing with audio, so including synchronized audio is difficult.

System Software

QuickTime is software that's based in the operating system. Huh? Well, *that* means programmers can incorporate QuickTime into their applications fairly easily, which means many Macintosh applications that you buy will be able to play QuickTime movies. It also means that QuickTime looks and acts the same way in almost every program that supports it, and that you can copy video data between many of these programs as easily as you move text between programs you already use.

The fact that it's system software also means that it's easier for you to upgrade your system as new developments arise in hardware and software. As improvements are made to QuickTime, you won't have to update all your applications; you'll just replace your QuickTime extension.

Furthermore, QuickTime has been developed to have what are called *plug-in* capabilities. These capabilities make adding on to QuickTime easy. For example, if a new hardware device is designed, QuickTime doesn't need to be updated. Rather, the hardware vendor provides a small file (another extension) to put in your System folder that QuickTime refers (or "plugs in") to in order to properly use that hardware.

Another example: software developers can write extensions that make QuickTime work more efficiently at compressing and decompressing data, which will mean larger window sizes and higher frame rates. In order for you to take advantage of an improved method of compression, you need only put such an extension in your System folder, and QuickTime will take care of the rest.

Potential Uses for QuickTime

So, now you know that the quality you get from a QuickTime movie isn't what you've come to expect from TV. Right now what you'll see are small movies that don't always play as fast or as long as you'd like. So why get excited? What can you do with QuickTime besides have lots of fun watching and editing movies?

One thing to remember is that you are still going to see a fairly good representation of video—*your* video if you make your own movies—on your Mac screen. And that's going to be good enough for communicating a lot of information that words and still pictures can't. Really, that's what it's all about—communication.

QuickTime gives you an additional tool in the bag of tricks you use for communicating. Sometimes video can show things that straight text, still images, or even a computer animation can't. Video also grabs people's attention and evokes an emotional response more effectively at times than other media. Often, however, the *most* effective way to communicate an idea is to use video (including audio), text, still images, and animation together. QuickTime makes it easy for you to merge all of these types of media.

The most obvious areas where people can use QuickTime are in training and education (see figure 1.12). For years, developers of computer-based training who wanted to use video in their courses either had to go the costly route of using laserdisc technology or sacrifice interactivity by using a "supplemental" videotape. Now they can incorporate interactive video into their computer-based courses for less money.

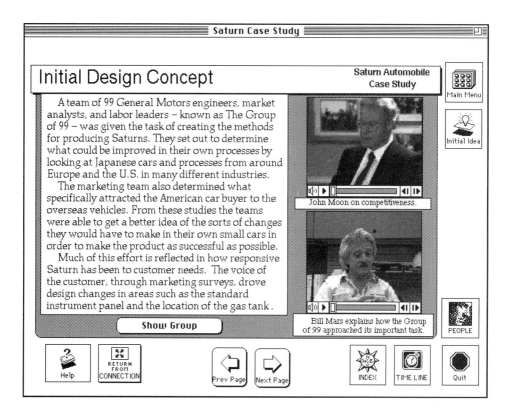

Figure 1.12   *QuickTime movies used in educational software (NSF Synthesis Coalition at U.C. Berkley)*

People who put together presentations also find QuickTime attractive. Again, it's a less costly and less complex way to incorporate moving images into presentations.

Just about any up-to-date piece of Macintosh software used to create instructional software or presentations should have a way to incorporate QuickTime movies. This type of software includes programs such as HyperCard, as well as animation programs such as Macromedia Director and presentation programs such as Aldus Persuasion.

If you look at commercial multimedia titles, such as interactive encyclopedias, travel guides, games, medical references, and textbooks, you'll see that many now incorporate QuickTime video.

Then there are categories of software that you wouldn't necessarily think of as including video. Word processing applications are one of these categories. Why? It may seem odd if you only print out your documents. But if you start thinking of documents as being online, then including QuickTime movies starts to make sense. You can create interactive documents, where people read some text and then click on an image that comes alive, illustrating the words (see figure 1.13).

Once you can imagine video as just another form of information like text and graphics, you'll think of other places where you can include QuickTime movies. For example, you can send video electronic mail. You can also put together a database where some of the information is in video form. And in many of these cases, the small window is an advantage.

Finally, the fact that QuickTime gives you a fairly good representation of your video means that if you are trying to put together a video production, you can test out your ideas with QuickTime before you use more expensive video editing equipment.

What Else is QuickTime?

Throughout this chapter we've emphasized digital video in our discussion of QuickTime. A more encompassing and accurate description given by Apple in their *QuickTime Technical Backgrounder* defines QuickTime as "a new architecture for the integration of dynamic data types." *Dynamic data* is anything that changes over time. Animation—moving images generated on the computer, rather than taken from video—fits in this category. So does audio and even text.

Behind the scenes, QuickTime stores all of these different types of data separately in what are called *tracks,* so that you can work with one type at a time. You can edit them, move them from one movie to another, or get rid of them, but ultimately you can have them play at the same time in your final production.

QuickTime also offers something for those working with still images. With its compression capability, QuickTime provides ways to make images take up less space on your computer.

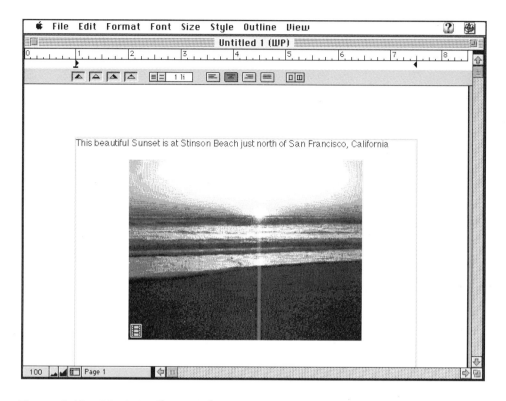

Figure 1.13   *Movie in ClarisWorks*

We'll explore animation, sound, tracks, and compression in more depth later in this book.

But before we do that, let's play some movies.

Playing Movies—
The Standard
Controller

*I*n the preceding chapter, we quickly showed you a QuickTime

movie. To play it, you pressed a

triangular-shaped button that was

located at the bottom of the movie

window. That button is part of a set

of buttons and controls called the

Standard Controller.

Any software developer whose application uses QuickTime is supposed to use the Standard Controller. That's because it's part of Apple's standard human interface; this interface is governed by a set of guidelines that Apple has established for all developers to follow so that all applications have a consistent look and feel. For example, the Quit command that you see in the File menu of all applications is part of these guidelines.

The Standard Controller is used to control what you're viewing. It also provides a simple set of editing tools that you can use to modify QuickTime movies (see figure 2.1). In this chapter, we'll describe the features of the Standard Controller that you'll use when playing a movie. (We'll discuss the editing features in Chapter 4.) We will also describe the different types of movies that exist, as well as where to find more movies and how to get the best performance while viewing them.

Figure 2.1   *Standard Controller*

Changing the Color of the Controller

In System 7, the Color control panel allows you to set the color of your highlight and windows. The Standard Controller reflects the window color selected, so changing the window color changes the color of the Controller.

Basic Controls

Let's go over the basic components of the Standard Controller:

In the Chapter 2 folder (within the Media folder on the CD), locate the movie file "Fruit Stand Scan" and double-click to open it (see figure 2.2).

You should see a window titled "Fruit Stand Scan" that shows an image of a bunch of fruit (see figure 2.3).

Figure 2.2   *Folder containing the movie "Fruit Stand Scan" on the CD*

Figure 2.3   *Movie "Fruit Stand Scan" in MoviePlayer*

Thank You BMUG

Many of the movies we use as samples in this book are from BMUG's TV-ROM™ Too and TV-ROM™ Too Update. Read Appendix B for more information on BMUG!

Once again, you have opened a movie file with MoviePlayer, the movie-playing application from Apple.

Play and Pause

1. Click on the triangle that's near the bottom of the left side of the Standard Controller. The triangle is called the *Play* button (see figure 2.4).

Figure 2.4   *Play button*

Once you click on the Play button, the movie will begin to play (see figure 2.5). Notice that while the movie plays, the button changes to a *Pause* button, which has two parallel bars (see figure 2.6).

Figure 2.5   *Movie while it's playing*

Figure 2.6 *Pause button*

If you find that the movie ends before you see the Pause button, click on the Play button again.

2. Click on the Pause button.

When you do, the button will change back to a triangle and the movie will pause.

The Pause button shows when the movie is playing, and the Play button shows when the movie is paused. Got it?

The Slider

1. Click on the Play button again.

As the movie plays, notice the rectangle that moves—it's to the right of the Play button. That little rectangle is called the *Slider*. It marks your place in time over the length of the movie. The area in which it moves is called the *Play bar* (see figure 2.7).

Figure 2.7 *Slider and Play bar*

2. You can manipulate the Slider yourself. Click on and drag the Slider to the right or the left and then back again (see figure 2.8).

Figure 2.8 *Dragging the Slider*

Continue dragging back and forth like this until you are tired of it. You will cause the movie to move forward and backward, though without audio and not necessarily at its normal rate.

Each time you move the Slider, you change the current viewing point in the movie. Moving the Slider all the way to the left sets the movie to the beginning. Moving it all the way to the right sets the movie to the end.

3. Click on the Play button.

If the Slider was at the left, the movie should play from the beginning. If the Slider was in the middle, the movie should start playing somewhere in the middle. If the Slider was at the far right, the movie will start over from the beginning.

One Frame at a Time

To the right of the Play bar are the *Step buttons*, each of which is marked with a vertical bar and a triangle (see figure 2.9). You use these buttons to play the video portion of the movie one frame at a time, either forward or backward.

Figure 2.9   *Step buttons*

Click a few times on each of the Step buttons.

Each time you click, you will see the image change only slightly. Remember that each frame represents a fraction of a second of time.

Audio Level

Now let's go look at what's at the far left side of the Controller. To the left of the Play button is the *Volume Control* button, which looks like a little speaker (see figure 2.10). You use this button to control the audio level of your movie.

Figure 2.10   *Volume Control button*

1. Click and hold on the Volume Control button.

A thermometer-looking image should pop up to the left. This is called the *Volume Controller* (see figure 2.11).

Figure 2.11   *Volume Controller*

Using the Sound Control Panel

The volume setting in the audio control portion of the Standard Controller is relative to the volume that is set on your Mac's Sound control panel (see figure 2.12). If you can't hear the sound in your movie, check the volume in the Sound control panel to make sure it is not turned off.

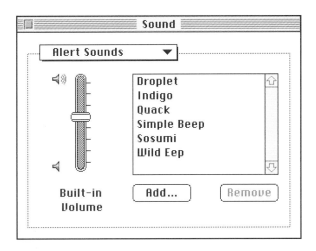

Figure 2.12   *Sound control panel*

2. Continuing to press down on your mouse button, move the *Volume Slider* on the Volume Controller up and down.

You'll see that you are moving a slider similar to the slider that you move to control your place in a movie, although this slider moves vertically in the Volume Controller. As you move it up and down, notice the lines emanating from the speaker (see figure 2.13). When you have the volume slider at the top, you should see two lines emanating from the speaker. When you have the

slider at the bottom, you should see no lines emanating from the speaker—
this means that the sound is turned off or muted or—you won't hear it
when the movie plays. Inbetween values are indicated by one or two lines
of varying sizes.

Figure 2.13   *Low volume*

3. Release the mouse when you have the slider near the top, and then click on the
   Play button to play the movie.

   Notice the volume level of the movie.

4. Click and hold on the speaker button again, slide the Volume Controller down,
   release the mouse, and then play the movie.

   This time the audio should be less loud.

Sometimes you won't see a speaker icon (see figure 2.14). This means that the movie
has no audio track.

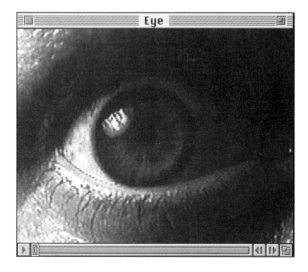

Figure 2.14   *Movie without audio*

Resizing Movies

You can resize movies to any size by clicking and dragging on the *Size box* located at the lower-right corner of the window (see figure 2.15).

Figure 2.15   *Size box*

1. Resize your movie to make it larger and then play it (see figure 2.16).

Figure 2.16   *Resizing a movie*

You will notice that the quality of the movie has degraded, giving you a very blocky effect. The motion is choppier because the computer cannot play as many frames.

Also, chances are that when you enlarged the movie, you changed its proportions, making it too wide or too tall (see figure 2.17).

Figure 2.17   *Movie stretched out of proportion*

2. Now click on the button in the upper right corner of the window (see figure 2.18).

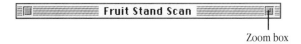

Zoom box

Figure 2.18   *Zoom box*

This is called the *Zoom box.* It will return the movie to its original size and proportions.

Where's the Zoom Box?

The Zoom box does not appear on movies without an image. You'll see some movies without images later in this chapter.

3. Resize the movie again, but this time hold down the Shift key while you drag the Size box.

This constrains the movie's proportions to their original ratio.

The Size box and the Zoom box are technically not part of the Standard Controller, but since you will frequently see them when you see the Standard Controller, we decided to discuss them here.

You've now seen the most important features of the Standard Controller. If you'd like, take some time to play with them.

4. When you're finished playing, quit MoviePlayer. Choose Quit from the File menu.

Although the Standard Controller looks simple, it is packed with controls. Just take a look at figure 2.19 and you'll see what we mean!

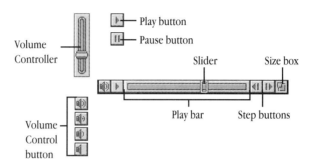

Figure 2.19   *Summary of the Standard Controller*

Applications that Use the Standard Controller

Let's take a break from playing with the Standard Controller to talk about where you will see it. There are many, many different types of applications that play movies using the Standard Controller.

We just used MoviePlayer, a movie playing application. Such applications let you control movies in various ways, and some enable you to do limited editing of movies. There are other simple movie playing applications. One is Popcorn, written by Leonard Rosenthol of Aladdin Systems. (Leonard originally wrote Popcorn for BMUG's TV-ROM, one of the first collections of QuickTime movies.) Others are Easy Play, written by Michael O'Connor and QuickMovie, written by Paul C.H. Ho; both of these are on the CD. Both are shareware and are available from user groups and online services, as are other simple players.

SimpleText as a Movie Player

You can even use SimpleText, the simple text editor provided by Apple, to open and play a QuickTime movie.

Since QuickTime was introduced, hundreds of application developers have updated their products to give them the ability to play QuickTime movies; playing a movie is just another function these other programs are capable of. Many word processors, spreadsheet programs, presentation programs, scientific modeling programs, and others enable you to play movies. Inserting a movie in most applications is a simple matter, just like other elements that you may use (see figure 2.20).

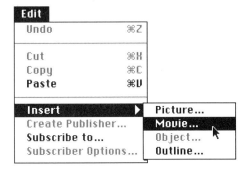

Figure 2.20   *Inserting a movie*

You may also come across *self-playing* (also called *standalone*) movies. These are QuickTime movies in which the movie and the movie playing application are folded together into one double-clickable application, alleviating the need for a separate movie playing application. When you open one of these self-playing movies, you'll see the movie, often with the Standard Controller. (See Chapter 5 for information on creating your own self-playing movies using VideoShop.)

Although most applications use the Standard Controller to play movies, most do not include the Standard Controller's editing features which we will cover a little later.

Sometimes, There's No Standard Controller

In certain applications a movie may appear without the Standard Controller, but it will have a small icon that looks like a piece of a filmstrip in the lower-left corner of the screen (see figure 2.21). This icon is called the *Badge*. The Badge is a way to hide the Standard Controller from sight. Clicking on it will make the Standard Controller reveal itself at the bottom of the window.

Badge

Figure 2.21   *Movie with a Badge*

Finally, there are programs for creating and editing QuickTime movies, which we'll talk about in the next four chapters. Many of these also provide you with the Standard Controller for playing movies even though the movie window may look slightly different than what you're used to seeing in MoviePlayer. See figure 2.22 for an example.

Figure 2.22   *Movie window in Avid VideoShop 3.0*

Some applications provide access to the Standard Controller features, but don't look exactly like the Standard Controller (see figure 2.23).

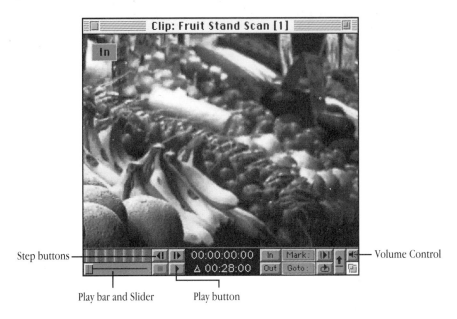

Figure 2.23   *Movie window in Adobe Premiere 4.0*

Remember, if you have a QuickTime movie file, there are many applications that will let you play it, and most will use the Standard Controller or something very similar.

Power Tricks

The Standard Controller has some features that aren't obvious and may or may not be documented in a Help file or the user manual for the software that you use to play movies. Some of these features are useful, and others are just fun. We can't promise that they'll be implemented in every application that uses the Standard Controller, but they're worth looking for.

Let's play with MoviePlayer again, so we can check out some of these features.

Open the file "Intro," which is in the Chapter 2 folder within the Media folder on the CD.

If you're not familiar with your keyboard, take a few seconds to locate your Command, Control, Option, and Arrow keys (see figure 2.24).

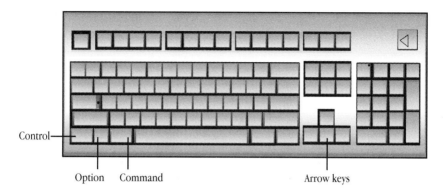

Figure 2.24   *Control, Command, Option, and Arrow keys*

Scratching

In our opinion, the neatest feature in the Standard Controller is the *jog shuttle* or *scratching* ability.

1. Hold down the Control key and click and hold on either of the Step buttons.

   A small slider will appear (see figure 2.25).

Figure 2.25   *Scratching slider*

2. Drag this small slider from the right to the left and then back again.

   This is a variable-speed adjustment for the movie. Normal speed is when the slider is in the middle. When the slider is all the way to the right, the speed is two-and-a-half times normal. When the slider is all the way to the left, the playback speed is the equivalent of two-and-a-half times normal speed backwards.

   Notice the difference between using this slider and the Slider that is on the Play bar. When you use the Slider on the Play bar, you don't get any audio.

3. Use the Control key again, clicking on the Step buttons, but this time, when you slide to the right, let go of the mouse button.

The movie will continue to play at that faster speed with sound. This technique will also work when you play the movie backward, although the movie won't play as smoothly.

QuickTime normally plays a movie so that one second of the movie happens in one second of real time. In order to keep up, it will drop out some video frames if a movie has more frames than QuickTime can show in a second. When you use the jog shuttle option to increase the speed of a movie beyond normal playback speed, you are telling QuickTime to play the movie so that each second of movie happens in *less* than one second of time. QuickTime may have to drop out a lot of frames to do this.

Playing All Frames

If you want to see every frame, regardless of how long it takes, QuickTime will do this, too.

Hold down the Option key while clicking the Play button.

All of the frames in the movie will be shown. If you have a slow Macintosh, the movie may play in slow motion.

When you force QuickTime to show all of the frames, it sometimes has to play each second of movie in *more* than one second of real time. For example, a 10-second movie may take 15 seconds to play if it has to show all frames on a computer that is too slow to play the movie at its true frame rate. If you use a fast computer or play a movie with a low frame rate, there will likely be no slowdown when you tell the system to play all frames.

Shortcuts with the Option Key

The Option key actually has several uses:

- Hold the Option key down while clicking either of the Step buttons.

  This will jump you to the beginning or the end of the movie.

- While dragging the Size box, hold down the Option key.

  The movie height and width jump to a new size, rather than gradually increasing or decreasing. Holding down the Option key causes resizing to dimensions that are optimal for QuickTime playback.

  You can return the window to its original size by clicking the Zoom box.

- Hold the Option key down while clicking the Volume Control button.

  This will mute the audio. You'll see that there are no lines emanating from the speaker, and when you play the movie, you'll hear no audio. Option-click again to reset the movie to its original volume.

Expect the Unexpected

There are many keyboard shortcuts in the Standard Controller. Be fore-warned, however, that some applications may use these keyboard shortcuts for other features; if you try these within an application other than MoviePlayer, you may get results different than those we are describing here.

The Arrow Keys

You can also use the Arrow keys as shortcuts.

- Press the Up or Down Arrow key.

  These arrows control the volume of the movie (Up is louder, Down is less loud). If you press on one of these enough times, you should see that the number of lines emanating from the speaker icon changes (indicating the volume level has changed).

- Press the Left and Right Arrows on the keyboard.

  These arrows will step you through a movie one frame at a time, just as if you had clicked the Step buttons (the Left Arrow moves you toward the front of the movie while the Right Arrow moves you toward the end).

Playing and Pausing Shortcuts

Here are some playing and pausing shortcuts.

- Press the Return key or space bar when the movie is paused.
  This will play the movie.

- Press the Return key or space bar when the movie is playing.

  This will pause the movie.

- Type Command-period (⌘–.) when a movie is playing to pause it.

- Double-click on the movie image to play it.

- Click once on a playing movie to pause it.

- Hold down the Shift key when you double-click on the movie image to have the movie play backward.

Looping

You can set your movie to loop, which means that the movie will repeat continuously until you pause it.

Choose Loop from the Movie menu and then play the movie (see figure 2.26).

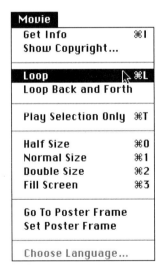

Figure 2.26   *Choosing Loop from the Movie menu*

Another fun (and somewhat silly) thing to do is to make your movie play forward, then backward. This is sometimes called *palindroming*.

Choose Loop Back and Forth from the Movie menu and then play your movie.

Looping and Looping Back and Forth are functions of the Standard Controller. Consequently, many applications that play movies will give you these abilities. You'll have to search in the application's menus for them, however.

Sound Overdriving

Often when you play a QuickTime movie, the audio is not as loud as you want it to be, even when you set the volume slider to its maximum. There is a way to make it louder, which is essentially like setting the audio to 11 when the scale only goes up to 10! In order to do this little trick, however, you must be running the Sound Manager 3.0 (which we had you install in Chapter 1) or be running System 7.5. As long as one of these conditions is met, you can do the following:

1. Hold the Shift key down when you click on the volume slider.

    If you look closely, you'll see that the Volume Controller now has two black horizontal lines through it (see figure 2.27). The lower line represents the normal maximum volume. The higher one represents double the normal maximum volume. The top of the slider represents three times the normal maximum volume.

Figure 2.27   *Clicking on the Volume Controller with the Shift key down (percentages of normal volume)*

2. While holding down the Shift key, drag the Volume Slider up, at least to that higher black line or higher, and release. Then play the movie again.

    You'll find that the audio level is quite a bit higher. Unfortunately, overdriving the audio may also cause poor audio quality.

Tracks

The movies you've played so far have contained both video and audio. As we mentioned earlier, the video and audio information is contained in separate tracks. You can think of a typical video and audio movie in this way:

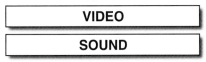

However, any QuickTime movie can have any number of tracks, including multiple video or audio tracks or even a single track of either type. It can also contain track types besides video and audio, such as text and music. The Standard Controller works in the same way, no matter what the track configuration.

Let's look at some files with different track configurations, all of which are in the Chapter 2 folder within the Media folder on the QuickTime Guide CD.

1. Start by opening and playing the movie "Crowd Applause."

    This movie has only a sound track and thus has no video window (see figure 2.28).

Figure 2.28   *Movie with only a sound track*

    You can think of a movie of this type like this:

2. Next, open and play the movie "Eye."

    This movie has only a video track. It has no sound track.

    A video-only movie looks like the QuickTime movies you've already seen, except that it has no Volume Controller (see figure 2.29).

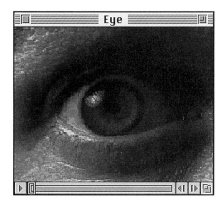

Figure 2.29   *Movie with only a video track*

It can be represented like this:

VIDEO

3. Open and play "Gettysburg Address."

This is a special kind of movie, one containing only a *text track* (see figure 2.30).

Figure 2.30   *Movie with only a text track*

In the next chapter, we'll show you how to search for specific chunks of text in a movie with a text track. You can think of a text-only movie like this:

TEXT

A fourth kind of track is a *music track*, a track type which is new to QuickTime 2.0. Unlike a regular QuickTime sound track, the music track stores data as a sequence of commands telling the system what notes to play and how long to play them. It relies on a music *synthesizer* to actually play those notes. For most users, their Macintosh will do the job of a synthesizer. With the right software, the commands can also be sent to any external synthesizer, if one is hooked up to the Mac, resulting in much improved audio quality. The storage space taken by a sequence of note commands is very small in comparison to digitized sound.

Of QuickTime Music and MIDI

QuickTime music tracks are very similar to MIDI (Musical Instrument Digital Interface) tracks. MIDI provides a standard way for computers and synthesizers to communicate, and it has been used in the electronic music industry for years.

As a matter of fact, QuickTime can import MIDI files. We'll discuss this in Chapter 7. Also the instrument samples contained in QuickTime are licensed from Roland Corp., a major player in the MIDI market.

4. Open and play "Reggae Groove Sample," a music track-only movie.

    Notice that when you open it, it looks like a sound track movie (compare figure 2.31 to figure 2.28).

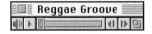

Figure 2.31   *Movie with only a music track*

Thanks Bruce!

Reggae Groove Sample is a portion of a music track movie composed by musician and Mac enthusiast Bruce Linde. The full movie can be found on BMUG's TV-ROM Too Update. Bruce can be contacted at bruce_linde@bmug.org.

It's particularly fun—and sometimes useful—to use QuickTime's scratching ability with Music movies because you can still hear the tune, just at a faster rate. You can only scratch forward, however.

If you compare a sound-only movie to a music-only movie in the Finder, you'll notice remarkably different file sizes.

Look at the sizes of the two movies "Reggae Groove Sample" and "Crowd Applause" in the Finder. You'll need to view the folder by name or by date and stretch out the window (see figure 2.32).

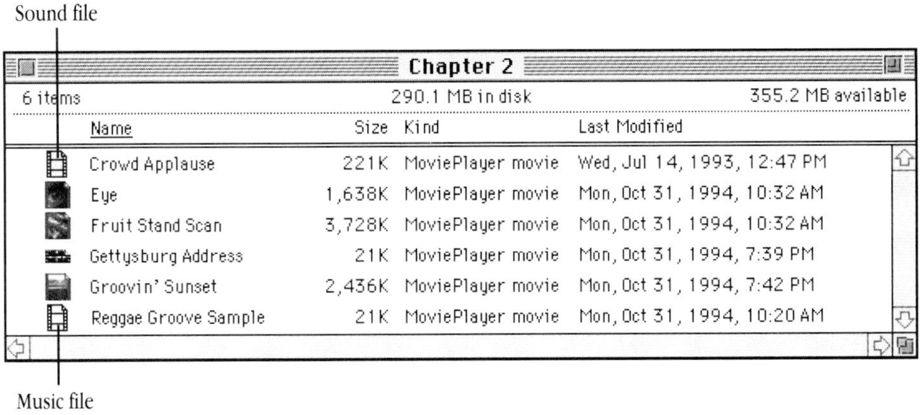

Sound file

Chapter 2			
6 items	290.1 MB in disk		355.2 MB available
Name	Size	Kind	Last Modified
Crowd Applause	221K	MoviePlayer movie	Wed, Jul 14, 1993, 12:47 PM
Eye	1,638K	MoviePlayer movie	Mon, Oct 31, 1994, 10:32 AM
Fruit Stand Scan	3,728K	MoviePlayer movie	Mon, Oct 31, 1994, 10:32 AM
Gettysburg Address	21K	MoviePlayer movie	Mon, Oct 31, 1994, 7:39 PM
Groovin' Sunset	2,436K	MoviePlayer movie	Mon, Oct 31, 1994, 7:42 PM
Reggae Groove Sample	21K	MoviePlayer movie	Mon, Oct 31, 1994, 10:20 AM

Music file

Figure 2.32 *Comparison of the size of a sound-only movie file and a music-only movie file*

You can, of course, think of music track-only movies like this:

MUSIC

5. Finally, open and play the file "Groovin' Sunset."

Here's a movie that has many tracks—one of each in this case. It has a video track and a text track that you can see (see figure 2.33).

Figure 2.33   *A movie with a video track, text track, sound track, and music track*

It also has a sound track and a music track that you can hear. It can be represented like this:

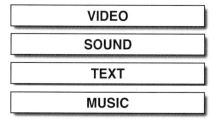

When you use the Standard Controller to play the movie, all tracks play at the same time.

There's no rule that says a movie can have only one of each type of track, either. You could have five different sound tracks, for example. In Chapter 4, we'll show you how to put together movies that are composed of multiple tracks.

More Types of Tracks

QuickTime can have many types of tracks, not just the four we've described here.

One new type of track is the *timecode track*. It's a track that will be useful if you're digitizing your own movies (see Chapter 6). You can store information in your QuickTime movie about what tape you digitized from and where on the tape (hours:minutes:seconds:frames) you grabbed your video data. Then, as you edit your movies, the timecode data is maintained correctly. You can cut data or put different movies together, and you'll still be able to tell where the original analog footage is located.

In the future, digitizing applications will enter the timecode into the timecode track as you digitize. Currently, you can enter the timecode using the unsupported application AddTimeCode (included on the CD). MoviePlayer enables you to see the timecode track information (see end of Chapter 4).

There will likely be even more track types in future versions of QuickTime. See Chapter 5 for information on a track type that is rumored to be close to being available, the *interactivity track*.

Playing More Movies

So far we've had you play only a few different movies. There are many sources for more movies.

Start with the CD that comes with this book. In the More Movies folder, we've included a bunch of clips for your viewing pleasure. Many of these come from existing QuickTime collections available on CD-Rom; others are movies produced from stock video footage houses. Information on how to contact vendors to get more clips is available in the folders that contain the movies.

Check ads in your favorite Mac or multimedia magazines to locate additional collections of QuickTime movies on CD-ROM.

There are also many bulletin boards and online services that have movies for you to download. Internet users can find QuickTime movies at particular ftp sites. Look on sumex-aim or any of its mirrors in /info-mac/art/qt.

Finally, ask around. Your friends or colleagues may have some movies that they will let you copy.

Improving Playback Performance

Do you wish that you could see movies playing at a higher frame rate, so that they're not so jerky? There are a few things you can do to improve performance, all of which relate to speeding up the playback of your movies.

Obviously, it would help to find a faster Macintosh or to speed up the one you already have with an accelerator card.

The media that the files are on matters as well. Different types of disks transfer data at vastly different rates. If you play a movie off of a CD-ROM, you won't necessarily get the best performance because CD-ROMs transfer data relatively slowly. If you have a CD-ROM with QuickTime movies and you have room on your hard disk, you may want to copy the movies you want to watch to your hard disk. Floppy disks are also slow, so if someone gives you a movie on a floppy disk, copy it to your hard disk to improve playback performance.

The QuickTime Guide Movies

Some of the movies on the CD that comes with this book have been optimized to play off of a CD, so you probably won't see much of a difference if you copy them to your hard drive. We'll talk more about optimizing QuickTime movies for CD-ROM playback in Chapter 9.

Hard drives can also have problems, however. Your hard drive may be *fragmented*, which means it has files in so many places that it has no contiguous free space large enough to hold a file as large as a QuickTime movie. If this is true, when a movie file is put on the hard disk, it has to be split into multiple pieces. Then, when you play the movie, QuickTime has to be jumping to different locations on the disk to gather the different pieces of the movie, which slows down the process enough to possibly degrade performance. The best thing to do is to defragment your hard disk with software such as Speed Disk (part of Norton Utilities).

Memory versus Hard Disk Space

If you don't understand the difference between memory and hard disk space, you're not alone. This is one of the most often confused issues for computer users. What's most often called memory is RAM, which stands for

Random Access Memory. RAM is your computer's temporary memory, and when the computer is turned off, everything in RAM is lost. Hard disk space is the place where your computer permanently stores data. Your Macintosh desktop is a visual representation of your hard disk's content. Hard disks access data more slowly than does RAM. Both RAM and hard disk use the same unit of measure, megabytes (MB), although the amounts of RAM are usually in the single digits (e.g., 4 MB or 8 MB) and the amounts of hard disk space are usually in the tens to hundreds (e.g., 80 MB or 230 MB). Having plenty of RAM *and* hard disk space is helpful when working with QuickTime.

If you have too little RAM, movies may not play as well as they could because QuickTime will have to go to hard disk more frequently in order to get more movie data. If you have 4 or fewer MB of RAM, you will probably see improved movie performance if you increase the amount of memory in your system.

PowerBook Playback

On some PowerBooks, the main processor can slow itself down in order to save power. This is known as *processor cycling*, and the PowerBook tries to do this every 15 seconds if there is no user interaction. Unfortunately, when processor cycling occurs during playback of a QuickTime movie, the performance of that movie declines. To turn off processor cycling, you can go to the PowerBook control panel, switch from Easy to Custom, and turn off "Allow processor cycling." Alternatively, you could just touch the track ball every 10 to 15 seconds.

Virtual Memory, a feature of most new Macintosh computers with System 7, fakes the computer into using the hard disk as RAM. However, QuickTime does not play back movies well if Virtual Memory is turned on. You should make sure Virtual Memory is turned off in your Memory control panel (see figure 2.34). A few older Macs don't use Virtual Memory, so you may not have to worry about this feature.

Ram Doubler, a system extension that effectively doubles your available RAM, can also cause performance problems because it's a form of virtual memory. To maximize performance, disable Ram Doubler when using QuickTime applications—especially video editors, which we will cover shortly.

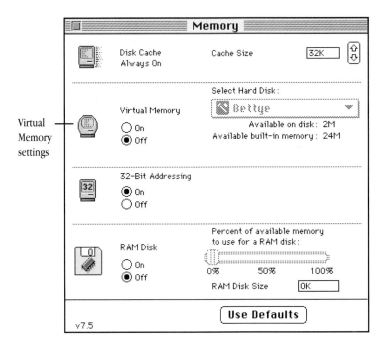

Figure 2.34 *Memory control panel*

Playback performance can also be affected by the number of colors that your monitor is set to show. For many of you, your Mac is only capable of showing 256 colors, so this section will not apply to you. Just make sure that you're using 256 colors, not fewer.

Those of you who have systems that can show more than 256 colors (thousands) will probably want to set your system to show all of these colors because the image quality will then be improved. In many cases, this simple adjustment will give you the best playback frame rate because your computer won't have to calculate what colors to use, a process called *dithering*.

However, if you are not using your computer's built-in video graphics capabilities because you installed an extra graphics card for a second monitor and/or you purchased a high resolution color graphics card, movies may play back at a better frame rate if you switch to 256 colors. Add-on graphics cards can't redraw the screen as quickly when set to a large number of colors because there's more color data to keep track of. In this case, dithering may actually result in better performance because it's reducing the color data that has to be put on the screen. There are other factors, such as the speed of your computer, that enter into the equation, so we recommend that you do some experimentation.

You can check or set the number of colors using the Monitors control panel (see figure 2.35).

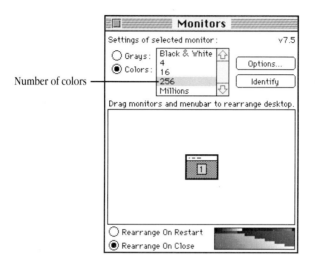

Figure 2.35   *Monitors control panel*

If you are running any version of System 7 earlier than 7.5, you will want to make sure that you have the Sound Manager 3.0 system extension. We had you install this extension in Chapter 1, when you installed QuickTime. Version 3.0 is more efficient than previous versions of Sound Manager. With System 7.5, the correct version of Sound Manager is built into the System. When playing QuickTime movies, Sound Manager 3.0 enables your computer to concentrate less on audio and more on video. As a result, playback of both audio and video is smoother.

Always make sure that you are using the latest version of QuickTime. QuickTime 2.0, the version we've provided on the CD that comes with this book, included significant performance enhancements over the preceding version, and we expect that future versions will include further enhancements.

For better performance you should also: turn off file sharing, use the optimal sizes for movie windows, and make sure your SCSI bus is properly teminated.

In the next chapter, we'll move beyond the Standard Controller to show you other ways to play.

Chapter 3

More Ways to Play

*I*n the preceding chapter, we showed you how you control movies using the Standard Controller. While the Standard Controller is used by many software applications, there are times when it's not the best choice or when some additional controls are needed.

In the first part of this chapter, we'll show you how to play movies without using the Standard Controller. After that, we'll show you applications that provide you with ways to use and control movies that go beyond the capabilities that the Standard Controller provides. We'll start by showing you QuickTime's text searching abilities and then move on to the use of QuickTime in interactive multimedia.

Playing without the Standard Controller

As we said, there are ways to play movies that don't use the Standard Controller. These methods give you very little control over how a movie is played. However, they're useful when you just want to show off a movie or have a little fun.

Playing QT Movies Upon Startup

To have a movie play when your computer starts up requires no software other than the QuickTime extension. Any movie named "Startup movie" that's in your System folder will play on startup. Let's try it now:

1. Copy the file "Sunset" from the CD to your hard drive (it's in the Chapter 3 folder within the Media folder).

   If you prefer to choose another movie file, feel free to do so.

2. Rename the file you just copied "Startup movie."

3. Move "Startup movie" into your System folder.

4. Restart your computer.

   The movie plays automatically when QuickTime loads (see figure 3.1).

Any movie named "Startup movie" that's in your System folder will play every time you start or restart your computer. (It must be in your System folder, not within any folder that's within your System folder; don't put it in the Startup Items folder or the movie file will simply open with MoviePlayer after the computer has started.)

This technique will work with System 7 aliases too. You can make an alias of any movie file, name the alias "Startup movie," and put it into your System folder. (As with any alias file, you must make sure that the original file doesn't get removed.)

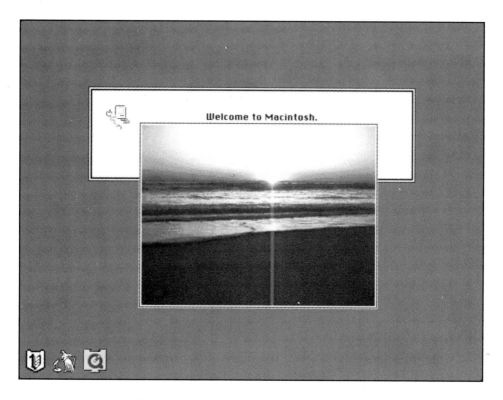

Figure 3.1   Movie playing upon startup

While it can be neat to have a startup movie, you should know that movies with music tracks won't sound quite right when played as startup movies. That's because QuickTime plays a startup movie before it loads the QuickTime Musical Instruments extension, which has all the musical instrument sounds in it. The QuickTime Extension contains only one musical instrument, the electric piano, which just isn't enough to make most music tracks sound like much of anything.

Movie Presentation

In some applications that play movies, you'll find an option that plays your movie on your monitor with nothing else around it (see figure 3.2). No menu bar or Standard Controller shows, and the movie simply plays from beginning to end. It's an effective way to show your movie on the screen as long as you have no need to control it.

Figure 3.2 *Movie shown using Present Movie option*

In some applications, this function is called Print to Video, presumably because it can be used when you want to record a movie to videotape. However, recording a QuickTime movie on videotape requires hardware to get the signal from your monitor out to a VCR; see Chapter 9 for details on how to do this.

Printing to Video

Most QuickTime editing packages, including Adobe Premiere, Avid VideoShop, and VideoFusion/Radius's QuickFLIX! (all of which we'll discuss in Chapter 5), have a Print to Video feature.

MoviePlayer has a Present Movie option, so you can see for yourself how it works:

1. Double-click on the file "Sunset" to open it.

   Again, since it's a MoviePlayer document, MoviePlayer is launched.

2. Choose Present Movie from the File menu (see figure 3.3).

Figure 3.3   *Choosing Present Movie from the File menu*

3. When you see a dialog box with the title "Present Movie," click on the Play button (see figure 3.4).

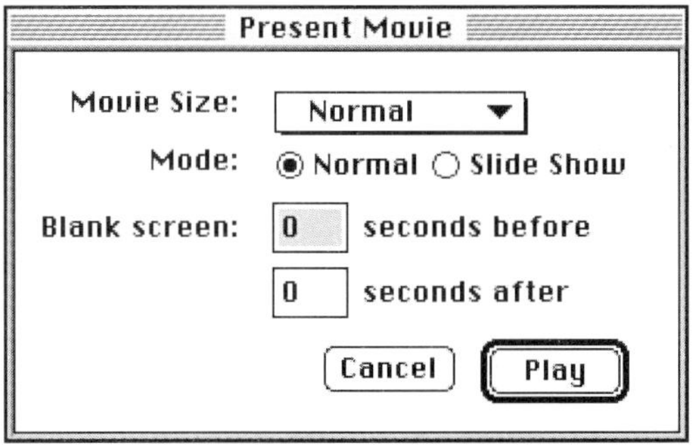

Figure 3.4   *Present Movie dialog box*

Your monitor will go black and then the movie will play in the center of it, as in figure 3.2.

If you want to stop the movie while playing, simply press the mouse button.

What's especially nice is that you can choose to enlarge the movie on playback. For example, you can enlarge a quarter-screen movie so it fills the screen. Even though the pixels are stretched out, it looks and plays much better than if you had simply stretched out a movie window in an application such as MoviePlayer. Of course, playback performance depends on your computer.

So let's try it again, but this time we'll double the size of the movie:

Choose Present Movie from the File menu, and this time when you see the Present Movie window, choose Double from the Movie Size popup (see figure 3.5).

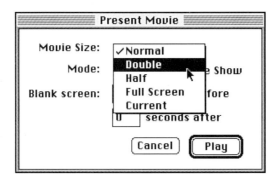

Figure 3.5   *Choosing to present a movie at double the size*

This time the movie will play at 640 x 480 because that is double the size of the movie's 320 x 240 dimensions.

As you probably noticed (or can see from figure 3.5), other size options are available to you.

In MoviePlayer, you can also choose to play the movie in *Slide Show* mode, which advances the movie from frame to frame only when you click. No audio is played. This option is better suited to QuickTime movies composed of a series of still images, rather than those meant to be played as motion video. Here's an example:

1. Open the movie file "New Mexico Movie" and play it using the Play button.

   You'll notice that the movie doesn't look like video because it shows single frames of completely different images.

2. Choose Present Movie from the File menu.

3. Click on the Slide Show radio button in the area labeled "Mode," and then click on the Play button (see figure 3.4).

   Again the screen will go black and the movie will appear, but this time you'll see only the first frame of the movie, a photograph from New Mexico.

4. Press the mouse button to advance forward in the slide show frame-by-frame through the photographs; double-click to go backward.

   You can also use the Arrow keys to step through the presentation both forwards and backwards.

5. To stop the presentation, use command-period.

While you can also use the step buttons on the Standard Controller to step through a movie frame by frame, the presentation won't be as dramatic—black background and all—as when you use a Present Movie or Print to Video option. However, with the Standard Controller, you have the ability to more easily jump around to images you might want to review.

Another option available in the Present Movie dialog box is the amount of time that the screen is black before and after the clip plays. Set the amount of time you want in the area labeled "Blank screen" (see figure 3.4).

Text Track Searching

In the last chapter, we introduced you to the QuickTime text track. The beauty of the text track is that its data is stored as text (i.e., not just as a graphic), so it is searchable. Being able to search for certain key words enables you to find precise points in the movie. It's a unique complement to the Standard Controller for navigating in movies.

MoviePlayer provides text track searching capabilities, so let's try them now with a movie that has a text track.

1. Open the file "Tom's Summary with Text" and play it.

This is a movie with a video track, an audio track, and a text track (see figure 3.6).

Figure 3.6   *Movie with a text track*

Credit Where Credit's Due

The movie "Tom's Summary with Text" is a VideoFusion demo clip to which we have added a text track.

2. Now choose Find from the Edit menu (see figure 3.7).

Figure 3.7   *Choosing Find from the Edit menu*

3. Type in the word "PowerPC" and click on Find, as in figure 3.8.

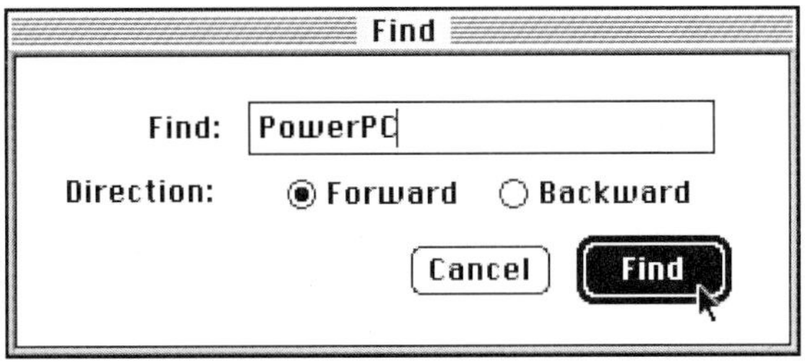

Figure 3.8   Typing text to search for PowerPC

The movie jumps to the point where the correct text is located.

This feature is particularly useful when analyzing movies. It also works well as an indexing method. In the next chapter, where we'll show you how to add a text track to a movie, we'll also show you how you can make the text track invisible so that you don't have to see it, but can still take advantage of it for searching for specific parts of a movie.

Interactive Playing

We move now into the realm of *interactive multimedia*, where QuickTime movies and presentations that use QuickTime can be controlled in ways that are more sophisticated than those the Standard Controller offers. QuickTime movies can be controlled by additional actions by a user, making them interactive in ways not available with videotape. In many ways, the ability to control what is played is the real beauty of QuickTime. We'll now describe some tools that let you use QuickTime interactively.

We've Only Just Begun

In this section, we just barely scratch the surface of interactive multimedia by focusing on QuickTime-specific concepts and software functions. There's much more to the field than just QuickTime, of course. For more thorough coverage, check out these other Hayden books:

Multimedia Starter Kit by Michael D. Murie (Hayden Books, 1994).

continues

Virtual Playhouse for Macintosh by Jonathan Price (Hayden Books, 1994).

Macromedia Director Design Guide by Lee Swearingen and Cathy Clarke (Hayden Books, 1994).

Including QuickTime in Interactive Presentations

While just about all presentation tools let you easily include QuickTime movies in your presentations, only a certain subset of them can be considered interactive presentation or authoring tools. Among those included in this subset are: Gold Disk's Astound, Roger Wagner Publishing's HyperStudio, Vividus' Cinemation, Apple Computer's Apple Media Tool, Macromedia's Authorware Professional, Passport Design's Passport Producer Pro, and Interactive Media's Special Delivery. We differentiate these tools from simple presentation slide show-type tools, such as Microsoft's PowerPoint, which are used to build linear, noninteractive presentations that work essentially the same way every time they are used.

On the CD

Vividus' Cinemation can be used for creating simple animations and presentations with interactivity. A demo version of the product—completely functional except for saving functions—is on the QuickTime Guide CD in the Demos folder.

Most of these interactive presentation tools provide dialog boxes and/or menus that make it relatively easy to add interactive buttons and other objects (including QuickTime movies) that link to another part of the presentation (such as a QuickTime movie) when clicked on. See figure 3.9 for an example of one of these dialog boxes.

Though the amount of control over playing the QuickTime movie is somewhat limited, the presentation itself is controlled directly or indirectly by the user. Depending on how the creator of the presentation has defined the links and what choices the user makes, the user may see different QuickTime movies. In applications that provide functions for keeping track of a student's progress—such as Macromedia's Authorware—a different movie might be shown depending on how well the student seems to understand certain concepts.

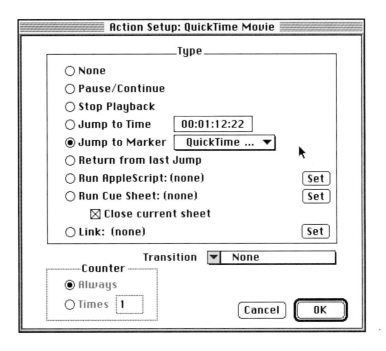

Figure 3.9   *Passport Producer Pro's dialog box for creating a link to a QuickTime movie*

Scripting QuickTime

The greatest flexibility you have in creating interactive presentations comes with software that has a *scripting language.* Scripting languages are similar to programming languages, but they are more like standard English and are easier to use. Applications that have scripting languages that include QuickTime commands enable you—as the creator of a multimedia file—the ability to program responses to user interactions. You can program how the actions of your users—where they click, when they click, what they type, or how long it takes them to do something—will determine what happens to the QuickTime movie. In other words, you can manipulate the movie by script, rather than by the Standard Controller. This programming ability makes QuickTime really useful for interactive instructional applications. Apple's HyperCard is the most widely used application that provides this power. Others include Allegiant's SuperCard and Macromedia Director.

In Chapter 5, we'll show you how to add interactivity directly to your movies. (Because this requires changing the movie files themselves, we consider it movie editing rather than movie playing.)

HyperCard

HyperCard is an authoring program that's been around for many years. It is relatively inexpensive and easy to learn to use. With HyperCard you produce *stacks*, which are files that are composed of a series of *cards*. Scripting using the scripting language HyperTalk is not required to build stacks, but it provides a great deal of power and extensibility, particularly when using QuickTime.

Imagine a HyperCard stack that shows different cards depending on what's happening in a movie that's playing. Visualize a QuickTime movie in which a user can click on a character in a scene and then watch the action from that character's point of view. You might create a HyperCard stack with a movie that asks a student a question; then it waits until the student answers that question (perhaps by clicking a button or typing a word) before continuing on, perhaps to another section of the movie, depending on the answer given. With HyperCard, you can provide students with a clickable index to the parts of a movie that you want them to review or analyze. Or better yet, you can give them the ability to index or annotate the parts that they find most interesting.

Such interactivity can be accomplished via scripts that control QuickTime. If you're using HyperCard, before you can write such scripts, you'll need an XCMD that enables you to play and interact with movies. An XCMD—pronounced "X command"—is a small program that can be installed into HyperCard stacks to extend the functionality of HyperCard. Some XCMDs work in programs other than HyperCard.

Movie Playing XCMDs

Where do you get one of these XCMDs? An XCMD called "Movie" is contained in the *QuickTime Tools* stack, which comes with HyperCard 2.2. Apple has an alternative QuickTime XCMD, written by programmer Ken Doyle. This XCMD is called "QTMovie," and you'll find it in a HyperCard stack called *QTMovie Stack*. This stack is on the CD that comes with this book. You may find additional Shareware QuickTime XCMDs on bulletin boards or online services.

More QuickTime XCMDs

Besides QTMovie, Ken Doyle has also created the QTEditMovie and QTRecordMovie XCMDs (also on the CD that comes with this book). While the XCMDs we discuss here only provide playing functions, these XCMDs enable you to create HyperCard stacks in which your users can actually edit movies (see Chapter 4) or digitize video (see Chapter 6).

Of the two XCMDs, QTMovie offers many more options and is far more powerful; in particular, it provides ways to control individual tracks in your movies. It is, however, an unsupported product and is probably best for people who are experienced programmers or HyperTalk scripters.

The Movie XCMD is a little more friendly. The QuickTime Tools stack (the one that contains the Movie XCMD) will automatically install the XCMD in your stack. It also has a special screen which will automatically write a script, build a button, and install it in your own HyperCard stack. You just have to tell it the name of the movie you'd like to play and pick a few options from the QuickTime Toolkit card (see figure 3.10).

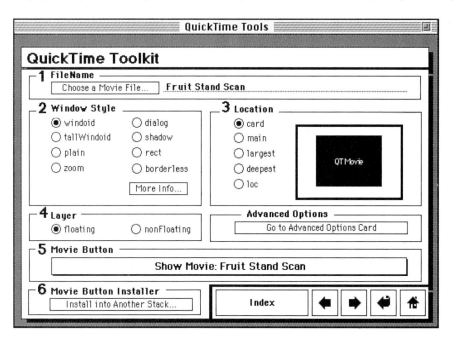

Figure 3.10   QuickTime Toolkit card in the QuickTime Tools stack

The button that is automatically created will have a script that looks like the one in figure 3.11.

```
Script of card button id 1 = "Show/Hide Movie"

Scripting language: [ HyperTalk ▼ ]

on mouseUp
   set cursor to watch
   -- Load the name of the movie window into TheMovieName
   put "Fruit Stand Scan" into TheMovieName --Δ
   --
   -- Check the status of the movie window
   if TheMovieName is in the windows then
      -- The movie window is open and this script will close it
      close window TheMovieName
   else
      -- The movie window is closed and this script will open it
      Movie TheMovieName,"Windoid","Card","visible","floating"
      put the result into TheResult
      if "Error" is in TheResult then -- Something went wrong
         answer TheResult
         exit mouseUp
      end if
      --
   end if
end mouseUp
```

Figure 3.11   *Script created with the help of the QuickTime Toolkit*

You can then modify this script if you want to change some of the specifics of how movies are played. This is a great way to begin learning about scripting QuickTime and to build your skills up so that eventually you will be able to write scripts for more complicated interactions. You might start to take advantage of many more of the options available with the Movie XCMD, which are shown in the index of the QuickTime Tools stack (see figure 3.12).

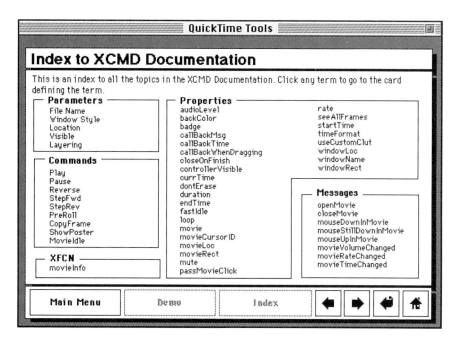

Figure 3.12 *Index card in the QuickTime Tools stack*

Each option is well documented on screens such as the one in figure 3.13.

Some Scripting Examples

To give you a feel for how these scripts are written and what they can do, we'll provide a few simple examples using the Movie XCMD. You'll find complete documentation in the QuickTime Tools stack, so we won't try to list every option.

You might use the following script in a button that, when clicked, would cause a movie called "Tennis Game" to appear, turn its audio level down low, and then play:

```
on mouseup
      movie "Tennis Game"
      set the audio level of window "Tennis Game" to 50
      send "Play" to window "Tennis Game"
end mouseup
```

Let's take apart this script. The line that starts with "movie" calls up the movie. You could, of course, replace "Tennis Game" with the name of any movie file.

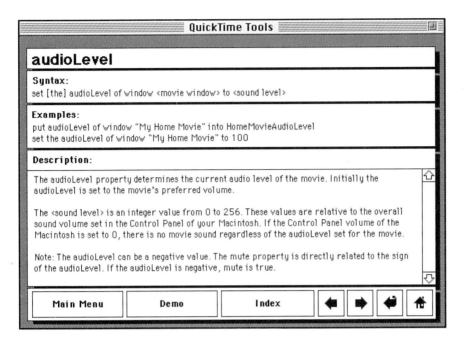

Figure 3.13   *Example of documentation in the QuickTime Tools stack showing the audioLevel property*

Below that, notice the line that starts with "set." "Audio level" is a *property* that you can set, and changing it has the same effect as changing the volume in the Volume Controller on the Standard Controller. You can also set:

- Whether the Standard Controller is visible (**controllervisible**)
- Whether a badge is visible (**badge**)
- The size and location of the window in which the movie plays (**windowrect**)
- The speed at which the movie plays (**rate**)
- What happens when the movie gets to a certain point (**callBackMsg**)
- Whether the movie window closes when the movie is done playing (**closeOnFinish**)

These are just a few of the features you can set (see the list of properties in figure 3.12).

Next, notice the line that starts with "send." This line causes the movie to play by sending "Play" to the window—in effect doing the same thing as if you clicked on the Play button on the Standard Controller. Play is a *command*. Other commands that you can send include Pause, StepFwd, and StepRev; as you might guess, these commands are equivalent to clicking on the Pause and Step buttons on the Standard Controller.

Here's another sample script, one that will react when a movie is clicked on and can recognize where the click was:

```
on mouseupinmovie moviename, movienum, location
      if moviename is "tennis game" then
             if item 1 of location < 160
             then movie "Navratilova"
             else movie "someothertennisplayer"
      end if
end mouseupinmovie
```

In this example, we check to make sure that the movie clicked is one called "tennis game," and if so, we open a different movie depending on whether the right side of the movie or the left side of the movie was clicked. The script language "item 1 of the location" gives the horizontal pixel location where the user clicked. If we assume that the window is 320 pixels wide, then anything less than 160 is the left side of the screen, and anything greater or equal to 160 is the right side of the screen.

There are many other interactions you can script that give you, as a multimedia developer, more power than simply putting a movie on the screen.

SuperCard

SuperCard is a product similar to HyperCard. However, unlike HyperCard, SuperCard has QuickTime controlling commands built into its scripting language, SuperTalk, so no XCMD is necessary. Besides using SuperTalk's built-in commands to call up a movie to be played onto a SuperCard card, you can control the following:

- Where on the screen your movie plays.
- What size and shape the movie should be played in. The shape could even be non-rectangular (see figure 3.14).

- The playback rate (normal speed or faster or slower) and direction (forward or backward).
- What point in the movie playback should start and end.
- Whether the Standard Controller shows.

Here's an example from a SuperTalk script that plays a movie:

```
play movie "My Hard drive:Eye" at loc of card graphic 5
➥ using card graphic 5 very fast with invisible controller and
➥ repeat 10 times until click
```

This script plays the movie "Eye" at the location of a graphic that's on the card and in the shape of that graphic at twice as fast as normal speed, with no Standard Controller showing. The movie will repeat 10 times or until the user clicks on it.

SuperCard's commands for dealing with QuickTime are currently quite limited compared to what can be done in HyperCard using the Movie or QTMovie XCMD, but we expect to see additional QuickTime support added to SuperCard in the future. In the meantime, if SuperTalk's internal commands don't give you enough flexibility, the QTMovie XCMD can also be used, although not all options will work (the Movie XCMD won't work at all).

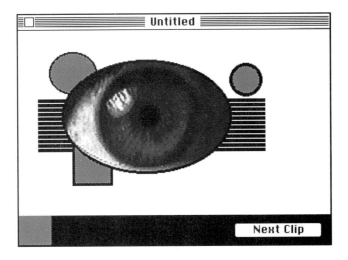

Figure 3.14   *Movie cropped to a shape*

Director

Macromedia Director is considered a more powerful multimedia authoring package than either HyperCard or SuperCard. Like them, however, Director (version 3.1 or later) enables you to easily incorporate a QuickTime movie. In Director, you import a QuickTime file, and it becomes a *cast member*. In Director, everything you want to place on the screen—all artwork, animations, sound, and text—is considered a cast member.

For each QuickTime cast member, you can set certain initial options for the movie using the dialog box shown in figure 3.15.

No scripting is required in order to use QuickTime in Director. However, like SuperCard, Director's built-in scripting language, Lingo, provides commands for controlling your movie during playback. Also like SuperCard, if the built-in commands aren't sufficient, you may opt to use the QTMovie XCMD.

Cross Platform Multimedia

One advantage to using Director is that there is a Windows version of Director. Since there's also a Windows version of QuickTime (which we describe in Chapter 9), it's relatively easy to move a Director project that includes QuickTime over to a PC.

Director 4.0 comes with a CD that has many Director examples for your examination. One of these is a file called "QT controller," which provides a demonstration of how to use Lingo to control a QuickTime movie.

Lingo has commands to control:

- Where on the screen your movie plays.
- The scale of the movie (it can be enlarged or shrunk).
- The rate and direction of playback.
- The playback start and end points.
- The visibility of the Standard Controller.
- The audio level of the movie.

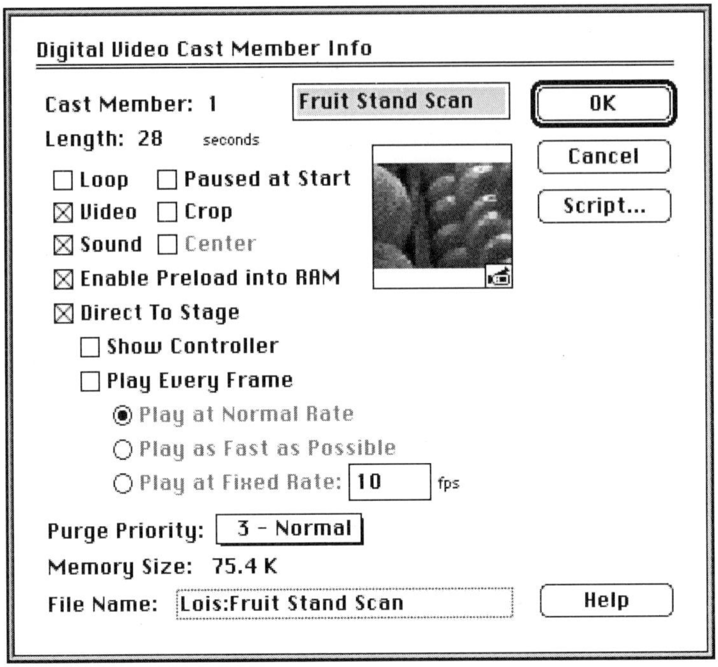

Figure 3.15   *QuickTime cast member information dialog box in Director 4.0*

Lingo also provides a property called *movietime*, which enables you to detect or set the current point of the movie. This feature is very valuable for interactive applications because you can cause other events to happen in your production depending on which point in the movie is playing, or you can set the movie to a specific point depending on the wishes, needs, or characteristics of the user.

Even though Director plays ordinary sound files, many people creating presentations with Director prefer to use audio-only QuickTime movies (both music and sound) because they can use Lingo's QuickTime commands to control the audio. This is very helpful when it comes to synchronizing audio with animations or other action happening on the screen.

Director also lets you export noninteractive animations as QuickTime movies. We discuss this feature in Chapter 7.

QuickTime and AppleScript

Because QuickTime is from Apple and AppleScript is from Apple you'd think they'd work together. However, currently neither QuickTime nor MoviePlayer provide support for AppleScript. We'll have to wait for future versions for that.

If you want an AppleScriptable movie-playing application now, check out EasyPlay 2.0. It's included on the QuickTime Guide CD, in the Shareware folder.

So How Do You Want to Play Your Movies?

We've shown you a number of ways to show finished movies to the public. You saw first how to simply present a movie. Then we shed some light on the interactive abilities of QuickTime-savvy authoring tools.

Less control or more control—it's up to you. We wanted you to see the whole spectrum. You'll use the methods that best suit your needs and time constraints.

In upcoming chapters, you'll learn about what goes into putting together those finished movies so that they're *your* movies, not somebody else's.

Chapter 4

Basic Editing— Cut, Copy, Paste, and Beyond

So far you've only played back files that were created by someone else, leaving no room for your own creativity. Now we move on to editing, where you can combine, refine, and shape movies into a finished product that you define.

Besides the element of creativity, you'll want to know how to edit movies you make from videotape (which we cover in Chapter 6), since what you first record is rarely what you want the final product to be.

There are two kinds of software for editing movies. One type enables you to do basic cut, copy, and paste editing with the Standard Controller. The other type includes more powerful, sophisticated editing tools that enable you to do functions that the basic editors can't, such as special effects.

In this chapter, we'll talk about how you can do simple editing of QuickTime movies—delete portions of them, combine them, and add new elements. We'll stick to the basics, using the application MoviePlayer. You'll find that the functions we discuss in this chapter are quite extensive, useful, and powerful; they may even be all you'll ever need.

We'll also explain *file dependencies*, one of the thornier issues of QuickTime, and *previews*, one of the time-saving features of QuickTime; you'll want to understand both when you save your edited movies in any program.

At the end of this chapter, we'll show you a number of editing techniques for working with individual tracks, many of which are currently only available with MoviePlayer 2.0.

In the next chapter, we'll discuss some more powerful editing tools.

MoviePlayer

We really want you to think of MoviePlayer as the prototypical QuickTime player and simple editor. Because it was developed by the same people who developed QuickTime, it's a good tool to use to show you all of QuickTime's capabilities. But remember that you'll see many of the same features in other QuickTime applications.

Simple Editing with the Standard Controller

If you've used the Macintosh before, you're no doubt familiar with the Cut, Copy, and Paste commands. These commands, part of the Macintosh standard human interface, are used in all types of applications, with all sorts of data. Open any Macintosh application and you'll see the Edit menu along with the Apple and File menus. Pull down the Edit menu and you'll always see Cut, Copy, and Paste (see figure 4.1). QuickTime applications are no exception.

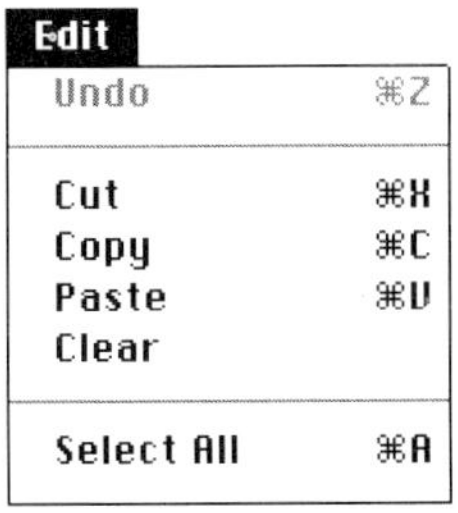

Edit	
Undo	⌘Z
Cut	⌘H
Copy	⌘C
Paste	⌘U
Clear	
Select All	⌘A

Figure 4.1   *The Edit menu*

Shortcuts

As in most other Macintosh applications, QuickTime applications enable you to use keyboard shortcuts for Cut, Copy, and Paste. Cut is ⌘-X. Copy is ⌘-C. Paste is ⌘-V.

Enough general stuff, let's do some editing. Start by opening the movies "Real Dinosaur" and "Jet Taking Off" located in the Chapter 4 folder within the Media folder. To open both clips at once, you can click on one movie and then hold down the Shift key and click on the other; both should be selected. Then release the Shift key and double-click on either file.

Thanks to WPA

The clips you're using in this exercise come from the WPA Multimedia Collection. On the CD that comes with this book are a few more clips from this collection, but the company has tons of really cool archival footage for sale. Their toll-free number is 1-800-777-2223.

When you double-click to open the movies, you open the application MoviePlayer, which you will be using to edit the movies.

To Copy or Not to Copy

We haven't asked you to copy these movie files to your hard disk because they're so large. However, if you have 11 megabytes of free hard disk space, you may want to copy the entire Chapter 4 folder to your hard disk to achieve slightly better performance.

Selecting and Copying Part of a Movie

When you're working with text on the Macintosh, you *select* or *highlight* the portion of the text you want to change (see figure 4.2). The process is only slightly less direct when you're working with QuickTime data. Recall that the Play bar represents the length of the movie. You select portions of the movie by selecting an area of the Play bar.

Lorem ipsum dolor sit amet, consectetuer adipiscing elit,

Figure 4.2   *Text selected in a word processing application*

Let's select part of the second half of the dinosaur movie now:

1. Click in the "Real Dinosaur" movie window.

   This makes it the active window.

2. Move the Slider to the point where the dinosaur grabs the tree, which is slightly past the halfway point.

3. Now, holding down the Shift key, move the Slider all the way to the right to the end of the clip; then release the mouse button and Shift key.

   As you drag, you should see the portion of the Play bar that you have dragged along turning black; when you release the mouse button, the entire portion you have selected should remain black (see figure 4.3).

The selected portion of the movie

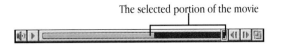

Figure 4.3 *Movie data selected in an application that uses the Standard Controller*

Once a portion of the movie is selected, you can, for example, copy that portion and paste it elsewhere. So, make sure the portion of the movie is still selected. If you clicked on the Play bar, you will have deselected what you just selected; if so, select it again.

Tip

You can clear your selection without moving the slider by holding down the Shift key and pressing the Clear key on the number pad of your keyboard.

---

4. Choose Copy from the Edit menu.

You won't notice any changes, but you pasted the copied portion of the movie to the clipboard.

Macintosh Drag and Drop

Drag and Drop is a new Macintosh feature that refers to the general ability to drag and drop data from one application to another or from one document to another. The data can be text, graphics, or sound. With QuickTime 2.0, it can also be QuickTime data. Macintosh Drag and Drop provides the same functionality as Copy and Paste, but it is a faster and more intuitive operation. In addition, there are a number of MoviePlayer advanced editing functions which can only be accomplished with Drag and Drop. However, in order to use Macintosh Drag and Drop, you'll need either System 7.1 with the Drag and Drop Extensions (which come with certain software products) or System 7.5.

To use Drag and Drop once you've made a selection, click on the selection you want to copy—the actual image in the case of a QuickTime movie— and, without releasing the mouse, drag to the window in which you want to

continues

paste, and then release the mouse. It's all one smooth action, instead of the several steps that comprise Copy and Paste. There's visual feedback, too: as you drag, you get an outline of what you're dragging; when your cursor moves into a window which can receive the data, the window becomes outlined.

Creating a New Movie

Now you will make a new movie into which to paste the portion you just copied.

1. Choose New from the File menu.

   This creates a new empty movie file called "Untitled 1" (see figure 4.4).

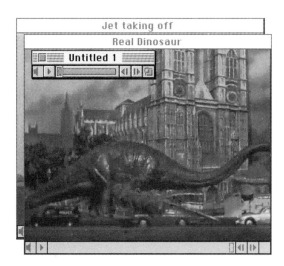

Figure 4.4   *An empty movie, "Untitled 1"*

2. Choose Paste from the Edit menu.

   Make sure that the Untitled 1 window is active; when you do the paste, it will be placed into whatever window is active.

   Your new movie is no longer empty; the image you see should be from the dinosaur clip. You will also see that the entire Play bar is now selected (see figure 4.5).

Figure 4.5   *"Untitled 1" after a portion of "Real Dinosaur" has been pasted into it*

Selecting with More Control

Let's now go get part of "Jet Taking Off." You may feel a little frustrated by the lack of fine control you have when you just click and drag on the Play bar. The Standard Controller gives you ways to fine-tune your selecting. We'll use these methods this time:

1. Click on the "Jet Taking Off" window.

    This makes it the active window.

2. If it's not there already, move the Slider to the beginning of the movie.

3. Holding down the Shift key, click on the forward Step button until you come to the first frame in which the jet is at its largest size (about halfway through the movie). If you step forward too far, hold down the Shift key and click on the backward Step button until you reach the correct point.

    You'll notice, again, that about half of the Play bar is selected.

Tip

You may recall that you can use the Left and Right arrow keys in the same way that you use the Step buttons. So you can, of course, use these keys when selecting parts of a movie.

---

4. Choose Copy from the Edit menu.

5. Paste what you've just copied into the movie "Untitled 1." To do this, click on the "Untitled 1" window and choose Paste from the Edit menu.

    Notice that you now see the jet instead of the dinosaur and that the second half of the Play bar is highlighted (see figure 4.6).

Figure 4.6 *"Untitled 1" movie after a portion of "Jet Taking Off" has been pasted into it*

When you pasted the clip of the jet, the Slider was at the end of the Play bar, so the copied movie frames were pasted after the movie frames from the dinosaur clip.

When you make a selection, the frame that you see when you're finished selecting is the first frame that follows the selection. In this case, you copied everything up to, but not including, the frame in which the plane appears largest. This selection was what was pasted.

Tip

If you have selected part of a movie, holding down the option key while clicking either of the Step buttons will jump you to the beginning or the end of that selection.

---

6. Play your newly created movie.

You'll see that it's composed of the other two movies. You've just edited two different movies into a single new one.

Saving Your Movie

Next, we'll save the movie you just created:

1. Choose Save from the File menu.

You should see a Save dialog box like that in figure 4.7.

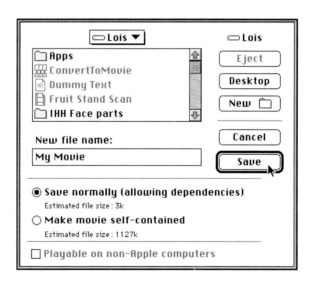

Figure 4.7 *Saving a movie file*

2. Name the movie whatever you'd like.

   Something creative like "My Movie" is okay.

3. Navigate to a location on your hard disk where you'd like this movie saved (remember that you can't save it on the CD because CDs are read-only devices).

4. Make sure Save normally is selected and then click on Save.

   We'll explain what this option means shortly.

   If you want to continue to experiment, try selecting a part of your movie, copying it, and then pasting it within the same movie. You should notice that the portion you select, copy, and paste plays twice. If you paste a few more times, you get an effect much like certain cat food (chow, chow, chow!), cereal, and chewing gum commercials that you may have seen on TV.

5. When you're finished, choose Quit from the File menu, or type ⌘-Q, to quit MoviePlayer.

Where Can You Do Simple Editing?

The editing you just did is a function of the Standard Controller, not MoviePlayer. This means that you will find the same capability in other QuickTime-savvy applications.

However, some applications that let you play movies won't let you edit movies because they haven't implemented the editing features of the Standard Controller. As long as a movie is open, you can tell at a glance whether the application will let you edit. You should look closely at the Slider. If you can see through the middle of the Slider to the Play bar, you can edit. If the Slider is solid, you can't edit (see figures 4.8 and 4.9).

You can edit this one

Figure 4.8   *Play bar when application allows editing*

You can't edit this one

Figure 4.9   *Play bar when application doesn't allow editing*

File Dependencies

In most applications that allow you to save QuickTime movies, you will be given a choice of saving your movie "normally" or saving it as a "self-contained" file (see figure 4.7).

Now in our way of thinking, the "normal" setting is not really normal. Here's why: when you save "normally," you are not necessarily saving exactly what plays. Instead, you are saving a file that contains information about what *should* be played. The saved file could contain less data than you actually see or hear, or it could contain more data than you actually see or hear.

Movie Files with Less Data Than It Seems

When does the file contain less data than you actually see or hear? This occurs when you have pasted frames into the movie and then saved "normally." Instead of containing those pasted frames, the movie file contains information about where the original version of those frames can be found. We can say that the file contains a *pointer* to the location of the original frames. We can also say that the file has a *dependency*: It depends on the files from which the original frames were copied. If you remove any of those original files, then the movie file into which you have pasted will no longer work. If you have used System 7 aliases, you will recognize that a dependent movie file, one that is saved normally, is very much like an *alias* file.

Once again, you'll understand this concept best if you explore with the software.

Looking at File Sizes

Let's start by looking at some file sizes in the Finder.

1. Open the Chapter 4 folder in the Media Folder and select both of the files you used for editing in the previous section.

2. Choose Get Info from the File Menu.

   Two windows will open, giving you information about the two files. Notice the sizes of the files (see figure 4.10).

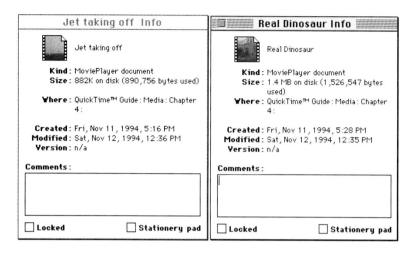

Figure 4.10 *Info windows for "Jet Taking Off" and "Real Dinosaur"*

3. Now locate the file you created and saved to your hard drive in the previous section; we'll refer to it as "My Movie." Once you've located it, check its size by selecting it and choosing Get Info from the File Menu (see figure 4.11).

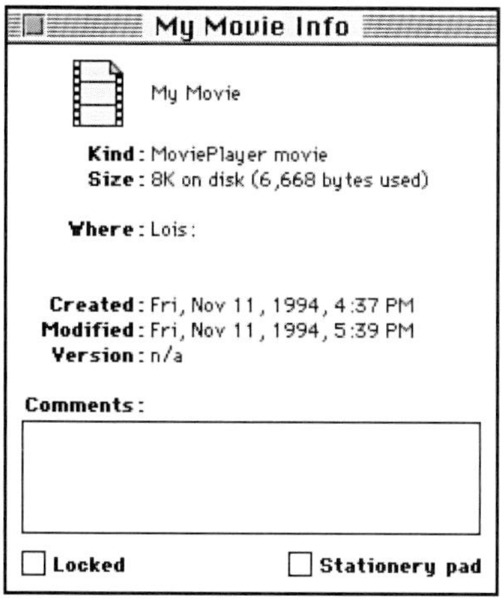

Figure 4.11 *Info window for "My Movie"*

"My Movie" is very small in comparison to both the "Real Dinosaur" and "Jet Taking Off" files. Remember that "My Movie" is composed of almost half of the other two clips; if you had pasted in all of the data, instead of references, "My Movie" would be more than two megabytes, rather than just a few kilobytes. However, because you saved the file "normally," it did not actually move all that movie data into the file.

Getting Movie Info

Now let's take a closer look at MoviePlayer.

1. Open the "My Movie" file.

2. Choose Get Info from the Movie menu.

   You should see a new window labeled "My Movie Info."

3. From the popup menu you see in the top right of the window, choose Files (see figure 4.12).

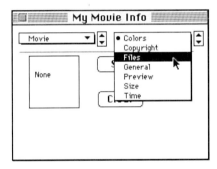

Figure 4.12   *Choosing Files in the Info window in MoviePlayer*

In the lower portion of the Info window, you should now see a scrolling field in which two file names are listed. This field tells you that the movie depends on these two files (see figure 4.13).

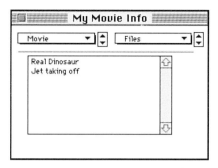

Figure 4.13   *File dependency info*

In order to play this movie, the files "Real Dinosaur" and "Jet Taking Off" must be available. These are called *reference files*. If you were to remove the CD that contains the reference files and then try to open the file "My Movie," you would see a dialog box asking you to insert the CD-ROM (see figure 4.14). You would not be able to open "My Movie" until you had reinserted the CD-ROM.

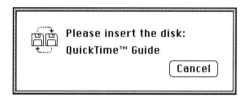

Figure 4.14   *Dialog box asking you to insert CD-ROM with reference files*

In the case where the files are not available—either because they've been deleted, or because they're on a CD-ROM or other volume that's not accessible—you won't be able to open the movie. QuickTime will first search for the files it needs, putting up a dialog box telling you that it's searching. Then you'll see a dialog box telling you that it can't find a file that it needs. It will give you the option of canceling or searching for the file in a standard open file dialog box.

For comparison's sake, now open the movie "Real Dinosaur," and check its file dependency information in the same way you did for "My Movie."

This time, notice that the only name in the list is the name of the movie itself (see figure 4.15). This is how all self-contained files will appear.

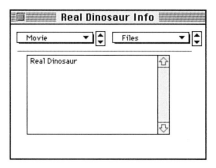

Figure 4.15   *Info window for a movie that has no dependent files*

QuickTime Scrapbooks

A special QuickTime-aware Scrapbook desk accessory comes with this book. It won't work with System 6. And it's not necessary with System 7.5— the Scrapbook that comes with System 7.5 is already QuickTime-aware. You can paste portions of your movies into and play them from a QuickTime-aware Scrapbook. However, you should know that Scrapbook entries are always dependent. That is, if you select and copy part of a movie, paste it into your Scrapbook, and then later delete the original file, the clip in your Scrapbook will not play.

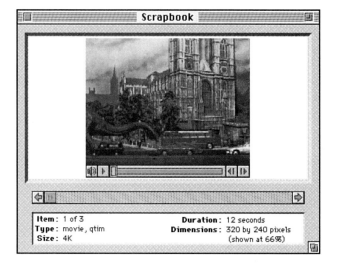

Figure 4.16   *QuickTime movie in the System 7.5 Scrapbook*

Movie Files with More Data Than It Seems

Now you have seen a movie, "My Movie," which contains *less* data than you actually see because it uses data from other files. When does a movie file contain *more* data than it seems? If you cut segments from a movie and then simply save it, using the Save command from the File menu, the data doesn't go away; instead, the file contains the information about what parts of the movie shouldn't be played. If you have a movie from which you have cut segments, you should make sure to save it as a self-contained file. In doing so, you will actually get rid of the data that you cut.

Why File Dependencies?

One of the reasons Apple chose this system of dependencies was to cut down on the time it would take to cut, copy, and paste a movie. If you selected a 3-minute, 20-megabyte clip and then copied it, you'd wait a long time for the system to handle that much data. So, instead, when you copy, all that you copy are the references to that data. When you paste into the new movie file, you paste in about 5 kilobytes of references instead of 20 megabytes worth of video. This saving speeds up the process of editing a movie. However, it can create a mess when it comes to storing movies.

So, when would you want a dependent movie? Well, if you are reusing parts of movies, it makes little sense to store them multiple times because movie data takes up so much space. Say, for example, your company logo is a gorilla, and you have a great 2-second, 1-megabyte QuickTime movie of a gorilla pounding its chest. You have 10 training movies, and you'd like to begin all of them with that same clip. For each of those 10 movies, you would copy the entire gorilla clip, paste it into the beginning of your movie, and then save the movie as a file that is *not* self-contained. This approach will save you 9 megabytes of storage space because you only have to store the gorilla movie once. Each of your training movies would have a pointer to the gorilla clip.

Confusing Terms

The terms that have to do with file dependencies can be somewhat tricky. Different people and different applications use different terms. For example, when you save a QuickTime movie in VideoShop, a QuickTime editing

continues

package, you'll be given an option to save the movie as a *reference movie*, which is the same as MoviePlayer's normal option. Both terms mean that you are saving the movie with dependencies to other files.

Then there is the term *flattening*, which is often used incorrectly. As originally defined by Apple, *flattening* means saving a movie as a self-contained file. If you take a movie that has dependencies and save it as a self-contained movie, you'll see a progress box saying "Flattening movie." However, many people use the term *flattening* to mean saving in a format that can be played back on non-Macintosh computers, a process that involves more than simply moving all of the data into a single file (see the section on QuickTime for Windows in Chapter 9).

Another point of confusion is the term *self-playing*. A self-playing movie, also called a *standalone* movie, is one that doesn't require a special movie playing application to play it; you can double-click on the movie file and it will open and play, as long as the QuickTime extension is installed. The applications VideoShop and Theater Maker are just a few that allow you to save QuickTime movies in this way. However, you can have a self-playing movie that is not self-contained—but it may still require movie data from another file to play.

Another example of when you may want a dependent movie is when you are using a network to share movie data. On your local machine, you might have your dependent file, and on the file server you could have the "real" file. However, you'd need a fast network (for example, one that uses Ethernet) to do this; otherwise, movie responsiveness will be so slow that you'll be frustrated and want to copy the file anyway.

Here's yet another example. You and a colleague are working on a project together. This project is going to be an amalgamation of QuickTime movies from a CD-ROM. You both have copies of the CD-ROM, which contains all of the original movies. You can create a new movie that contains pieces of the movies from the CD-ROM. If you save this movie so that it is *not* self-contained, it will be a very small file, one that you can easily send over a network or put on a floppy disk. Your colleague can open this file on her computer system, and it will refer to the same files on her CD-ROM. Again, you avoid storing and moving large quantities of data.

Previews

Most of this chapter is devoted to showing you how you can edit the content of your movies. We'd like to quickly show you how to set a special portion of your movie file, called a *preview*, which enables you to get an idea of what's in your movie before you open it.

When you are using an application that enables you to play QuickTime movies and you open files from within that application, you'll see a dialog box that is probably slightly different from what you're used to when you open files from other applications.

Seeing a Preview

Let's take a look:

1. Open MoviePlayer. To do this, double-click directly on the MoviePlayer application.

2. Choose Open from the File menu.

   You'll see an Open dialog box that differs slightly from Open dialog boxes you may have seen in the past; it has a preview area to the left of the file list. Apple altered its Human Interface Guidelines to include this dialog box when it introduced QuickTime.

3. Click on the file "My Movie" in this dialog box.

   On the left side of the box, you should see a small picture that looks like one of the frames of "My Movie" (see figure 4.17).

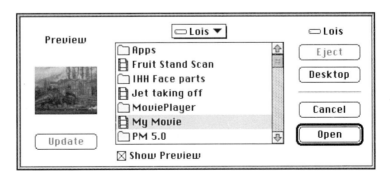

Figure 4.17 *Open dialog box showing preview for "My Movie"*

The image shown is called the *poster*, and, for most files, it is a scaled-down version of the first frame of the movie.

Some movies, however, will have a sequence of frames as a preview. We call this a *dynamic preview* to differentiate it from a poster. Think of the poster as the cardboard poster you see outside the theater and the dynamic preview as the "Coming Attractions" you watch inside the theater before the feature film starts.

Let's see a dynamic preview:

1. From within the Open dialog box, locate the file "Real Dinosaur" on the CD and select it.

    This time you should see a truncated movie controller—one that's missing the step buttons—below the preview area (see figure 4.18).

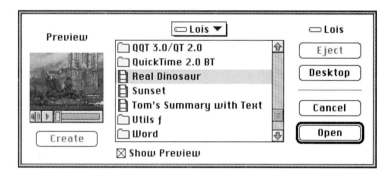

Figure 4.18   *Dynamic preview*

2. Click the Play button on the controller.

    The preview sequence plays.

The ability to see a preview of a movie, whether it's a single frame or a sequence of frames, can save QuickTime users a lot of time because it's no longer necessary to open the file to be reminded of what's in it.

Tip

If there's no preview defined for a particular movie, you'll see an active Create button. Click on it to create a poster based on the first frame of the movie.

Changing the Poster

What if the first frame of a movie is not indicative of what's in the movie? MoviePlayer gives you a way to change the poster.

1. Go ahead and open the file "My Movie" if it's not already open.

2. Use the Slider to move to a frame of the movie that contains the jet.

3. Choose the Set Poster Frame command from the Movie menu.

   You have now chosen a new poster frame.

4. Choose Save from the File menu.

   You have saved the file with its new poster.

5. Close the file by clicking on the close box.

6. Choose Open from the File menu and click on the listing for the file "My Movie."

   Notice that the preview image in the dialog box now shows the frame that you just set as a poster (see figure 4.19), whereas earlier it showed the first frame of the movie (see figure 4.17).

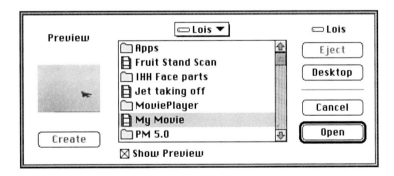

Figure 4.19   *Open dialog box showing new poster for "My Movie"*

7. Click on Open in this dialog box.

   We want the file open so that we can use it for the next section.

Creating a Dynamic Preview

The steps for setting a preview that's composed of a sequence of frames are somewhat different than the steps for setting a poster frame. Create a preview composed of a sequence of frames by following these steps:

1. If it's not already open, open the file "My Movie."

2. Select a portion of the movie that shows both the dinosaur and the jet.

3. Choose Get Info from the Movie menu.

4. From the popup on the right, choose Preview.

    You'll see several buttons (see figure 4.20).

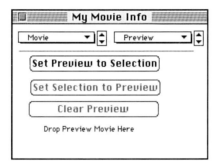

Figure 4.20   *Preview options in Info window*

5. Click on the button "Set Preview to Selection."

6. Close the Info dialog box.

7. Choose Save from the File menu so that the preview is saved.

8. Choose Open from the File menu, locate "My Movie," and click on it.

    Notice this time that you have a dynamic preview, one that you can play; it's not just a poster.

Tip

If you have a Mac using Drag and Drop, you can even define a portion of a completely different movie as a preview. As with previews for some major motion pictures, your preview can be more than just a particular segment from the actual movie; it can be a complete, edited piece of its own.

Other Types of Previews

If, in the Open dialog box of applications that can show QuickTime movies, you click on a QuickTime movie file that has only audio and no video, you will see only a truncated controller in the preview area. Click on the play button if you want to hear the sound before opening the file.

Also, QuickTime applications will even provide a preview for non-QuickTime files in the Open dialog box. If you click on a standard Macintosh sound file, you will see an icon of a speaker and a button that says "Play Sound," which you can click on to hear the sound (see figure 4.21). A standard Macintosh still image file will show a small version of the image (see figure 4.22). A standard Macintosh animation file will show a small version of the first frame of the animation. In Chapter 7, we'll talk about how and why you'd convert files such as these to QuickTime movies.

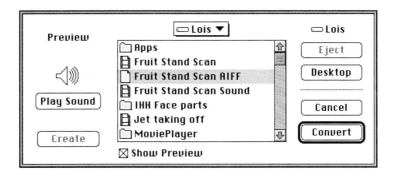

Figure 4.21   *Previewing a non-QuickTime audio file*

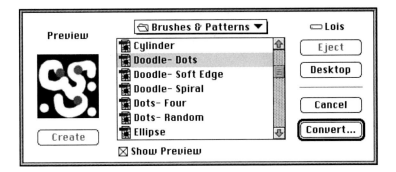

Figure 4.22   *Previewing a still image*

Note

If a file has no defined preview of any type, but does have a custom icon, that icon will show in the preview area in the Open file dialog box.

Track Editing

Earlier in this chapter we pasted portions of one clip into another, just as you might paste text from one word processing document into another. However, QuickTime movies are more sophisticated than word processing documents in that they may have multiple types of data that are, in a sense, layered. We return here to the concept of *tracks*—the idea that QuickTime plays multiple types of data synchronously. As you saw in Chapter 2, a QuickTime movie can have multiple video and audio tracks, as well as other types of tracks, such as text and music tracks.

Putting Tracks Together

In Chapter 2, we showed you different single track movies: a video movie, a sound movie, a text movie, and a music movie. We also showed you a movie that contained one of each type of track. Now we'll show you how you can combine data from different movies to create a new multiple-track movie of your own.

Adding a Second Video Track

We'll start by taking one clip and adding an extra video track to it.

1. Open and play both "Hypnotic Lips" and "Eye" (they're in the Chapter 4 folder in the Media folder).

   What we're going to do here is add a blinking eye at the point where the lips say the word "heavier."

2. Select the portion of the "Eye" movie where the eyelid goes down, which is located slightly before the middle of the clip (see figure 4.23).

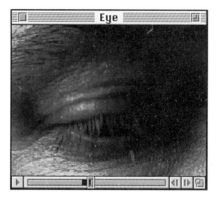

Figure 4.23   *Selection of "Eye" clip that contains eye closing*

3. Choose Copy from the Edit menu.

4. Click over to the "Hypnotic Lips" window, play the movie, and locate and move the slider to the point (close to the beginning) where you hear the word "heavier" (see figure 4.24).

5. Holding down the option key, pull down the Edit menu and choose Add.

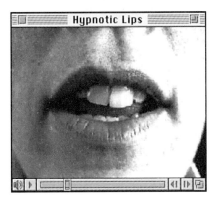

Figure 4.24   *Slider at point in "Hypnotic Lips" where she says the word "heavier"*

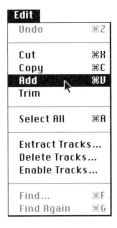

Figure 4.25   *Choosing Add from the Edit menu*

You may have noticed that Add replaces Paste in the Edit menu when you hold the option key down.

6. To see the difference between Add and Paste, move the slider to the beginning of the clip and then play it.

The eye blinks *at the same time as* the voice says "heavier." The Eye video hides the Hypnotic Lips video for the few seconds that it plays.

Tip

When you hold down the Option key while pulling down the Edit menu, Trim replaces Clear in the Edit menu. Trim will cut away everything but the selection.

7. Save the file to your hard drive as "Hypnotic Lips with Eye" (you can save "normally").

When you use Add rather than Paste, the result is the addition of a video track.

Earlier in this chapter, you pasted from one movie into another. However, when you did that, you pasted data *after* the data that was already there. The result can be represented like this:

From Clip 1	From Clip 2	**VIDEO TRACK 1**
From Clip 1	From Clip 2	**SOUND TRACK 1**

What we just did with the "Hypnotic Lips" and "Eye" clips can be represented like this:

From Clip 1	**VIDEO TRACK 1**
From Clip 1	**SOUND TRACK 1**
From Clip 2	**VIDEO TRACK 2**

Tip

When you hold down the Shift key when pulling down the Edit menu and if you have something on the clipboard from a previous copy and something selected in the current movie, you'll see Replace rather than Paste or Add. This option will replace the selection with what's on the clipboard, making the movie smaller or larger, depending on whether what's on the clipboard is smaller or larger than what's in the selection. Replace, like Add, actually adds extra tracks to the movie.

Adding a Music Track

Let's continue adding more tracks to this movie.

1. Open the music track movie "Reggae Groove Sample."

2. Select and copy the entire movie (an easy way to do this is to choose Select All from the Edit menu and then choose Copy).

3. Now click on the movie "Hypnotic Lips with Eye" again and move the slider to the beginning of the movie.

4. Hold down the Option key, pull down the Edit menu, and choose Add.

   You have just added another track to the movie.

5. Play the movie.

   Notice that you can hear both the music track and the voice from the pre-existing sound track. Also notice that the music is longer than the video, so nothing but white shows at the end.

6. Select the portion at the end that contains only music, and choose Clear from the Edit menu.

Tip

Rather than choosing Clear from the Edit menu, you can press the Delete key on the keyboard.

You can think of the movie so far as follows:

From Clip 1	**VIDEO TRACK 1**
From Clip 1	**SOUND TRACK 1**
From Clip 2	**VIDEO TRACK 2**
From Clip 3	**MUSIC TRACK 1**

Adding a Text Track

What's missing? Well, we haven't yet added a text track. If you had a text track movie with the desired text, you could add it to the movie, just as you added music. However, you usually don't already have such a movie. Fortunately, with QuickTime, you can get data into a movie by copying and pasting from other applications.

1. Launch SimpleText (in the "Utils" folder), or your own word processor.

2. Type "Your eyelids are getting heavier," and then select and copy those words.

3. Click on the movie window "Hypnotic Lips with Eye" to make it active.

4. Move the slider to the beginning of the movie.

5. Hold down the Option key and choose Add from the Edit menu.

   Your movie will have a white bar added below the video (see figure 4.26). Text was added but only in the area of the selection. Your cursor is now at the end of the selection, so you don't see the text.

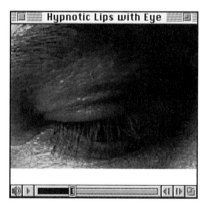

Figure 4.26   *Movie window after adding text*

6. Move the slider to the beginning of the movie, where you will see your text (as in figure 4.27) and then play it.

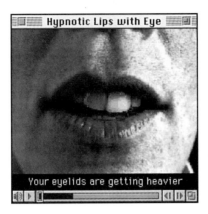

Figure 4.27   *Movie with text added*

The text is displayed for two seconds along the bottom of the movie image.

The movie can now be represented like this:

From Clip 1	**VIDEO TRACK 1**
From Clip 1	**SOUND TRACK 1**
From Clip 2	**VIDEO TRACK 2**
From Clip 3	**MUSIC TRACK 1**
From Clip 4	**TEXT TRACK 1**

The text style, size, font, and color of the text you copy from most text editors and word processors will be maintained when you paste the text into a movie. Though only one style, size, font, and color can be used on each movie.

Unfortunately, you have no control over the location or background color of the text you add when you use MoviePlayer. If you don't like the default location (bottom of window) or background color (black), you'll want to use VideoShop's title track (we'll take a look in the next chapter).

You can copy a graphic from a graphics program and add it to a movie in the same way that you copy and add text from a text processor. Graphics are stored in an additional video track.

To alter the amount of time that text or graphics appear, select a portion of the clip into which you're adding material, and then hold down both the Shift key and the Option key when pulling down the Edit menu. You'll see Add Scaled, rather than just Add, which, when chosen, will result in the text or graphic being put into the movie for the length of the selection. You can use the same technique for time-based data (video or audio), and that data will be squeezed or stretched to fit into the duration of the selection. This technique can be used to produce a fast- or slow-motion effect.

Now close all of the files that are open in MoviePlayer. Make sure that you save any files that you want to use again.

Motion video usually requires a great deal of disk space, as does sound. On the other hand, text, music, and still image graphics are relatively small. A QuickTime movie with just text, music, and graphics can easily be distributed on floppy disk, even if it's several minutes long. Not a bad way to provide a small and simple, but dynamic, presentation!

Text Replace

Text Replace is a choice in the right popup menu when you have chosen a text track in the left popup menu of the Info window. It currently provides the only way to change the text in your text track. This is one of the features in MoviePlayer that you can use only if you have Macintosh Drag and Drop. You'll also need a Drag and Drop-aware text or word processor. SimpleText fits the bill.

To use Text Replace, select a portion of the movie that has the text you want to replace, and drag the replacement text from the text processor to the area of the Info window that reads "Drop Text Here" (see figure 4.28). When you drop the text, it will replace what was selected.

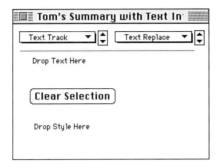

Figure 4.28   *Text Replace Options and Info window*

If you drag to the area that reads "Drop Style Here," the text style of the entire text track changes to match the style, font, and size of the text you dragged. Any one text track can have only one text style.

Burnt Text

In QuickTime 2.0, a text track can be turned into graphic data, or "burnt." Doing so results in a smoother playing movie, as well as one that doesn't require the font to be installed (which is helpful if you've used a specialized font). The text is still searchable, however. Presently, burnt text can be created by using a developer tool called Text Movie Converter, which can be found on the CD that comes with this book.

Pulling Tracks Apart

The exercise that you just completed was artificially easy because we provided single-track movies for you to practice copying techniques with. However, sometimes you want to copy a track from a movie that has multiple tracks. To do this, you will need to pull the movie apart into its separate tracks.

Extracting Tracks

What you may want to do is *extract* a track—to pull a single track out of a movie. Extracting a track leaves the original movie file intact and produces a new file. Let's say we want the surf sound from the file "Sunset" for use in another movie.

1. Open the file "Sunset," which is in the Chapter 4 folder (within the Media folder) on the CD.

2. Go to the Edit menu and choose Extract Tracks.

   You are given a list of all of the tracks in the movie (see figure 4.29).

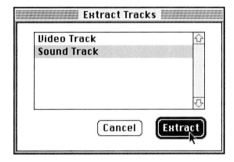

Figure 4.29   *List of tracks to extract*

3. Click on the Sound Track.

4. Click on Extract.

   This results in a sound-only movie in a new untitled window.

If you want to save a file created by extraction, you probably should save it as a self-contained movie; otherwise, it will still depend on the original file.

Tip

If the movie has multiple tracks, you can select more than one track, and they will be extracted into a single new movie file.

Deleting Tracks

Sometimes you may want to simply remove a track from a movie. The process of deleting tracks is similar to extracting tracks, but it removes the track from the movie file and doesn't create a new file. Let's delete the video from a movie:

1. Click back on the "Sunset" window.

2. Go to the Edit menu and chose Delete Tracks (see figure 4.30).

Figure 4.30   *Choosing Delete Tracks from the Edit menu*

Again you are given a list of all of the tracks in the movie.

3. Click on the Video Track.

4. Click on Delete (see figure 4.31).

Figure 4.31   *List of tracks to delete*

Now you have another sound-only movie.

Tip

If the movie has multiple tracks, you can select more than one, and all selected tracks will be deleted.

Again, if you wanted to save this sound-only movie, you should save it as a self-contained movie. Otherwise, the file will still contain all of that video data and will be much larger than it needs to be.

Enabling and Disabling Tracks

You can turn different tracks on or off. This gives you the ability, for example, to switch between two different audio tracks. Unlike adding, extracting, or deleting a track, enabling and disabling tracks is a temporary action. A disabled track can always be enabled, and vice-versa.

Warning!

While QuickTime movies can theoretically have any number of tracks, you should know that memory use and playback performance is impacted by each additional track. However, if a track is disabled it has virtually no impact.

There are a number of reasons for turning a track on or off. In the following example, we'll turn off the text track of a movie. By turning off the text track, you can still search for text (as described in the previous chapter), but the text doesn't have to appear in the movie window.

1. Open the movie "Groovin' Sunset."

   This movie has four separate tracks: video, sound, music, and text.

2. In the Edit menu, choose Enable Tracks (see figure 4.32).

Figure 4.32   *Choosing Enable Tracks from Edit menu*

A dialog box will appear with all tracks listed. On the left side of each is an "On" icon (see figure 4.33).

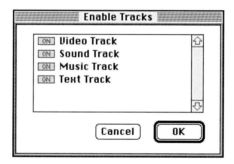

Figure 4.33   *Enable Tracks dialog box*

3. Click once on the Text Track line.

The icon should now be an "Off" icon (see figure 4.34).

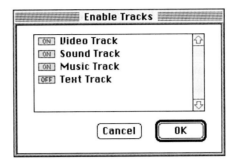

Figure 4.34   *Enable Tracks dialog box with Text Track turned off*

   4. Click on OK.

   Notice that the text track in the movie has disappeared.

The movie can be saved this way, and when subsequently opened, it will appear not to have a text track. Of course, the track still exists and can always be enabled later.

Naturally, you can disable or enable any track in a QuickTime movie.

Note

Macromedia's Sound Edit 16 provides the capability to add, delete, enable, and disable sound tracks in a QuickTime movie.

Alternate Tracks

A QuickTime movie can have a set of tracks; within a set, the tracks can be alternates for one another. The most common use of this function is for multilingual situations. For example, you may want to provide both an English and a German version of a text track and/or a sound track. Anyone who opens the movie with MoviePlayer can use the Choose Language command in the Movie menu to show a dialog box that enables him to choose a language (see figure 4.35).

Figure 4.35   *Choose Movie Language dialog box*

Also, when the movie is first opened, it will automatically enable the track that matches the current system language and disable any other tracks that have been designated as alternates for that track. For example, if you are running the French version of the Macintosh operating system, and one track in a set of tracks has been designated as a French track, the French track will be enabled when the movie is first opened.

Note

HyperCard, SuperCard, and Director developers should know that the QTMovie XCMD (see Chapter 3) has functions for track control, such as the ability to enable and disable tracks, set the language and alternates for a track, and search in a text track. Another XCMD, QTEdit, provides additions for cutting, copying, pasting, and extracting tracks, as well as setting posters and dynamic previews—in short, just about anything we've discussed in this chapter.

So how do you designate tracks as belonging in an alternate group? And how do you designate a particular language for a track? We'll show you now.

1. Open the movie "Liberty with Text."

    This is a movie with three tracks, one video track and two text tracks. Text Track 1 contains text in English, and Text Track 2 contains a German translation.

Credit

The clip "Liberty" is from the Fabulous Footage collection (see its folder on the CD).

2. Choose Get Info from the Movie menu.

3. Hold down the left popup menu in the Info window.

   You'll see for yourself that the movie has one video track and two text tracks (see figure 4.36). If you'd like, you can practice the track enabling and disabling skills that you learned in the previous section to prove to yourself that the text tracks really do contain what we say they do.

Figure 4.36   *Popup menu in Info window showing the tracks in the movie*

4. Choose Text Track 1 from the left popup.

5. Choose Alternate from the right popup, if it's not already listed.

   The window should now look like the one in figure 4.37.

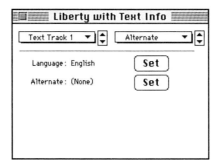

Figure 4.37   *Info window showing Alternate track settings*

6. Click on the top Set button.

A dialog box appears in which multiple languages are listed (see figure 4.38).

Figure 4.38   Picking a language for a track

7. English is probably already selected because you are probably running the English version of the Macintosh operating system. If not, click on English to select it. Then click OK to close this dialog box.

Now we'll designate an alternate for this track.

8. Click the bottom Set button.

A different dialog box appears in which all the tracks of the movie are listed (see figure 4.39).

Figure 4.39   Picking an alternate track

9. Choose Text Track 2 and click on OK to close the dialog box.

10. Next, choose Text Track 2 from the left popup in the Info window.

    Notice that Text Track 1 is already listed as the alternate to this track.

11. Set the language of this track to German, using the top Set button (see steps 6 and 7).

12. To test what you've done, use the Choose Language command that's in the Movie menu, select German, click OK, and play the movie.

    The German text should show.

13. Switch to English, again using the Choose Language menu item in the Movie menu.

If you were to open this movie on a Macintosh running the German system, you would first see the German track, regardless of which track was last visible. On an English system, you'd first see the English track.

___

Tip

You can set multiple alternates for a track, even though you'll only see one listed in the Get Info dialog box. This limitation will probably be fixed in the next version of MoviePlayer, but for now you'll have to live with not being able to see all the alternates you've set for a track.

Musical Instrument Changing

With QuickTime music tracks, you have a special type of editing ability—you can actually change the way the music sounds by changing the instruments that are played. Remember that the information stored in a music track is a series of commands telling the Mac (or whatever synthesizer is connected to the Mac) what notes to play. Also stored is information about which instrument should play each particular sequence of notes. It's quite simple to change instruments.

1. Open the file "Reggae Groove Sample."

2. From the Movie menu choose Get Info.

3. Click and hold on the left popup and choose the Music Track.

4. Now that the Music Track is selected, click and hold on the popup on the right and choose Instruments.

Notice that the information in the bottom of the window now shows a list. The items in this list are the General MIDI instruments that are currently used in this movie (see figure 4.40).

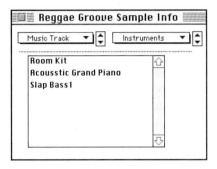

Figure 4.40   *Picking an Instrument from the list*

Memory Note

More instruments in a movie mean that more memory and computer power are required to play them back.

---

5. Now double-click on the on the third instrument in the list, Slap Bass 1.

   This brings up the *Standard Instrument Picker* dialog box, which you'll also see in other applications (see figure 4.41).

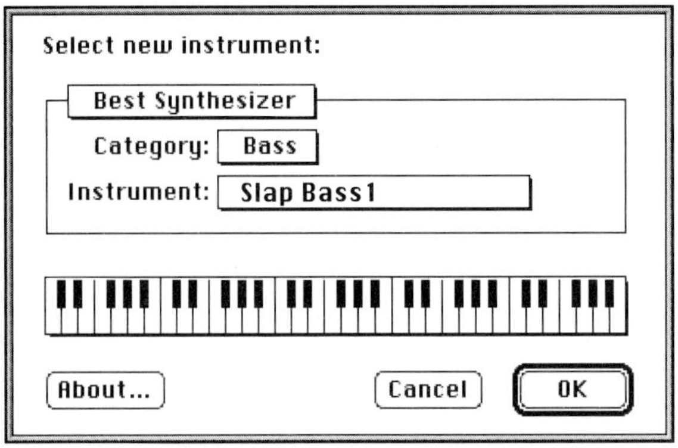

Figure 4.41   *Standard Instrument Picker dialog box*

The popup menu closest to the top is used for choosing the synthesizer. In almost all situations, you should leave this set to Best Synthesizer, which causes QuickTime to choose the best synthesizer for playing back the musical notes. Currently, the best synthesizer is always the *only* synthesizer—the Mac itself, using the sound samples stored in the QuickTime Musical Instruments extension, which you installed in Chapter 1. On the CD, we include Apple software (Music Configuration) that, in the case of an external synthesizer being connected, will cause QuickTime to automatically use the external synthesizer when Best Synthesizer is chosen.

Below are two more popups. The first is the *category*; these are the families of instruments. The category chosen has a direct effect on the next popup, labeled *Instrument*. With the instrument popup, you actually choose the instrument that will be played by the musical notes stored in the movie file.

Notice also that there is a piano-like keyboard at the bottom of the screen. You can sample the instrument that is selected by clicking on the piano keys.

1. Now choose the category "Percussive," which is near the bottom of the list.
2. Pick the instrument "Steel Drums."

   You have switched an electric bass for steel drums.

Note

The instruments that are in italics in the Instrument popup menu are the ones that are NOT included in the QuickTime Musical Instruments extension. If you choose one of these instruments, QuickTime will substitute an instrument that is near it in the list. If QuickTime uses an external synthesizer, it may not have to do such a substitution, because it does not have to rely on what's in the QuickTime Musical Instruments extension.

3. Click on OK and then play the movie, listening for the change in the way it sounds.

Custom Color Tables

In Chapter 1, we pointed out that QuickTime movies don't always look their best because the Macintosh they're playing on may show only 256 colors, and the 256 colors that a Mac normally uses are probably not the right colors for any particular movie. The Mac's standard system colors, for example, don't have many flesh tones. Fortunately, with QuickTime 2.0, you can designate a custom color table for a movie so that when it plays, the Macintosh on which it is playing switches to a better set of 256 colors. A movie with a custom color table still doesn't look as good as it would if more colors were available, but it looks better than it would if using the standard system colors.

Two of the movies that you've been using in this book, "Fruit Stand Scan" and "Sunset," have custom color tables. If you are using a Macintosh that shows only 256 colors, you may have noticed the strange color flashing when they are opened and closed. This occurs as the Mac is switching from one color table to another. You can see the custom color table in the Info window (see figure 4.42).

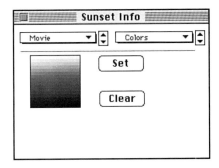

Figure 4.42   *Info window showing Colors option*

To define a custom color table for your own movie, you need software that can analyze your movie and figure out which 256 colors to use. On the CD that comes with this book are two unsupported applications, MakeMovieColorTable and ConvertToMovie, either of which will build a custom color table for a movie. Debabelizer is a commercial product that can create a custom color table for a movie. It can also analyze a group of movies and pick the 256 colors that will work best for the whole set.

Sometimes you may have an existing custom color table that you want attached to your movie. To do this, you'll use the Colors option in the Info window (see figure 4.42). You click Set and locate the file that has the custom color table. The file must have a clut resource.

More Info

Throughout this chapter, and particularly in the section on manipulating tracks, we've had you access MoviePlayer's Info window. This window is where you can really see all that QuickTime is capable of doing; it is where MoviePlayer exhibits QuickTime capabilities that no other currently available application has.

However, we've only shown you a few of the many things you set or check in this window. Here you can get information and set options on the entire movie or on any track in the movie. For each of these, there are now between five and seven options. The number of options is likely to grow, too. More than half of the options are provided by plug-in files, "Authoring Extras" and "Goodies," that reside in the same folder as MoviePlayer. QuickTime developers will probably write additional plug-ins to provide even greater access to QuickTime's capabilities.

Table 4.1 lists which options are available for a movie and each track type. Following the table we briefly describe what each option shows or does.

Table 4.1   Summary of Options in MoviePlayer's Info Window

	Movie Track	Video Track	Sound Track	Text Track	Music Track	Timecode Track
Files	✓	✓	✓	✓	✓	✓
Size	✓	✓	✓	✓	✓	✓
Time	✓					
General	✓	✓	✓	✓	✓	✓
Color	✓					
Copyright	✓					
Preview	✓					
Alternate		✓	✓	✓	✓	✓
Format		✓	✓			
Preload		✓	✓	✓	✓	✓
Volume			✓		✓	
Instruments					✓	
Frame Rate		✓				
Text Replace				✓		

- **Alternate**—Enables you to pick a set of tracks which will be alternates for each other and assign languages to these tracks (we explored this topic in the section on Alternate Tracks in this chapter).

- **Color**—Used for setting custom color tables. Only applicable to the whole movie, not individual tracks.

- **Copyright**—Used for adding the information that appears in the copyright dialog box, which is shown when you choose Show Copyright from the Movie menu. The only way to add copyright information, however, is using Drag and Drop.

- **Files**—Shows the file(s) upon which the movie or specific tracks depend (we explored this topic in the section on File Dependencies in this chapter).

- **Format**—Has various information about the format of the data in individual tracks. For example, for video tracks, it shows the compressor used to compress the movie, the width and height of the movie frame, and the number of colors that the movie can show (we'll explain what all the information here means in later chapters).

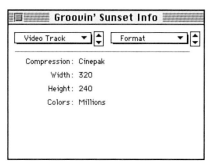

- **Frame Rate**—Shows the frame rate that is actually being played (as compared to the actual number of frames per second that are in the movie). You'll only see a number here if the movie is currently playing.

- **General**—For the entire movie, tells the number of tracks in the movie, how much data is being used by the movie and its data rate (we'll discuss data rate in Chapter 8).

  For individual tracks, it also tells where in the movie this track starts and how long it lasts. It also tells the track type, how much data is being used by that track, and its data rate.

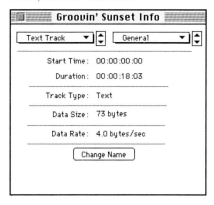

At the bottom is a button that enables you to give the track a name, so that when you pull down the left popup in the Info Window, you might see "French text track," for example, rather than the more generic "Text Track 1."

- **Instruments**—Enables you to change the instruments of a music track (we discussed this topic in the section on Changing Musical Instruments in this chapter).

- **Preload**—If you check the Preload checkbox, it loads the entire track into RAM when the movie is opened. This is good for tracks such as music and text, which are usually small enough to fit into RAM, allowing for better playback, and, in the case of text tracks, fast text searching. If you check the Cache hint checkbox, QuickTime will keep movie data in RAM after it has played it. This works well only for very small movies that you have set to Loop. In most cases, it will degrade playback performance. Use both of these options with care because they may cause your system to crash.

- **Preview**—Used for setting a dynamic preview that appears in the Open file dialog box (we discussed this topic in the section on Previews in this chapter).

- **Size**—Shows actual visual dimensions of the movie and each track. If you have resized the movie, it also shows the current dimensions.

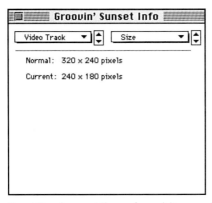

- **Text Replace**—Allows for adding and changing of text tracks.
- **Time**—Shows current time of the movie (i.e., where the slider is located), length of the movie, and time the selection has started and ended, if any. This information is only available for the entire movie.

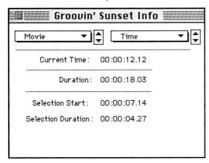

- **Volume**—Enables you to set the default volume for audio (both sound and music) tracks. For stereo tracks, you can also set balance here.

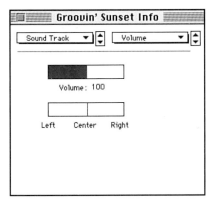

Well, that's a lot of editing functionality for one little program, isn't it?

Now go on to the next chapter, where you'll learn about editors that let you add various special effects to your movies.

Chapter 5

Power Editing—
Special Effects
and More

*N*ow you will see what you can do with editing tools that
are more sophisticated than those
provided by MoviePlayer. These sophisticated tools enable you to do the
"fancy stuff" that you see on TV and in
the movies. Indeed, TV and movie
producers use some of these very tools
for prototyping their work and sometimes even for final production.

Because this book is only a few hundred pages long, we can't go into too much detail on the specifics of all of the editing applications, but we do want to let you know something about what's available. In this chapter, we provide an overview of the effects you can achieve, followed by descriptions of specific products. We also walk you through a number of hands-on exercises.

Though this market is rapidly changing, it is currently roughly divided into two categories: first, there is QuickTime editing software, such as Adobe's Premiere and Avid's VideoShop (included on the QuickTime Guide CD); and second, there is software for creating special effects, such as VideoFusion/Radius Inc.'s VideoFusion and CoSA's After Effects.

However, you can use the special effects software to do some editing, and you can use the editing software to do plenty of special effects. So, in discussing what you can do, we won't differentiate between these two categories. We'll refer to them all as editing software or special effects editors.

The Effects

The special effects that are possible with these tools are a major part of what makes them so desirable. After all, simple editing can be done with less expensive tools, such as MoviePlayer. (However, we provide two of these tools—QuickFLIX! and VideoShop—with this book, so for you they're no more expensive than MoviePlayer.)

We'll start by going over the different types of effects that are possible with these tools.

It's actually not a bad idea to try a little exercise before continuing in this chapter. Go watch TV (but not for too long!). Notice the transitions, special effects, text on the screen, and anything else that doesn't seem like just straight camera shooting. As you read through this chapter, try to imagine how you'd use the features that we describe to achieve similar effects.

Transitions

In the video world, people talk of straight-cut edits versus transitional edits. The copying and pasting you did using the Standard Controller in MoviePlayer gives you straight cuts: one clip ends and another begins. Transitional edits are those in which one clip begins before the other ends, with some kind of visual effect happening during the overlap. Almost any transition you see on TV can be done by at least one of the QuickTime editing applications. A typical visual effect is a dissolve, but there are many others possible, including some which are considered somewhat tacky, such as venetian blinds and page turns. Take a look at figures 5.1 and 5.2 to see a couple of examples of transitions.

Figure 5.1   *Dissolve or fade transition*

Figure 5.2   *Iris transition*

Even the effect where one movie melts and merges into another, called *morphing*, can be accomplished with some of these editing products.

Editing Individual Frames

You can paint on individual frames of a movie; in traditional film production, this is called rotoscoping. You usually don't do rotoscoping using QuickTime editing software. Rather, you use high-end painting applications, such as Fractal Design Painter or Adobe Photoshop (see figure 5.3).

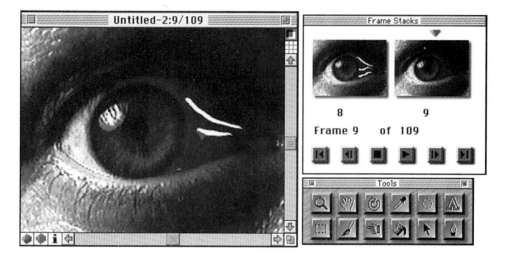

Figure 5.3   *Using Fractal Design Painter for rotoscoping*

Fractal Design Painter enables you to open a QuickTime movie and convert it to a Fractal movie. After it's a Fractal movie, you can step through individual frames, painting on each (see figure).

If you want to use Adobe Photoshop for rotoscoping, you first use a QuickTime editor to export a movie in a special format called a filmstrip, which Photoshop can then open so that you can paint on individual frames. With a special plug-in, available with VideoShop, you can use Photoshop's Acquire command to directly import a QuickTime movie without going through the intermediary filmstrip format.

Any application you use for rotoscoping will let you save the painted-on movie as a normal QuickTime movie.

Filters

Filters are used to alter an image. Graphic artists apply filters to still images using programs such as Adobe Photoshop. The same filters can be used by movie making artists on their QuickTime productions.

A filter can be applied so that it affects each frame in a similar way. Or a filter can be applied with different options at the beginning and ending frames; the editing software interpolates the effect of the filter on the frames in between the beginning and end, resulting in an edit in which the filter changes over time.

Most QuickTime editing packages support plug-in filters developed for Adobe Photoshop, but they also have their own filters. Many of these filters are specifically designed to work over time.

Some filters change color aspects of a clip, such as shifting the hue, inverting colors, or increasing color saturation. Others add artistic or texturing effects, such as pixellating, pointillizing, posterizing, or embossing the image (see figures 5.4 and 5.5). Still others come from a technological bent—they make the movie appear as if you were viewing it through some kind of camera lens—warping it, spherizing it, blurring it, flipping it, or changing its brightness and contrast. Premiere even has filters that add video noise and simulate the viewfinder of a camcorder!

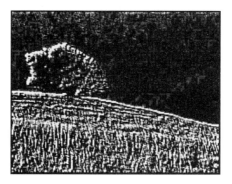

Figure 5.4   *Clip with emboss filter applied*

Figure 5.5   *Clip with wave filter applied*

Compositing

You can also create a movie that is composed of several movies playing on the screen at the same time. You can put movies side by side, or you can put one movie in front of the other to get a "movie-in-a-movie" effect (see figure 5.6).

Figure 5.6   *Movie-in-a-movie effect*

Another compositing effect is to have one movie play within selected segments of another. Tools to do such things as alpha channeling and chroma keying give you the ability to have one movie play through another by defining certain parts of the top movie as transparent (see figure 5.7).

Figure 5.7   *Two clips composited using transparency*

Note

A transition is a special case of compositing because during the time of the transition, both movies are on the screen together. For example, in Adobe Premiere, certain transitions are used to create a movie-in-a-movie effect.

Motion

While movies typically play as if on a flat, two-dimensional plane, filling the entire movie window, several of these applications let you move your movies on the screen. That is, you can have a movie fly into place, rotate as it plays, zigzag across the screen, or zoom in or out (see figure 5.8). There are a great many possibilities.

Figure 5.8   *Clip with motion settings*

Often these applications come with predefined motion paths and settings that you can adapt for your productions, rather than having to define each motion from scratch.

Cropping and Resizing

Often, digitized video contains "noise" around edges, particularly at the bottom of the frame. Or, sometimes the most interesting part of a movie is in the center of the frame, or at the right, left, top, or bottom. In any of these cases, you may want to crop the clip, leaving only the portion of the frame that's "good." Most editing software provides this capability.

A resize option in editing software enables you to make your final movie's frame size smaller or larger than the frame sizes of the movies of which it's composed. If you enlarge the movie, however, you will have degraded image quality because the information is stretched out.

Titling

When you create your own movies, you will often want to add some text, whether to point things out or to add a title or credits (see figure 5.9). Some editing packages have this ability built in. Some will even enable you to animate titles.

Figure 5.9   *Clip with a title*

Adding a title in these packages is different from adding a text track in MoviePlayer. The text in the title typically does not become a separate, searchable QuickTime text track, but is converted into graphic data and becomes part of the video track. VideoShop provides an exception to this rule—it gives you to the option of saving a title as a true QuickTime track (see tip later in this chapter).

Audio Control

These more sophisticated packages give you more extensive control over the audio than the simple editors, such as MoviePlayer. They give you a visual time-based representation of the audio track, making it easy to move or delete portions of the audio.

Like MoviePlayer, they also let you bring in audio from elsewhere. You can import many different types of sound files that have been recorded or created with other Macintosh applications.

These editing packages also give you multiple tracks for audio so that you can view, for example, both music and voice simultaneously.

Just So You Know

While all editors let you import sound files, only some editors let you import a QuickTime music file. The current version of Premiere won't. The current version of VideoShop (3.0) will.

You'll find that you have control over the audio level, enabling you to fade audio in or out. A common use of an audio fade is when there's music playing in one track that needs to be lowered so that someone's voice can be heard in another track.

Some editing packages also have filters for audio. They provide some of the same effects that audio editing packages, such as Macromedia's SoundEdit, do. For example, you can add an echo or make the sound play backwards to look for that Satanic message. QuickTime editing applications that don't provide ways to edit audio often let you export a QuickTime audio track. This enables you to edit the audio with a sound editing package and then re-import the altered sound track.

Note

Macromedia's SoundEdit 16 is an audio editing package that has the ability to directly edit QuickTime movie sound tracks. If you really want extensive control over the sound in a movie, you're better off editing your sound tracks in SoundEdit 16 and saving the special effects editors for working on your video tracks.

Time Scaling

Because part of what QuickTime does is define time inside the computer, you can change the definition of time within a movie. That is, with editing packages, you have the ability to have a clip play in different amounts of time.

You can change the length of a QuickTime segment to almost any time you want. Let's say that you have a QuickTime movie that's ten seconds long. You can speed it up by having the ten seconds-worth of movie play in less than ten seconds. Or, you can specify that you want it to play for longer than ten seconds, which will slow the movie down.

People often speed up movies when they want to show a long process happening more quickly than it ordinarily would. A sunrise or sunset is a good example of a process that is often edited to seem faster. On the other hand, people slow down movies when they want viewers to be able to view a motion that happens very quickly, as in a slow-motion version of some action in a sporting event.

The Tools

We now look at some specific pieces of software. We'll give you an overview of all and then describe specifics of each.

Overview

The major editing tools with special effects abilities that are currently on the market are listed here for you:

- After Effects (Aldus/Adobe)
- VideoFusion (VideoFusion/Radius)

- Premiere (Adobe)—Tryout version on the CD!
- VideoShop (Avid)—Full version on the CD!
- QuickFLIX! (VideoFusion/Radius)—Full version on the CD!

Aldus After Effects is priced substantially above the others (around $2,000) and is currently the most powerful special effects and compositing tool around. VideoFusion is priced under $500 and is also a very powerful special effects editor. Adobe Premiere and VideoShop are excellent editors with many special effects functions; some people swear by one, some by the other, but VideoShop is the less expensive of the two. QuickFLIX! is an introductory editing tool that's easy to use and provides most of the commonly used special effects functions; it's essentially a reduced-features version of VideoFusion.

Note

These applications are constantly being upgraded, so don't make any purchasing decisions solely on what you read here.

While each of the tools has a different interface, they have a few features in common.

All provide a *timeline view* for editing. In all of the applications but After Effects, the timeline view enables you to spread a movie out over time, seeing a frame next to a frame, as with a filmstrip. Compare these tools to simple editors, such as MoviePlayer, which have just one window; they enable you to step through each frame, one at a time, but not to see all of the frames lined up in sequence.

When you have a timeline view, you can specify the scale at which you would like to view your movie as you work. That is, you can set it to show every single frame, one frame for every second, one frame for every ten seconds, and so on.

Many editors also provide a *storyboard view*, where you can lay out the clips you want to use in the order you want them to appear. Unlike a timeline view, each clip uses the same amount of space. Amazingly enough, Premiere does not provide a storyboard view.

All of the tools provide *tracks* where you can place, view, and work on different types of data—video, audio, and titles—separately. Typically, more than one of each track type is provided. For example, Adobe Premiere starts with two video and three audio tracks, but it enables you to add additional tracks, up to 99 of each. Avid VideoShop opens with one track of each type and lets you add as many tracks as you want.

These tracks are for the purpose of editing only and do not usually bear a direct relationship to the QuickTime tracks we've discussed in previous chapters. When you finish editing and tell the software to create a final edited movie, multiple tracks of the same type are usually merged into a single track, so you will end up with a movie with only one video track and one sound track.

Note

Of all of these editing applications, VideoShop is the only one that respects QuickTime tracks—you can actually save a movie so that it maintains multiple tracks as QuickTime tracks. See the section on VideoShop later in this chapter.

All of the editors enable you to import and use various types of files, not just QuickTime movies. For example, you can import sound files and still image files. However, in many cases, only certain formats are supported—AIFF for sound and PICT for still images.

Making a Theater with Theater Maker

Theater Maker is a cool shareware program written by Mark Adams that's included on the QuickTime Guide CD. This application creates a movie that's a compilation of any movie you choose and a picturesque background image, which is called a *frame* (not to be confused with the frames of a QuickTime movie). You have a choice of several elaborate frames, including a movie theater, TV screen, drive-in movie theater, and computer (see figure 5.10).

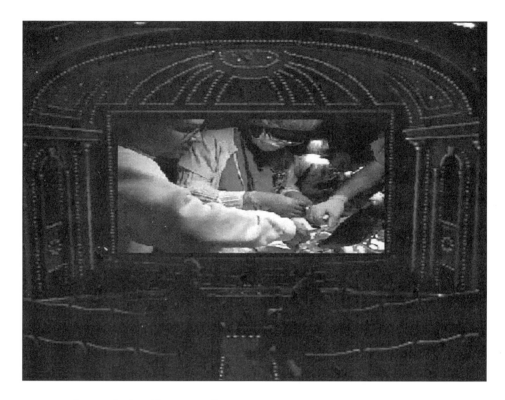

Figure 5.10   *Theater Maker movie*

The movie that Theater Maker creates is a *standalone* file—that is, it will play just by double-clicking on it; you won't need MoviePlayer or any other application to play it.

Save Theater Maker for showing off movies of momentous occasions.

Also, all of these tools provide the basic editing capabilities—cut, copy, and paste—but if that's all you need to do, you might want to stick with MoviePlayer.

Now let's look at the specifics of each tool.

VideoShop

On the disc that comes with this book, we provide you with VideoShop 2.0.3. This is a full, working version of the application, but not the currently shipping one. The version currently shipping is VideoShop 3.0, and you can update for only $79 (see the VideoShop folder on the CD). In this chapter, we'll describe the basics of VideoShop 3.0, which are quite similar to those of 2.0.3.

VideoShop provides a desktop much like your Finder, giving you quick access to your media (see figure 5.11). It saves you from having to use the Open File dialog box to locate files, and you never have to "import" clips—they're always available in windows within VideoShop. You can double-click to open folders within folders, click in the close box to close any window, and generally navigate around as if you were working in the Finder. However, you'll only see files that are useful in a QuickTime production. Also, unlike file icons in the Finder, the icons for QuickTime movies can be animated when clicked, showing a mini-preview of the movie. VideoShop calls these movie icons *Micons*™ and enables you to add them to any movie file using a simple menu command.

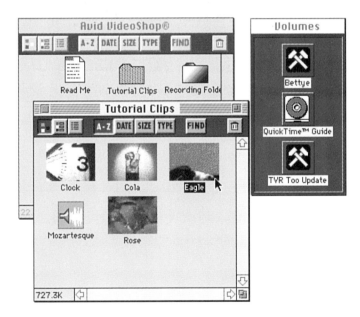

Figure 5.11   *VideoShop desktop windows*

To put together a new QuickTime movie, you drag the icons from the desktop windows to the *Sequencer* window. The Sequencer is where you work on the sequential aspects of your movie, defining which clip goes before what. It can be switched from a storyboard view (see figure 5.12) to a timeline view (see figure 5.13).

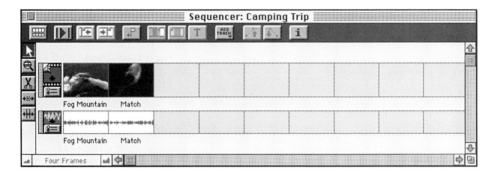

Figure 5.12   *VideoShop Sequencer window in storyboard view*

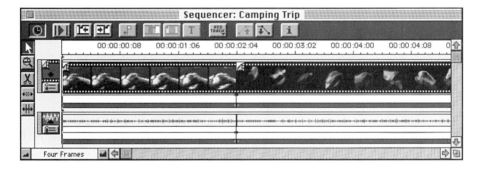

Figure 5.13   *VideoShop Sequencer window in timeline view*

When the clips have been put in the Sequencer window, you can view what you've put together in the *Canvas* window, which is a player where you can play your production using the standard controls (see figure 5.14).

Figure 5.14   *VideoShop Canvas window*

Transitions are applied by first selecting an area in the Sequencer at the junction of two clips and then calling up, via menu or button, the Apply Transition dialog box, which enables you to pick a transition and set options for that transition (see figure 5.15). VideoShop comes with almost 50 different transitions from which you can choose.

Note

Don't be intimidated by the seeming complexity of the dialog boxes we show. Almost all will work with default settings, enabling you to apply effects easily when you're just learning these tools. As you work with them more, you can start experimenting with the various options.

Filters are applied by selecting a portion of a video track and then picking a filter from the Apply Filter dialog box, also selected via menu or button (see figure 5.16). VideoShop comes with almost 40 different filters, and additional plug-in filters can also be used.

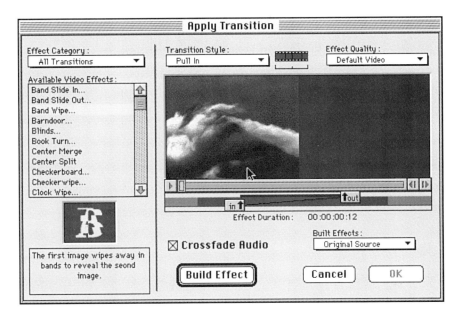

Figure 5.15   *Apply Transition dialog box*

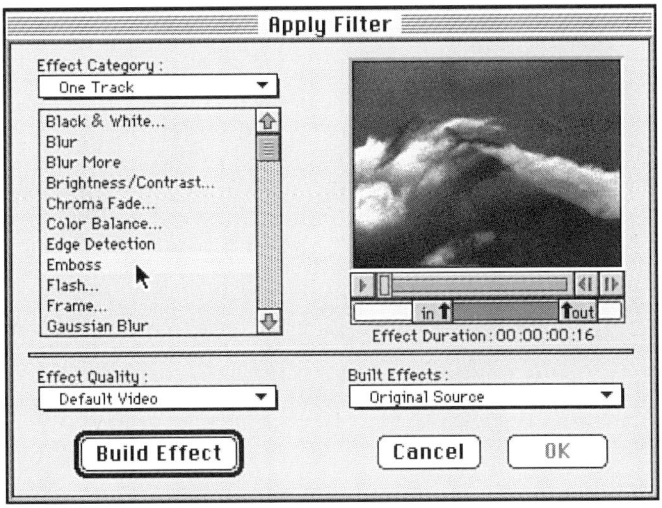

Figure 5.16   *Apply Filter dialog box*

Both filters and transitions can also be applied quickly by choosing them from pull-down menus in the menu bar rather than by using the dialog boxes described here.

To composite movies, clips need to be placed in separate tracks. VideoShop enables you to add additional tracks from a pull-down menu in the Sequencer window (see figures 5.17 and 5.18).

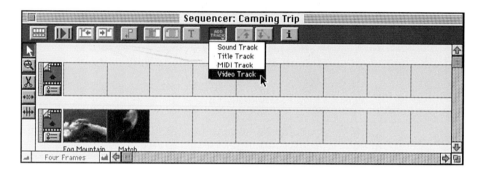

Figure 5.17   *Adding an additional track in VideoShop*

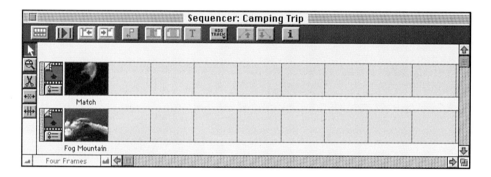

Figure 5.18   *Sequencer window with a second video track*

MIDI

With VideoShop 3.0, there's even a MIDI track for QuickTime music movies. VideoShop is the only editor at this time that can handle QuickTime music movies.

In the Canvas window, clips can easily be resized and positioned in order to set movie-in-a-movie or tiling effects (see figure 5.19).

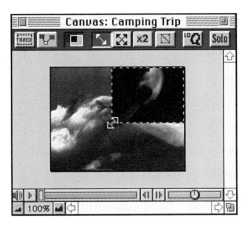

Figure 5.19   *Resizing a clip in the Canvas window to show clip underneath*

Transparency effects are applied to clips by using the Video Transparency dialog box (see figure 5.20) or, to have the degree of transparency change over time, by adjusting rubberbands in the Sequencer time view (see figure 5.21).

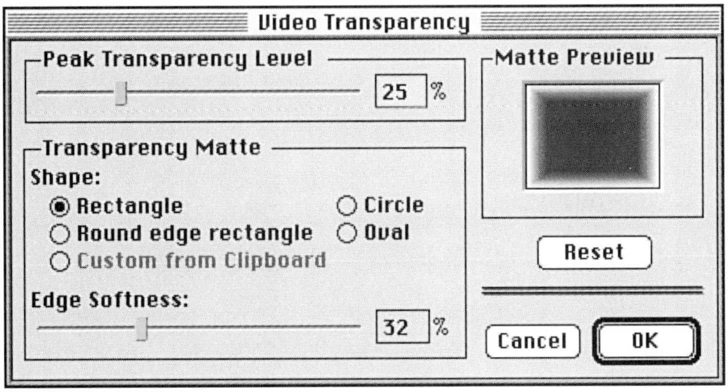

Figure 5.20   *Video Transparency dialog box*

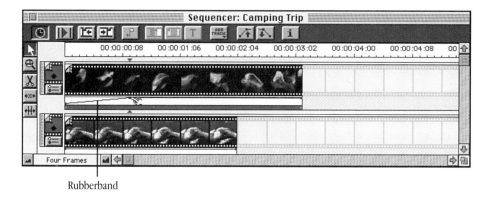

Rubberband

Figure 5.21   *Setting the transparency of a video track using a rubberband*

To have clips move across the screen as they play, you define a path in the Canvas window (see figure 5.22).

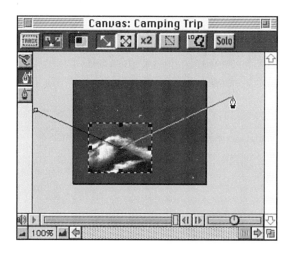

Figure 5.22   *Setting a path for clip movement in the Canvas window*

Titles go in a title track (see figure 5.23). They are entered, positioned, and edited for style, color, and font in the Titling window (see figure 5.24.). You can also have the text scroll on the screen.

Title Track

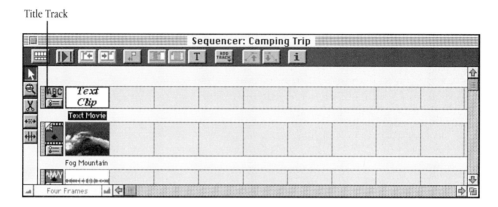

Figure 5.23   *Sequencer window with title track added*

Figure 5.24   *Titling window*

Titles can later be repositioned in the Canvas window. You can even have characteristics of a title change over time by selecting portions of the title clip in the Sequencer and then using the Titling window.

Audio volume can be adjusted—faded in or out—using rubberbands located below each audio track in the Sequencer window (see figure 5.25).

When it comes to saving your production as a QuickTime movie, VideoShop provides many options that other editors don't (see figure 5.26). You can save your movie as a standalone file so that no application is required for playback. You can also save the file so that separate tracks are maintained as QuickTime tracks and not *mixed-down*, which enables later control of the tracks via playing applications, such as MoviePlayer, and authoring tools, such as HyperCard.

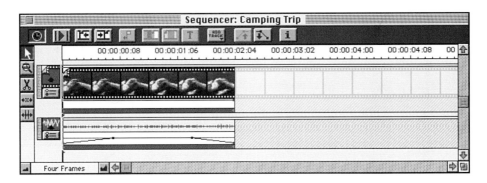

Figure 5.25   *Audio track with fade in and fade out set by rubberbands*

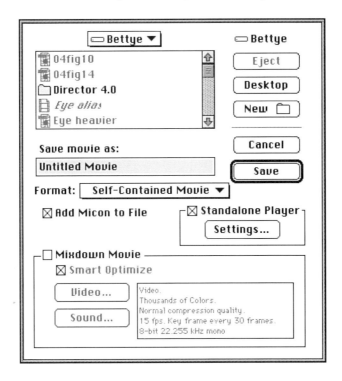

Figure 5.26   *Save as Movie dialog box*

Text Tracks and Foreign Language Tracks

VideoShop enables you to add text tracks to a movie. VideoShop calls these *transcript tracks*. Unlike the title tracks in other applications, these are true QuickTime tracks that can be searched. Unlike MoviePlayer, VideoShop provides extensive control over the way the tracks appear. To create a searchable text track, you add and style a standard VideoShop title track, but then you specify that the track should be a transcript track.

You specify that a track is a transcript track by selecting it and choosing Track Settings in the Sequence menu, which brings up a dialog box where there's a Transcript Track checkbox (see figure 5.27).

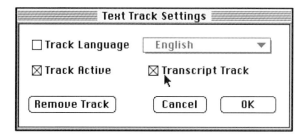

Figure 5.27   *Specifying that a title track is a transcript track*

VideoShop also enables you to assign a language to any audio or text track, which you can also do in MoviePlayer. To specify the language of an audio or text track, you again use the Text Track Settings dialog box.

If you save your movie as a standalone movie file, you won't need any movie playing application to play it. When a user opens your saved standalone file, if it has a transcript track, she'll be able to choose Movie search from the Play menu, where she can type in a word to search for (see figure 5.28). If it has tracks with multiple languages, she'll be able to choose the language by pulling down a menu in the menu bar (see figure 5.29).

continues

Figure 5.28   *Searching for text in a VideoShop standalone movie*

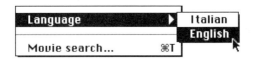

Figure 5.29   *Choosing a language in a VideoShop standalone movie*

Alternatively, the VideoShop file can be saved as a normal QuickTime movie file, which means that any application that enables text track searching or access to multiple language tracks can take advantage of the edits.

Premiere

There's a Tryout version of Premiere 4.0 included on the QuickTime Guide CD. It's almost the same as the real version, but doesn't enable you to save your work; it also puts a red box in any effects you add.

In Premiere, you start with a Project window into which you import, via standard open dialog boxes, the clips and other media you want to use in a production (see figure 5.30).

You then drag clips from the Project window and drop them in the Construction window (see figure 5.31). The Construction window provides a timeline view with multiple tracks. Premiere has no storyboard view.

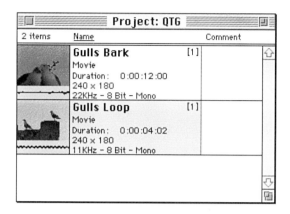

Figure 5.30   *Premiere Project window*

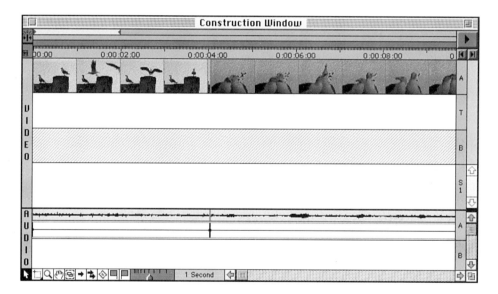

Figure 5.31   *Premiere Construction window*

To create transitions, you put two clips in separate tracks so that they overlap in time. You then drag and drop a transition from the Transitions window to the overlapping area in the transitions track, labeled "T" (see figure 5.32).

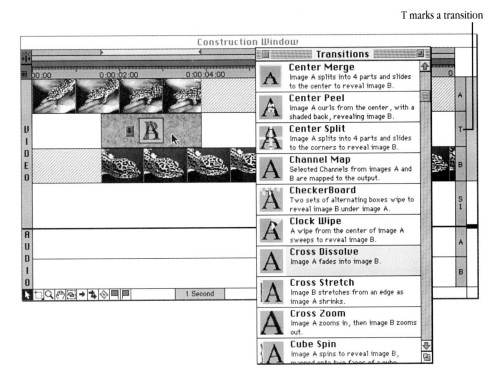

Figure 5.32 *Adding a transition*

Filters are applied by selecting a clip and choosing Filters from the Clip menu. From the resulting Filters dialog box (see figure 5.33), you can choose from among many different filters, most of which, when chosen, provide an additional dialog box for settings adjustments (see figure 5.34).

To set a transparency, you put the clip that you want to be transparent into the SuperImposition track in the Construction window. The SuperImposition track is the one labeled "S1" (see figure 5.32). You set the transparency via a rubberband, as in VideoShop, or, for more control, with the Transparency Settings dialog box, also accessed from the Clip menu (see figure 5.35).

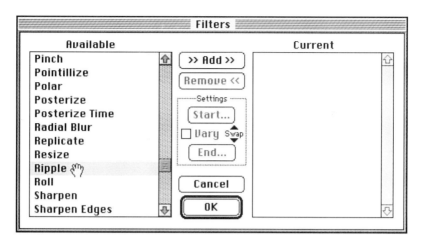

Figure 5.33   *Filters dialog box*

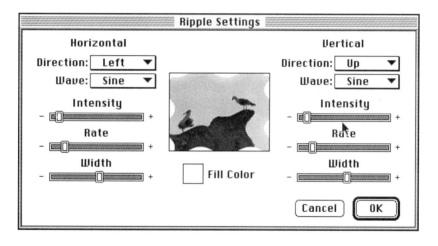

Figure 5.34   *Settings dialog box for a specific filter*

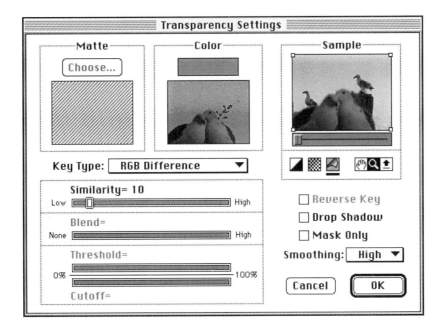

Figure 5.35   *Transparency Settings dialog box*

To show a movie-in-a-movie, you actually use a transition, such as iris square or zoom. Instead of using default settings, which change from showing one clip in its entirety to showing the other in its entirety (see figure 5.36), you alter the transition settings so that the clips have the same spatial relationship to each other at beginning and end (see figure 5.37).

Motion effects are accessed by choosing Motion from the Clip menu, which brings up the Motion dialog box in which you can rotate, zoom, distort, and move clips along a path (see figure 5.38).

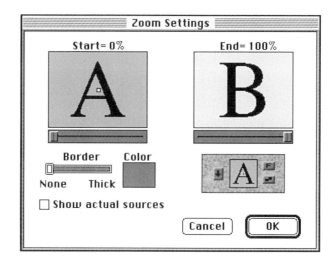

Figure 5.36   *Zoom transition settings for a normal transition*

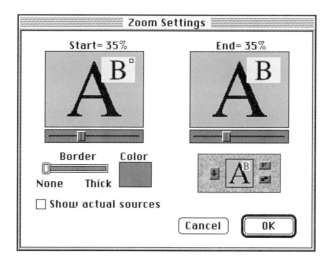

Figure 5.37   *Zoom transition settings so that movie in track B will play inside movie in track A*

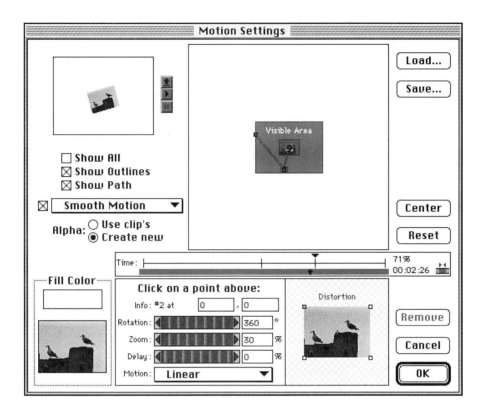

Figure 5.38   *Motion Settings dialog box*

Titles are created in a special title editor, which gives you basic text editing choices—font, size, style, color—as well as the ability to add a soft shadow, kern, draw simple shapes, and specify an animation path for the text (see figure 5.39). When created, titles are saved and placed in the Construction window, usually in the SuperImposition track so that transparency can be set to have the title appear on top of video.

Audio control is probably more extensive in Premiere than in any other QuickTime editor. Not only can you do rubberband fading as in VideoShop, you can also apply a handful of audio filters in much the same way you apply video filters (see figure 5.40).

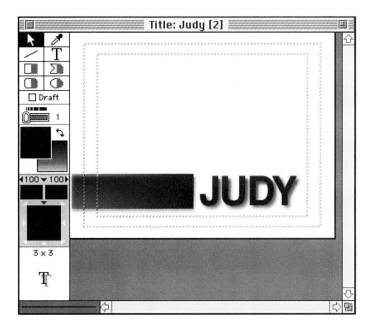

Figure 5.39   *Title editor*

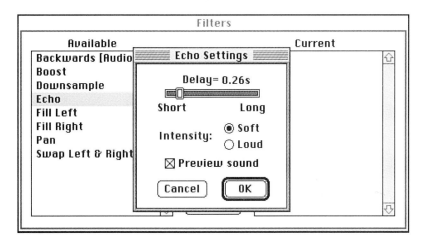

Figure 5.40   *Choosing and setting parameters for an audio filter*

Edit Decision Lists

Edit Decision Lists (EDLs), used primarily for professional video production, are beyond the scope of this book, but you should know that, simply put, an EDL is a list of the clip segments, transitions, and effects that go into a final video production. Such a list can be read by traditional video editing equipment in order to assemble the final video from the source videotapes.

You can use Premiere to create EDLs if the digitized clips you work with have timecode. Timecode can be added during digitizing using special hardware. (For more on this, see the section on controllable decks in Chapter 6.)

VideoFusion and QuickFLIX!

Of these two products, both from VideoFusion/Radius, VideoFusion has many more features. However, they have similar interfaces, so we'll discuss them together in this section.

QuickFLIX!

QuickFLIX! comes on the CD with this book. If you just need a basic special effects editor, it may be all that you need. If you like the way it works, however, you may want to upgrade to the much more powerful VideoFusion. One nice feature: VideoFusion will let you open and further edit any projects you create with QuickFLIX!

In both products, you work with three windows: the *Storyboard* window (see figure 5.41), the *Time View* window (see figure 5.42), and the *Player* window (see figure 5.43). Notice that this arrangement is different from VideoShop, in which there is a single Sequencer window that switches between time and storyboard views. The Player window is somewhat similar to VideoShop's Canvas window in that it provides a Standard Controller for playing your work.

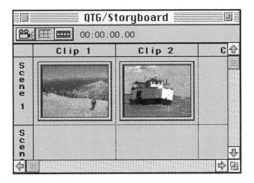

Figure 5.41   *QuickFLIX! and VideoFusion Storyboard window*

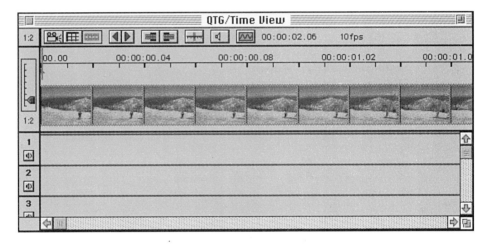

Figure 5.42   *QuickFLIX! and VideoFusion Time View window*

Figure 5.43   *QuickFLIX! and VideoFusion Player window*

When you work with these products, you open movie files and place them in the Storyboard window. When they are in the Storyboard window, they'll also show up in the other two windows. The three windows provide three different representations of the same data. When you do something to one, it affects the other two.

Transitions are added by first selecting adjacent clips in the Storyboard window, or by making a selection in the Player window (via the Standard Controller) or the Time View window, and then picking a transition in the Transitions dialog box, which you call from the Combine menu in VideoFusion or the Effects menu in QuickFLIX!. The dialog boxes are similar in the two applications, but VideoFusion has more options and controls (see figures 5.44 and 5.45).

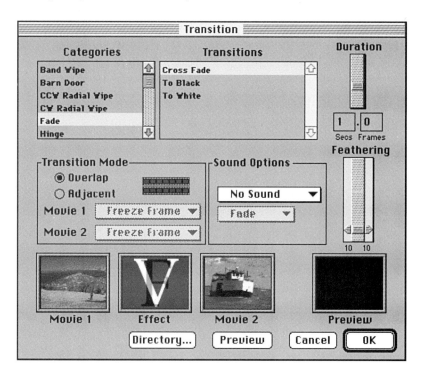

Figure 5.44   *Transition dialog box in VideoFusion*

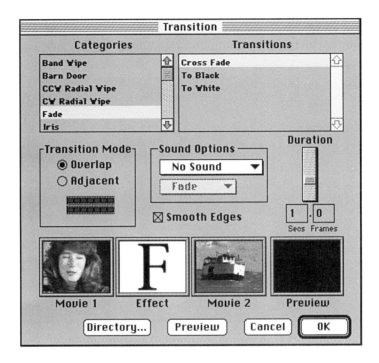

Figure 5.45 *Transition dialog box in QuickFLIX!*

To add a filter, you also start by selecting a clip or portion of a clip in any of the windows. Then you choose a filter from a menu: in VideoFusion you'll find them in the Filters menu, whereas in QuickFLIX!, which has only a few filters, you find them listed in the Effects menu. Both applications use similar dialog boxes to adjust settings for individual filters. For example, the Mosaic filter is available in both applications; its settings dialog box is identical in the two applications (see figure 5.46).

When it comes to compositing movies, both applications enable you to layer movies. Of course, VideoFusion has many methods and options for compositing. One such method is accomplished using the Chroma Key dialog box, in which a range of colors is made transparent in one clip so that the other can show through (see figure 5.47). In QuickFLIX!, the Layer dialog box is used for all compositing functions other than transitions. This dialog box works fine for movie-in-a-movie effects (see figure 5.48), but when you try to use it for chroma keying, it's not very effective because it only lets you pick a single color to be transparent, rather than a range of colors.

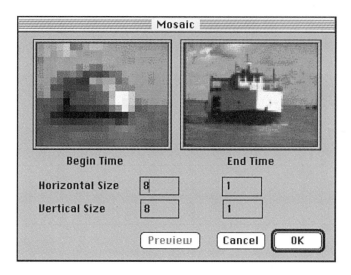

Figure 5.46   *Mosaic dialog box*

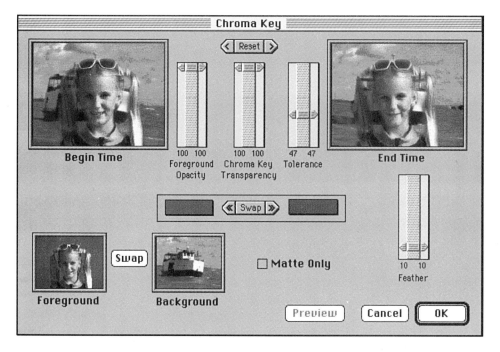

Figure 5.47   *VideoFusion Chroma Key dialog box*

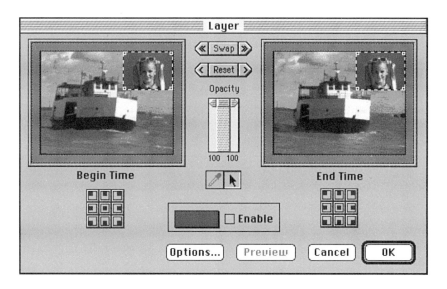

Figure 5.48   *QuickFLIX! Layer dialog box*

Motion is added in VideoFusion by selecting in any of the windows and using the Pan Zoom or Pan Zoom Rotate dialog boxes, found in the Filter menu (see figure 5.49).

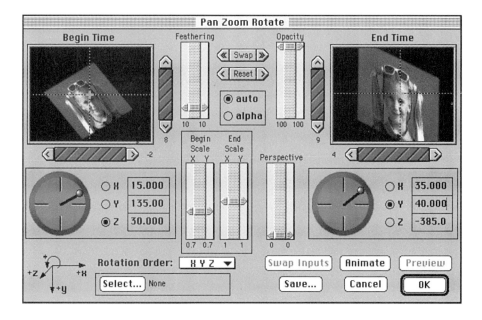

Figure 5.49   *VideoFusion Pan Zoom Rotate dialog box*

In QuickFLIX!, limited motion can be added using the Layer dialog box and setting a different size and/or position for the clip at beginning and ending points (see figure 5.48).

In both applications, you can add a title to any clip or portion of a clip by making a selection and then choosing Titling from the Movie menu. The dialog box that you use to specify the title in both applications looks like the one in figure 5.50.

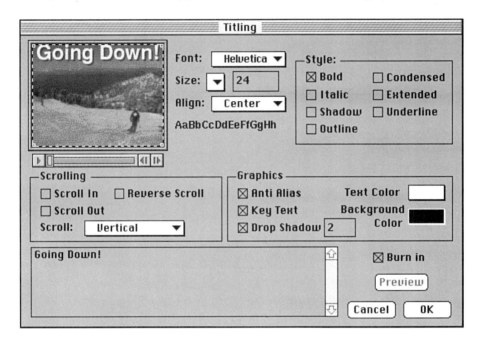

Figure 5.50 · *Titling window*

Also, in both applications you alter audio levels by making a selection and choosing Fade In, Fade Out, or Set Track Volume in the Edit menu.

After Effects

After Effects, the most powerful special effects editor available, has a learning curve to match its power. It's very complicated, so we'll hardly scratch the surface of the tool as we briefly describe its interface.

After Effects has a Project window, like Premiere, where you import your media (see figure 5.51). After that, the interface similarities end.

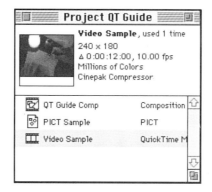

Figure 5.51   *After Effects Project window*

In After Effects, you move media from the Project window into a Composition window (see figure 5.52). You can play what's in the Composition window with a floating VCR Controls window (see figure 5.53).

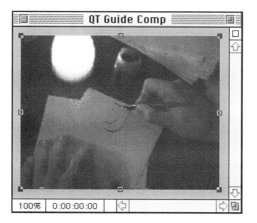

Figure 5.52   *After Effects Composition window*

Figure 5.53   *Floating VCR Controls window*

When you put anything in the Composition window, the name of the item appears in a *Time Layout* window, along with a bar to represent the length of the clip (see figure 5.54). Unlike the timeview in the other applications we've looked at, After Effects' time view does not use a filmstrip-like representation.

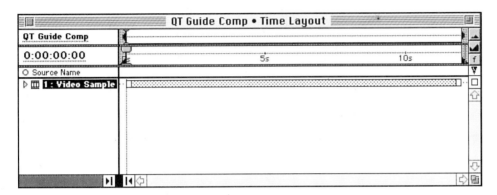

Figure 5.54   *After Effects Time Layout window*

Effects are added via the Effect menu (see figure 5.55), and options are picked in a floating Effect Controls window (see figure 5.56).

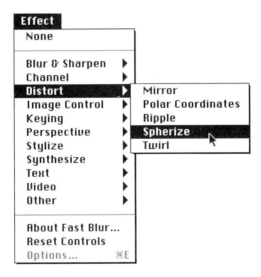

Figure 5.55   *Effect menu*

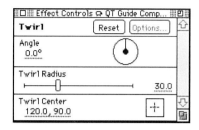

Figure 5.56 *Floating Effect Controls window*

The Time Layout window reflects effects you've added and enables you to change parameters of the effects over time, adjust the timing and layering of different media elements, and add additional properties, such as motion. It's a complicated window, using lots of symbols and numbers, but people who need the power of this tool appreciate this window (see figure 5.57).

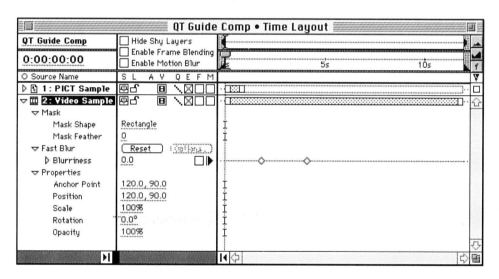

Figure 5.57 *Time Layout window after a number of elements have been added and parameters have been set*

Editing for Interactivity

In Chapter 3, we described authoring tools that let you create interactive presentations that incorporate existing QuickTime movies. However, there are ways to edit QuickTime movies so that the movies themselves respond to user interactions, rather than have an authoring tool do the work.

MovieClick is a small program from Motion Works International—part of their Multimedia Utilities package—that enables you to add *hot spots* to movies. A hot spot is an area that, when clicked, causes some other action. A simple action would be to have a different movie—perhaps a zoomed-in version of the object clicked—appear and play. More complicated actions can also be initiated because MovieClick enables you to make calls to HyperTalk, Lingo, and AppleScript.

While it's possible to program hot spots using HyperCard movie playing XCMDs, it's somewhat easier to use MovieClick. In MovieClick, no programming or scripting is required. Special editing windows are used to specify the time and location of hot spots (see figure 5.58).

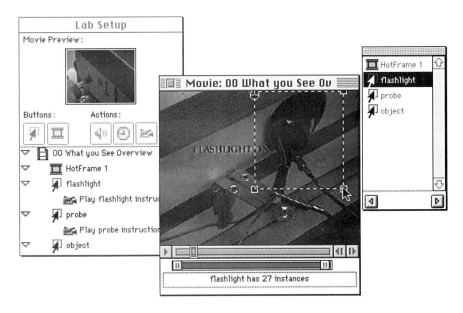

Figure 5.58   *MovieClick interface*

A movie edited with MovieClick can be opened and played in any application that plays QuickTime movies.

A product from Apple, currently called QuickTime Interactive, is expected in 1995. Using this tool, you'll be able to add an interactivity track to a QuickTime movie and do many of the same kinds of things that you can do with MovieClick—that is, initiate actions depending on where and when a user clicks.

For information on a special kind of interactive QuickTime movie, see Chapter 7, where we talk about QuickTime VR.

Now It's Your Turn

It's time for you to actually work with some of these products. Since the QuickTime Guide CD contains full working versions of QuickFLIX! 1.1.1 and VideoShop 2.0.3, as well as a Tryout version of Adobe Premiere 4.0, we'll walk you through some of the basics of using these applications. We'll show you how to apply the same kinds of effects with each, so you can see how they're all similar, yet different.

Using VideoShop

While the currently shipping version of VideoShop is 3.0, we'll be showing you version 2.0.3, since that's what we include on the CD. The interface differs slightly between the two programs so you may notice some differences in the figures in this section and those in the previous section. However, the way the two versions function is very similar.

Installing and Opening VideoShop

In steps 1 through 5, we're going to have you use an Installer program, which automatically installs all the VideoShop files you could possibly need—but requires 18 megabytes of hard disk space.

If you don't have that much space, read the Read Please file that's in the VideoShop folder—it will tell you how to install VideoShop so less disk space is used. If you install it this way, skip to step 6.

1. In the VideoShop folder that's within the FX Editors folder on the QuickTime CD, double-click on the file "Install VideoShop."

   You'll see a splash screen with the VideoShop logo.

2. Click on OK.

   A window appears welcoming you to VideoShop and explaining how you can upgrade to version 3.0.

3. Read the information and click on Continue.

   An installation dialog box appears asking you to choose a hard disk for installation.

4. Use the Switch Disk button or the pop-up menu to pick the hard disk on which you'd like the software installed, and then click on Install.

   A progress dialog box appears as the installation occurs.

5. When you see a dialog box that tells you installation has occurred successfully, click on Quit.

6. Double click to open the file "Avid VideoShop® 2.0.3," which you'll find on your hard drive in a folder of the same name.

7. When a dialog box titled "Canvas Size" appears, enter 240 for the horizontal dimension and 180 for the vertical dimension, as in figure 5.59, and click on OK.

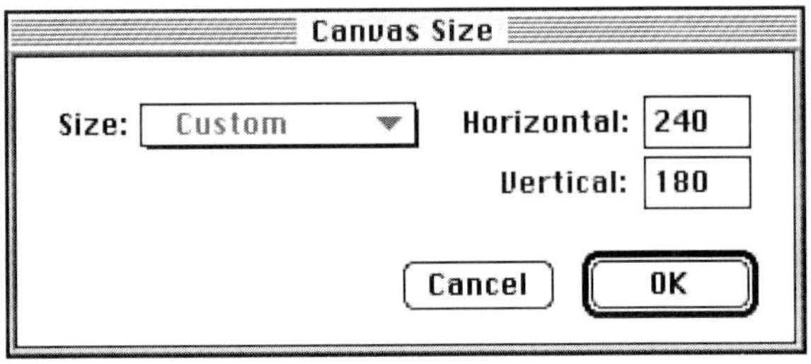

Figure 5.59   *Entering a custom Canvas Size*

Putting Two Clips Together

1. Using the Volumes window in the upper right of your screen, double-click to open the QuickTime Guide CD, then open the Media folder, and then open the Chapter 5 folder.

2. Drag the movie "Gulls Loop" from the Chapter 5 folder to the Sequencer window, dropping it in the top track.

   You'll see the first frame of the clip in the Sequencer window as in figure 5.60. The video portion of the clip is in the video track where you dropped it, and the audio portion is in the audio track directly below the video track.

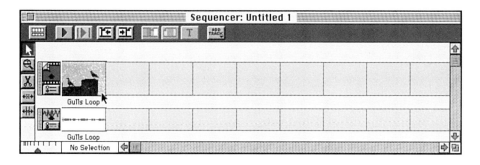

Figure 5.60   *Gulls Loop in Sequencer window*

3. Now click on and drag the movie "Gulls Bark" to the Sequencer window, dropping it to the right of Gulls Loop.

   You've just put one clip after another, a straight cut, just like you did in MoviePlayer.

   To see what you've done, use the Canvas window, which is in the upper left of your screen.

4. To change the frame size of the movie in the Canvas window, click and hold where it says "50%" at the bottom of the Canvas window, and use the resulting popup to choose 100%.

5. Click on the Play button—the right-facing triangle on the right side of the center of the controller at the bottom of the screen (see figure 5.61).

Play button

Figure 5.61   *Canvas Window in VideoShop 2.0.3*

Your newly edited movie plays. (In VideoShop 3.0, a real standard controller is used. Refer to figure 5.22 earlier in this chapter.)

Transitions

Let's make this a little more interesting by adding a transition:

1. Choose Time View from the Sequence menu.

   The representation of the two clips changes to one in which the clips appear more like filmstrips, with each frame representing a certain amount of time—VideoShop's default is 2 seconds per frame. These are short clips, so the filmstrips don't take up much of the space available in the track.

2. In the lower left of the Sequencer window, locate the little triangle (pointing up), and drag it to the right.

   As you drag, the words to the right of the area in which you're dragging the triangle change from "2 seconds" to "1 second."

   When you release the mouse button, the filmstrips lengthen. You have just changed the scale of the window so each frame of the filmstrip represents one second. This makes it easier to work with the clips.

3. On the left of the Sequencer window are a stack of small buttons. Click on the bottom-most button, which selects the *mirrored selection tool* (see figure 5.62).

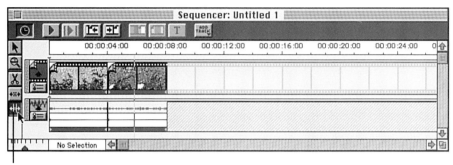

Mirrored selection tool

Figure 5.62   *Mirrored selection tool*

4. Click where the two filmstrips meet and drag left or right—whichever way you drag, you are selecting equal portions, one a mirror image of the other—until you have selected an area like that shown in figure 5.63. When the correct area is selected, release the mouse button.

Figure 5.63   *Using the mirrored selection tool*

5. In the Sequence menu, choose Apply Transition, and then in the submenu choose Dissolve (see figure 5.64).

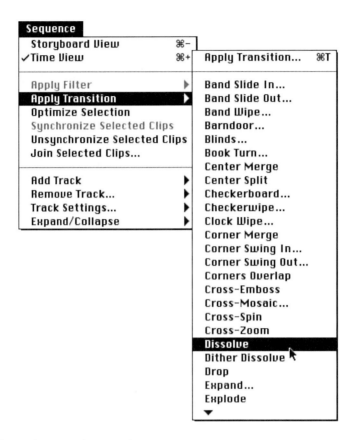

Figure 5.64   *Choosing the Dissolve transition*

(You could also have chosen Apply Transition in the submenu in which case you would have been given an Apply Transition dialog box, similar to the one in figure 5.15, from which to choose the type of transition and various other settings.)

A progress dialog box will appear, and you'll have to wait while your effect is built.

(VideoShop 3.0 is considerably faster than this version!)

6. Use the Canvas window to see what you've done.

By the way, notice how a line moves along the Sequencer window as you play the clip. This line shows you where you are in your clip.

Filters

Next let's try a filter:

1. With the pointer tool, click and drag from the beginning of the first clip, Gulls Loop, to somewhere in the middle of that clip.

2. From the Sequence menu, choose Apply Filter and then in the submenu choose Pixellate.

    A dialog box appears in which you set options for this filter (see figure 5.65).

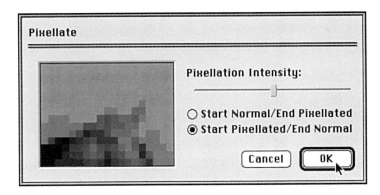

Figure 5.65   *Options for Pixellate filter*

3. Click on the second radio button to select "Start Pixellated/End Normal" and then click on OK.

    A progress dialog box will appear, and you'll again have to wait while the filter is applied to the clip.

    (Again, VideoShop 3.0 is considerably faster than this version.)

4. Use the Canvas window to check the results of your work.

Titling

Let's add a title:

1. From the Sequence menu choose Add Track and then from the submenu choose Title Track as in figure 5.66.

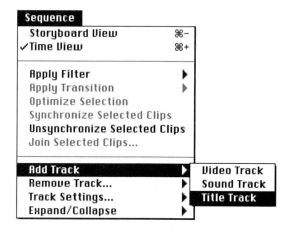

Figure 5.66   *Adding a Title Track*

A new track will appear in the Sequencer window. That's your title track.

2. In the title track, click and drag to make an 8 second selection, one that's as long as the two clips put together.

Warning!

You have to be in Time View in order to make this selection. When you first open the Sequencer window, you will probably be in Storyboard view. To change to the Time View, select Time View from the Sequence menu. If you have quit the program—for whatever reason—since the earlier steps, you will have to go back into the Time View to complete step 2.

---

3. From the Windows menu choose Title Window.

    The Title window appears.

4. Type "Seagulls" or any words of your choosing.

    The text will appear on top of the gulls image.

    There are various text options you can set here—feel free to click on the buttons along the top to change text size, style, color, and so on. You might also want to play with the scrolling options menu.

5. From the Title menu, choose Insert into Sequencer.

   The title track in the Sequencer window fills with a series of the letter "A" in the area that you selected in step 2 (see figure 5.67).

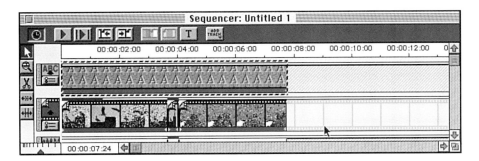

Figure 5.67   Title track after adding the text

6. Close the Title Window by clicking on its close box.

7. Play your movie in the Canvas window.

Saving Your Work

Finally, let's save this as a QuickTime movie.

1. Choose Save as Movie from the File menu.

   A fairly extensive Save dialog box appears (see figure 5.68). The default options are fine.

2. Enter a name for the file and navigate to a location on your hard drive where you'd like to save the file; then click on Save.

   A progress dialog box appears. When it's done, you'll have a new QuickTime movie.

3. Go ahead and experiment on your own for a while. When you are done using VideoShop, quit the program.

You should now have a feel for how VideoShop works. There's also a complete tutorial for the product on the QuickTime Guide CD—you'll want to go through that next. Then, check out the upgrade offer!

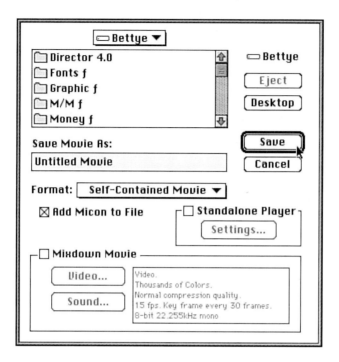

Figure 5.68   *Save dialog box*

Using QuickFLIX!

Now let's try accomplishing the same basic tasks—applying a transition, a filter, and a title—using QuickFLIX!.

Installing and Opening QuickFLIX!

1. Copy the QuickFLIX!™ 1.1.1 folder (in the FX Editors folder on the QuickTime Guide CD) to your hard disk. (You'll need about 4 megabytes on your hard disk to copy this folder, but a total of about 12 megabytes to complete this exercise.)

2. Open the folder you just copied and then open "QuickFLIX!."

   You'll see the QuickFLIX! splash screen for a few seconds, but you won't see any additional windows.

3. Choose New from the File menu to create a QuickFLIX! document. Name and save the new document to your hard drive.

You'll see the Storyboard window on the screen (see figure 5.69).

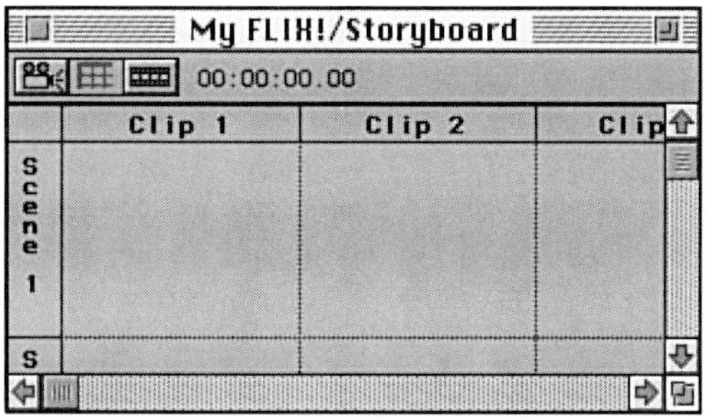

Figure 5.69 *Storyboard window in QuickFLIX!*

4. In the upper left corner of the Storyboard window are three icons; the first on the left is an icon that looks like a projector. Click on this icon.

You'll see the Player window. At the bottom is the standard controller. Along the top, on the left, you see the same set of three buttons as in the Storyboard window.

5. Click on the middle of the three icons, the one that looks like a grid.

This is the icon that represents the Storyboard window, and it brings that window to the front.

6. In both of the windows, the third icon is one that looks like a filmstrip. Click on this filmstrip icon.

You'll see the Time View window.

It also has all three icons at its top left.

7. Move the three windows around so that all three are visible.

Importing and Putting Two Clips Together

Now let's get some clips:

1. Choose Open from the File menu, navigate to the Chapter 5 folder within the Media folder on the CD, and choose "Gulls Bark" and open it.

2. Repeat the process to open "Gulls Loop."

   You should now have a window on the screen for each of the movies you just opened. They may overlap a bit.

3. Move the two windows so you can see the Storyboard window.

4. Click and hold on the image in the Gulls Loop window, and drag it to the Storyboard window, letting go of the mouse when your cursor is in Scene 1, Clip 1.

   The clip appears in the Storyboard window and the Gulls Loop window disappears.

   Notice that Gulls Loop now fills the Player window. It's also represented in the Time View window.

5. Follow the same steps to add Gulls Bark to Scene 1, Clip 2 in the Storyboard window.

   You've just done a straight edit; you put one clip after the other, just as you did with MoviePlayer.

6. To play your creation, first choose Play in Selection in the Movie menu (to remove the checkmark), and then click on the Play button in the Player window.

   The edited movie plays, switching from Gulls Loop to Gulls Bark about a third of the way through.

7. To see how your new movie is represented in the Time View window, click the filmstrip icon to bring the Time View window to the front, and then use the scroll bar at the bottom to scroll right until you get to the point where the clips meet (see figure 5.70).

Point where clips meet

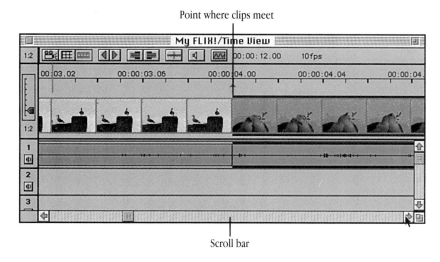

Scroll bar

Figure 5.70   *The scroll bar and the point where the clips meet*

Transitions

Now that you've seen how to put clips together, let's add a transition:

1. Shift-click to select both clips in the Storyboard window.

2. Choose Transition from the Effects menu.

    The Transitions dialog box appears (see figure 5.45). As we mentioned earlier, dialog boxes like this usually have many options, but we can ignore most of them to add basic effects.

3. In the Categories list, click on Fade, and then click on the OK button at the bottom right of the dialog box.

    A progress window appears, as the transition is generated (see figure 5.71).

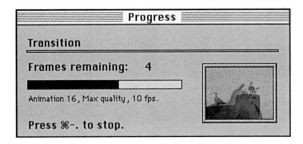

Figure 5.71   *Progress window*

4. Now use the Player window to rewind and play your clip.

   Notice that Gulls Loop now fades to Gulls Bark, rather than just abruptly switching to it.

   Notice also that the Storyboard window has changed. The transition that was just built was placed in Scene 1, Clip 2, pushing Gulls Loop into the Clip 3 spot. You can double-click to play any of the three clips in their little windows in the Storyboard window.

   ## Warning!

   In QuickFLIX! you can undo or change any special effects you've added, such as a transition, only immediately after adding it, so it's a good idea to play the clip and make sure you like the effect right away. If you don't like what you see, you should choose Undo from the Edit menu.

Next we'll make use of those additional Scenes in the Storyboard window. We'll create a new scene composed of altered versions of the clips in scene 1.

Filters

First we'll apply a filter to the Gulls Loop clip:

1. Click on Clip 1 in the Storyboard window to select it.

2. Choose Posterize from the Effects menu.

   The Posterize dialog box appears.

3. In the center you'll see a slider. Grab the arrow on the left side and drag it down until the number below the slider reads 4 (see figure 5.72). Then click on OK.

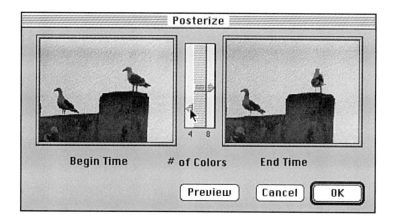

Figure 5.72 *Posterize settings*

Again you'll see a progress dialog box, and eventually a new window. The new window is a posterized version of Gulls Loop.

4. Play this new clip.

5. Drag this new clip to Scene 2, Clip 1 in the Storyboard window.

Titling

Now let's apply a title to the Gulls Bark clip:

1. Click on scene 1, clip 3.

2. Choose Titling from the Movie menu.

You'll see the Titling window.

3. Type "Don't they sound like dogs?" in the box on the lower left, and then click on OK.

There are a number of options in this dialog box that you might have used to color and style the text; experiment with them later.

Again, you'll see a progress window and finally a new window shows up in which you can play your newly titled clip.

4. Put the titled clip in Scene 2, Clip 3.

Constructing a New Scene

We're ready to put all three parts—the filtered clip, transition, and titled clip—together as one scene.

1. Drag the transition that you created earlier from Scene 1, Clip 2 to Scene 2, Clip 2.

2. Click once in the rectangle on the left side of the Storyboard window that reads "Scene 2."

    All the clips in that row are selected (see figure 5.73).

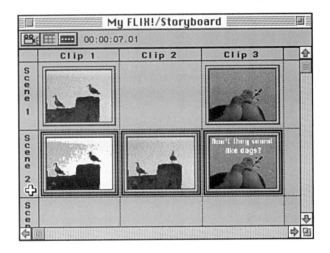

Figure 5.73   *Selecting the three clips in the Scene 2 row*

3. Switch to the Player window.

    The right half of the Play bar is selected. This is what we want to view.

4. In the Movie menu choose Play in selection.

5. Click on the Play button on the controller.

    You'll see what you have. Don't worry if the titled portion plays poorly. When we create a final QuickTime movie, it will be fine.

Saving

Finally, let's save what you have as a standalone QuickTime movie.

1. Choose Save As from the File menu, enter a filename, choose Self-contained QuickTime movie from the File Format pop-up, and click to check Save Selection Only. The dialog box should look like the one in Figure 5.74.

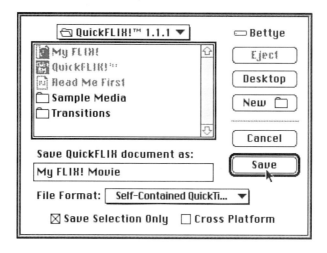

Figure 5.74   *Save dialog box with the correct settings*

2. Click on Save.

   A new QuickTime movie is created.

3. Go ahead and experiment on your own for a while. When you are done using QuickFLIX!, quit the program.

Like any QuickTime movie you've seen so far, the one you just created can be opened in MoviePlayer or any other application that plays or uses movies.

Using Premiere

With the Tryout version of Adobe Premiere 4.0 that's on the QuickTime Guide CD, you won't be able to save what you do. However, we can still show you how to apply a transition, filter, and title.

Installing and Opening the Tryout Version of Premiere

1. Copy to your hard drive the folder "Adobe Premiere™ 4.0 Tryout" that's in the Demos folder on the QuickTime Guide CD. It requires about 11 megabytes of disk space.

2. Double-click to open the file "Adobe Premiere™ 4.0 Tryout" that's in the folder you just copied to your hard drive.

   You'll see a splash screen, and you'll have to wait a few seconds while filters and transitions are loaded.

3. When you see a window titled "New Project Presets," click in the scrolling list on the left on the line that says "Presentation - 240 x 180" and then click on OK.

   You should see a bunch of overlapping windows.

Putting Two Clips Together

1. Choose Import from the File menu, and on the submenu, choose File.

   You get a standard open file dialog box.

2. Navigate to the Chapter 5 folder that's within the Media folder on the QuickTime Guide CD, choose "Gulls Loop," and click on Import.

3. Repeat the process to import "Gulls Bark."

   Now you have two files in your Project window (see figure 5.30 earlier in the chapter).

4. Drag the image of the Gulls Loop clip from the Project window to the top track of the Construction window. (The track is labeled "A" on the right side of the window.)

   The clip spreads out, showing thumbnail size frames of different points in the movie over time, like the timeviews in VideoShop and QuickFLIX! (Premiere doesn't have a storyboard view). As with VideoShop, there's a scale with a slider at the bottom of the window which you can use to change the window so that each frame represents more or less than the one second default.

   (You may want to close the Commands window; we're not going to use it in this exercise. You may also want to click on the Construction window to bring it in front of the Project window.)

Notice that the A track in the bottom of the window is now filled. That's a representation of the audio portion of the clip.

5. Drag the Gulls Bark clip into the A track next to the Gulls Loop clip, as shown in figure 5.75.

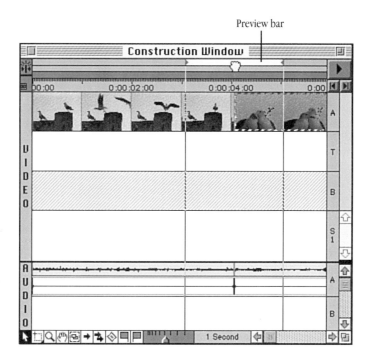

Figure 5.75   *Two clips joined using Premiere*

You just completed a very simple editing job: you put two clips together.

To see what you've done, you want to *preview*.

6. Use the scroll bar at the bottom of the Construction Window to move to the beginning of the clips; then locate the yellow bar at the top of the construction window and drag it so it covers at least a few seconds before and after the point where the two movies come together (see figure 5.75).

7. Press the Enter key.

A Preview window appears, showing you what you've done.

(You may also want to move or close the Info window.)

Transitions

Now let's make use of a transition:

1. Take the Gulls Bark clip, and drag it down to the B track, sliding it so that there are a few seconds where the two clips overlap in time (see figure 5.76).

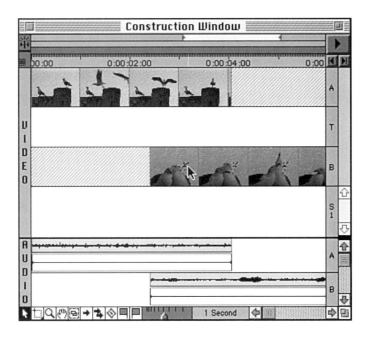

Figure 5.76   *Construction window with overlapping clips in the A and B tracks*

2. From the Windows menu choose Transitions.

The Transitions window comes to the front.

3. Scroll down to find the *Cross Dissolve* transition in the Transitions window, and click on it and drag it to the T track in the Construction Window. Place it in the area where the end of your A track movie and the beginning of your B track movie overlap (see figure 5.77).

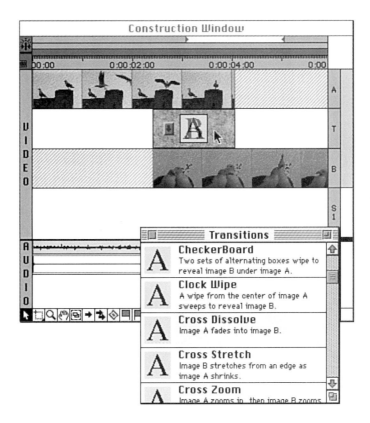

Figure 5.77 *A Cross Dissolve transition added to the T track*

4. You can preview what you've created by pressing the Enter key. (You may first need to move the preview bar.)

A progress dialog box appears while the preview is being built and then the clip is played in the Preview window (see figure 5.78).

A bright red box appears over the frame during the transition. (This is something the demo version does; of course, the complete version doesn't add this box.)

Figure 5.78   *Previewing a cross dissolve transition*

Filters

Filters are another powerful feature of Premiere that we can quickly show you:

1. Click on the Gulls Loop clip in track A of the Construction window to select it.

2. Choose Filters from the Clip menu.

   A dialog box appears.

3. Scroll down in the field on the left until you see "Posterize," and select it.

4. Click on the Add button.

   A smaller window appears which shows a frame from Gulls Loop. Below the image is a slider.

5. Drag the slider to the left, until the number to its right is a 6 (see figure 5.79).

6. Click on OK in this window and then click on OK in the Filters window.

7. Move the yellow preview bar so it's over some portion of the Gulls Loop clip in the Construction window and preview your creation by pressing the Enter key.

   Again, you'll see a progress dialog box, followed by your clip playing in the Preview window with a red box in the middle of it.

Figure 5.79   *Setting posterize options*

Titling

Since this is a save-disabled version of Premiere, and creating a title in Premiere requires saving, we won't show you how to create a title. Instead, we'll have you import a title we've already created, and show you how to add it to your production.

1. Choose Import from the File menu, and on the submenu, choose File.

2. Navigate to the Chapter 5 folder that's within the Media folder on the QuickTime Guide CD, choose "Seagulls Title," and click on Import.

    The title appears in your Project window.

3. Drag the title from the Project window to the beginning of the S1 track in the Construction window.

4. Click on the title clip that you just placed in the S1 track to select it, move your cursor to the right edge of the clip, and then click and drag to the right, stretching the clip out so it covers at least 4 seconds.

5. Select the title clip again and from the Clip menu choose Transparency.

    The Transparency Settings window appears.

6. From the Key Type popup, choose White Alpha Matte and then click on OK (see figure 5.80).

7. Hit Enter again to preview the clip.

You can't save with this demo version, but if it was the real version, you'd choose Movie from the Make menu and proceed to save your work as a QuickTime movie as we have with the other programs.

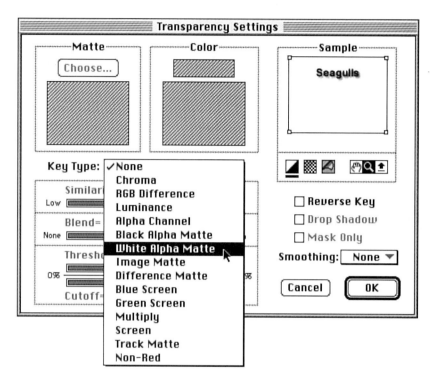

Figure 5.80   *Choosing a transparency type in the Transparency Settings dialog box*

The Power to Make a Masterpiece or a Mess

We hope that after this brief overview, you realize that, with all of these editing packages, you can let your creativity flow.

However, a warning is in order. In the early days of desktop publishing, when a large number of fonts were first made available, people with little design experience created eyesores by producing short documents that used too many different fonts. Don't make the same kind of mistake with QuickTime movies; an abundance of transitions and special effects do not necessarily make a better movie.

Remember that you can learn a great deal by watching movies or TV and noticing what works and what doesn't. For example, notice what kind of transition is used most often. That's right—a straight cut, the kind you can do with even a simple editing application. Sometimes you'll see a dissolve, as well. These transitions are popular because they work. Our point? For best results, keep it simple.

But go ahead and play. This stuff can be a blast!

Chapter 6

Recording Movies—Digitizing Your Video

In this chapter, we'll show you how to make a QuickTime movie from videotape. The basic idea is that you're converting the information on your videotape into digital data, information that can be stored on your computer's hard disk and used just like any other digital data. We'll discuss both the software and hardware you need, explain how to set them up, and show you what to do to make a movie. We think you'll be amazed at how easy it is to record a digital video movie.

Having covered the basics, we'll go into more depth about the range of options you have when recording a QuickTime movie and what you can do to make better movies.

What You Need

There are essentially four pieces of equipment you need for making a simple QuickTime movie from video: a Macintosh, a video source, a video digitizer, and an audio digitizer.

Macintosh

Almost any Macintosh model can be used to make QuickTime digital video movies (see chart later in the chapter for a detailed list).

You need a very large hard disk if you plan to make many movies, but for purposes of making your first movie, make sure that you have a minimum of 20 megabytes free on your hard disk.

You need a minimum of 5 megabytes of RAM—the more RAM the better.

You need System 6.0.7 or higher. Contrary to a popular myth, you do not need System 7 to run QuickTime; however, in some cases, the software you use to digitize may require System 7.

Video Source

What can you use as a video source? Well, anything that sends out a video signal. Playing a videotape from a VCR is the most obvious choice, but you can play a videotape straight from your camcorder as well.

The VCR (or camera) can be one that uses any one of a number of tape formats: VHS, VHS-C, S-VHS, 8mm, Hi-8, Betamax, 3/4-inch, or any other. Additionally, you can use either NTSC (the video format that is standard in the U.S. and Japan) or PAL (the standard European format). You may also be able to use SECAM (the standard in France).

You can also digitize from a laserdisc, using a laserdisc player.

You can even digitize "live" video: put your camera on standby and send the signal straight to your computer, without even using a tape.

In the same way, you can digitize from a TV program, again without tape, if you have a VCR that can tune in a channel (most can) or a TV that has a video out port (most don't).

Video Digitizer

To convert the visual portion of your video into digital data that can be stored on and used by your computer, you need a device to digitize video. Such devices are referred to as *video digitizers, video digitizing boards or cards*, or *video capture boards or cards*.

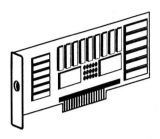

If you're lucky enough to have a Macintosh AV, you already have a video digitizer; it's built into the computer.

For a Macintosh 630 (Performa 630, LC 630, or Quadra 630), you can add the optional Apple Video System Card (it's only $149). This card digitizes both video and audio. You can also purchase the Apple TV/Video System card, which includes a TV Tuner card, enabling you to view and digitize TV on your Macintosh.

If you don't have an AV or a 630, you'll need to purchase a video digitizer, which will probably cost more than $500.

Where Have All the Inexpensive Digitizing Cards Gone?

As we write this book, it seems that the two lowest-priced Mac digitizing cards on the market—the SuperMac VideoSpigot and the Sigma Designs Movie Movie card, both available for under $500—are being discontinued (the Spigot's rusted out and Movie Movie is dead dead!). You may still be able to buy these cards, but they won't work with QuickTime 2.0. You can continue to use these cards if you switch back to QuickTime 1.6.2 or earlier when digitizing, but that's a less than optimal solution since you'll want to use the latest version to get optimal playback. Maybe the future will bring new inexpensive cards or updates to these classics.

One way to differentiate boards is by whether they digitize audio in addition to video. Many don't. If you get one that does, you won't have to get a separate audio digitizing device.

Digitizing without a Digitizing Card

Connectix's QuickCam is a great little digitizing device. It's an all-in-one video camera (not a camcorder—you can't put anything on tape!), video digitizer, and audio digitizer that lists for $149. This device, which is about the size and shape of a tennis ball, hooks to the modem or serial port on a Macintosh. Both audio and video come through this port. The QuickCam comes with easy-to-use software for digitizing and basic editing. With this camera and a PowerBook, you can digitize anywhere you go. It's also ideal for video conferencing or video email. The only drawback is that the video it shows and records is only gray scale. However, Connectix is planning to introduce a color version within the year. If you can get your hands on a QuickCam—they're in high demand—you'll find that it makes your Mac even more fun!

Some people want to know the frame size or frame rate that a digitizer will produce. Most basic digitizing cards will digitize *up to* quarter-screen movies (320 x 240), with a frame rate of *up to* around 15 frames per second, but the size and rate are *very* dependent on other factors, such as the speed of your Macintosh and hard drive. For example, an average system—such as a Quadra 660AV using its internal hard drive—can do a 240 x 180 capture at 10 frames per second, but only under optimal conditions. (You'll learn more about optimal conditions later in this chapter.)

However, there are cards that provide hardware compression and decompression capabilities, making faster recording and thus 30-frames-per-second, full-screen movies possible (see the section on hardware compression cards at the end of the chapter).

Most boards have the ability to be used as full-color graphics display boards. This means that they can show millions of colors, showing much richer and less splotchy images than would result if you relied on the standard color capabilities of your Macintosh, which may show only 256 or perhaps thousands (but not millions) of colors. Less expensive boards, such as SuperMac's Spigot II Tape, often don't have full-color display capabilities. However, having a card that only shows 256 colors doesn't prevent you from making movies with more than 256 colors.

Radius Mergers

SuperMac and Radius have merged; the company is called Radius, but some products that were previously SuperMac's still carry the SuperMac label. Also, Radius recently bought VideoFusion Inc., the makers of QuickFLIX! and VideoFusion software packages.

Audio Digitizer

Don't forget about the sound! Remember that your video source outputs both sound and images. One of the great things about QuickTime is that it takes care of both video and audio. When you record a QuickTime movie that has audio, the information about the audio is stored with the information about the video (remember the audio track?).

However, you'll still have to worry about providing a channel to get that audio information into the computer. Many video digitizing boards only take care of the video.

So, if you don't have one of the boards that takes care of the audio, how do you pump in the audio signal? Almost all new Macintosh computers have built-in audio digitizers, but most require an inexpensive adapter that you can purchase from Radio Shack or other electronics stores.

If you have no built-in recording capability, you must use an add-on audio digitizer. These range in price from $200 to a few thousand dollars. Sound quality differs between these devices, and if you are an audiophile, you will want to do extensive research on the differences between them.

Regardless of whether your audio and video digitizing capabilities come from one device or two, you'll still get synchronized audio and video when you record. QuickTime takes care of that!

Can Your Macintosh Be Used to Make Movies?

To see if your Macintosh can be used to make movies and, if so, which digitizers need to be added, look for the model name in Table 6.1.

Table 6.1   Macintoshes and Their Movie-Making Capabilities

Mac Model	Ready to Digitize	Needs Video Digitizer	Needs Audio and Video Digital Digitizer	Can't Digitize*
Mac XL (1)				✓
Mac 128k (1)				✓
Mac 512k (1)				✓
Mac 512k (1)				✓
Mac Plus (1)				✓
Mac SE (1)				✓
Mac SE/30			✓	
Mac Classic (1)				✓
Mac Classic II				✓
Mac Color Classic				✓
Mac Color Classic II				✓
Mac LC	✓			
Mac LC II	✓			
Mac LC III	✓			
Mac LC 475	✓			
Mac LC 520	✓			

continues

Table 6.1   Continued

Mac Model	Ready to Digitize	Needs Video Digitizer	Needs Audio and Video Digital Digitizer	Can't Digitize*
Mac LC 550		✓		
Mac LC 575		✓		
Mac II			✓	
Mac IIx			✓	
Mac IIcx			✓	
Mac IIvi		✓		
Mac IIvx		✓		
Mac IIsi		✓		
Mac IIci			✓	
Mac IIfx			✓	
Mac Centris 610		✓		
Mac Centris 650		✓		
Mac Centris 660AV	✓			
Mac Quadra 605		✓		
Mac Quadra 610		✓		
Mac Quadra 650		✓		
Mac Quadra 660AV	✓			
Mac Quadra 700		✓		
Mac Quadra 800		✓		
Mac Quadra 840AV	✓			
Mac Quadra 900		✓		
Mac Quadra 950		✓		
Mac Portable (1)				✓
Mac PowerBook 100 (1)				✓

Mac Model	Ready to Digitize	Needs Video Digitizer	Needs Audio and Video Digital Digitizer	Can't Digitize*
Mac PowerBook 140				✓
Mac PowerBook 145				✓
Mac PowerBook 145				✓
Mac PowerBook 150				✓
Mac PowerBook 160				✓
Mac PowerBook 165				✓
Mac PowerBook 165c				✓
Mac PowerBook 170				✓
Mac PowerBook 180				✓
Mac PowerBook 180c				✓
Mac PowerBook 520				✓
Mac PowerBook 520c				✓
Mac PowerBook 540				✓
Mac PowerBook 540c				✓
Mac PowerBook Duo 210 (2)		✓		
Mac PowerBook Duo 230 (2)		✓		
Mac PowerBook Duo 250 (2)		✓		
Mac PowerBook Duo 270c (2)		✓		
Mac PowerBook Duo 270c (2)		✓		

continues

Table 6.1   Continued

Mac Model	Ready to Digitize	Needs Video Digitizer	Needs Audio and Video Digital Digitizer	Can't Digitize*
Mac PowerBook Duo 280 (2)	✓			
Mac PowerBook Duo 280c (2)	✓			
Mac Performa 200 (1)				✓
Mac Performa 275				✓
Mac Performa 400		✓		
Mac Performa 405		✓		
Mac Performa 410		✓		
Mac Performa 430		✓		
Mac Performa 450		✓		
Mac Performa 460		✓		
Mac Performa 466		✓		
Mac Performa 467		✓		
Mac Performa 475		✓		
Mac Performa 476		✓		
Mac Performa 560		✓		
Mac Performa 550		✓		
Mac Performa 575		✓		
Mac Performa 577		✓		
Mac Performa 578		✓		
Mac Performa 600		✓		
Mac TV				✓
Power Mac 6100/60		✓		

Mac Model	Ready to Digitize	Needs Video Digitizer	Needs Audio and Video Digital Digitizer	Can't Digitize*
Power Mac 7100/66		✓		
Power Mac 8100/80		✓		
Power Mac 6100/60AV	✓			
Power Mac 7100/66AV	✓			
Power Mac 8100/80AV	✓			
Power Mac 8100/110		✓		
Mac Quadra 630 (3)		✓		
Mac Performa 630 (3)		✓		
Mac Performa 635 (3)		✓		
Mac Performa 636 (3)		✓		
Mac Performa 638 (3)		✓		
Mac LC 630 (3)		✓		
Performa 6110		✓		
Performa 6112		✓		
Performa 6115		✓		
Performa 6117		✓		
Performa 6118		✓		

(1) QuickTime does not work on these Macs.

(2) You need to have a Duo Dock in which to install the video digitizer.

(3) You could add the Apple Video System to these machines.

* Even though you can't add a digitizing card to these Macs, you can digitize using the Connectix QuickQam on many of them.

Digitizing Software

In addition to having hardware that can digitize, you also need an application for digitizing your video.

The software that you use sometimes depends on the hardware that you're using; some boards include digitizing software that is designed to work specifically with their hardware. SuperMac/Radius's Spigot cards, for example, come with software called ScreenPlay for recording.

Then there are digitizing applications that work with a variety of boards. For example, just about any board can be used with Apple's Movie Recorder software. FusionRecorder, a digitizing application from VideoFusion/Radius, comes installed on Macintosh AV computers, but it can be used with many video digitizers, not just the one that comes built into AV Macs. Almost all of the advanced editing applications (see Chapter 5) also have digitizing capabilities and can work with many different boards. As a matter of fact, we'll be using QuickFLIX! for digitizing in this chapter.

If you're using a Macintosh 630, you'll probably use the Apple Video Player digitizing software because that's what comes with the Video System digitizing card, although almost any digitizing application will work, too.

System Extensions

There are a few files that need to go into your Extensions folder in order for your recording software to work properly.

Obviously, you need QuickTime and the other extensions you installed in Chapter 1.

For any video digitizer that you install, you should have a *VDig*, which stands for Video *Digitizer* and is essentially a *device driver*—a file that contains information about the specifics of a piece of hardware. For QuickTime to work correctly with your specific hardware, it needs to have that information.

The only time you don't need a VDig in your System folder is when the information that would be in the VDig is already built into software you are using. It can be built into your system software, which is the case with the Macintosh AV computers. Or, it can be built into digitizing software that is designed to work specifically with that board. For example, if you use SuperMac/Radius's ScreenPlay recording software for digitizing with the SuperMac/Radius VideoSpigot digitizing board, you won't need the VideoSpigot VDig. But, if you want to use QuickFLIX! with the Spigot, you will need the VideoSpigot VDig.

RasterOps VDig

For RasterOps digitizers, the VDig code is in the file called "RasterOps Drivers."

In the same way that you need a VDig to tell QuickTime the particulars of the video digitizer that you use, you also need a special extension to tell QuickTime the particulars of the audio digitizer that you have hooked up. These extensions are not called ADigs, but we think they should be! Instead, they're typically referred to as *audio device drivers*. The most commonly used example of an audio device driver is the file called "MacRecorder Driver" for use with the MacRecorder. If you get a single board that digitizes both audio and video, it should come with both a VDig and an audio device driver.

However, if you're using the Mac's internal audio recording capabilities, as you will with most Macintoshes, you won't need to install an audio device driver because the device driver is built into the Macintosh system software.

If you purchase digitizing hardware, it will come with appropriate VDigs and audio device drivers, along with instructions for installation. You may want to get in touch with the device manufacturer to make sure you have the most current versions of these extensions—they seem to get updated at least once a year, especially when new versions of QuickTime are released.

Setting It Up

As with setting up a stereo, connecting all of the pieces can be the most frustrating part of making a QuickTime movie, but it's really quite straightforward if you understand the individual parts and the role they perform in the system.

The first thing you want to do is plug in your video digitizing board, unless it's already installed or built in. Plugging in this board will essentially mean opening up your computer and snapping the board into place. To do so, you should follow the manufacturer's instructions.

You will also need to plug in your audio digitizing device if the Mac or the video digitizing board you're using doesn't do audio. This may mean plugging in a board in the same way that you plugged in the video digitizing board. Or it may mean simply plugging an external device, such as a MacRecorder, into your modem or printer port.

When your video and audio digitizers are in place, you'll need to connect your video source to them.

On the back of your video source, you should find ports labeled *video out* and *audio out* (see figure 6.1). Start your cables here and connect them to your digitizing devices, which may or may not be labeled *video in* and *audio in*.

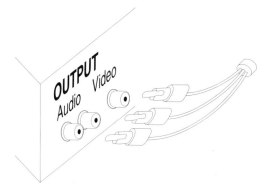

Figure 6.1   *Plugging RCA cables into your video source*

You will probably have all of the cabling that you need. Most likely you will use RCA cables or S-video cables, unless you have older video equipment or high-level equipment. Some adapters or special cables may be necessary. For example, if you use a MacRecorder, the "in" port (labeled "line") takes a mini jack. So you'll need either a cable that has two RCA jacks at one end and a mini jack at the other, or an adapter.

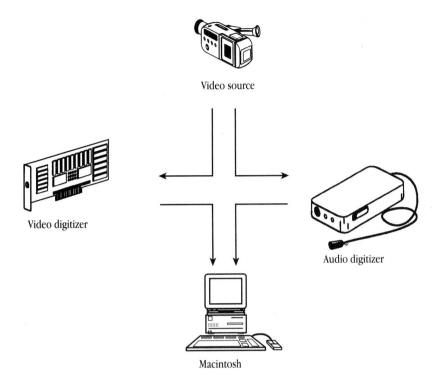

Figure 6.2   *How it's all set up: your video source is connected to your video and audio digitizer, which are in and/or connected to your Mac*

Cables, Connectors, and Adapters

Not having appropriate cables, connectors, and adapters can stop a multimedia production dead in its tracks. The most common connectors are shown in the following list:

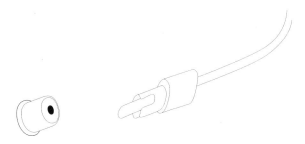

- **RCA**—This is the most common connector style; it's sometimes called a phono jack. It's used for both audio and composite video connections.

- **S-Video**—This is for S-video only. It's also just like the keyboard connector, so be careful plugging this one into the back of your computer. Shown is a 4-pin S-video connector; there is also a 7-pin style.

- **BNC**—The BNC is the Bayonet Nut Connector; it's for video and more common on professional equipment for use with component video connections.

- **Mini**—This connector is just like the connector on most personal stereo headphones. It's 1/4 inch long and used for audio in and out on your computer.

- **Coaxial**—The female end has threads and the male end usually just pushes over the threads; some are threaded. This connector is used for equipment such as cable TV.

Adapters are needed when your video source uses different connectors than your digitizers.

The built-in Mac audio digitizers, in particular, present challenges. Only a few take the standard RCA-style connector that most video sources use. Most take a mini jack, so you'll need an RCA-to-Mini adapter. To further complicate matters, some of the internal digitizers are, to put it simply, over-sensitive—they require *attenuation,* which reduces the amplitude of the signal without distorting it—for these you'll need an attenuating adapter. A simple RCA-to-Mini adapter will work for only a few Macintoshes. You'll need to look in the manuals that come with your Macintosh to find out if attenuation is needed; this information is usually found under "Specifications" in a section called "Microphones/Sound."

Doing It

Explaining how to "do it" when all of the pieces are in place means explaining how to use your digitizing software.

Just about any software that you use for digitizing video will have the same basic components. In this section, we'll introduce you to the things to look for and show you specific examples of how they're implemented in the QuickFLIX! recording software that we supply on the CD. What you learn about QuickFLIX! can be applied to other QuickTime recording software if you need or want to use something else. Other recording software may be slightly different; you should read the manual that comes with it.

When you first open your digitizing software, you will probably see a window that shows you what is coming through to your computer from your video source. Other than the size, what you see will be just about the same as what you would see if you were connecting your video source to a television set. That is, you'll see black if the video is stopped, or a blur of images if you are fast forwarding. Some recording software has a menu choice or button that you click on to start monitoring your video, but most do it automatically.

Figure 6.3 shows what some of the most common recording applications look like.

There is a button, usually labeled *Record*, that you click on to start digitizing video.

There usually is a button that you click on to stop digitizing video, but some applications let you click anywhere to stop recording.

When you stop recording, a window will appear in which you can play back the movie that you have recorded. In most cases, this window is an implementation of the Standard Controller or is something quite similar to it.

And, of course, as with any Macintosh program, you will find a Save choice in the File menu.

Besides the basic components we just described, all QuickTime recording applications will have additional buttons or menus that let you set various options, but you won't necessarily need to use them, at least not at first. We'll tell you more about them after we walk you through the basics.

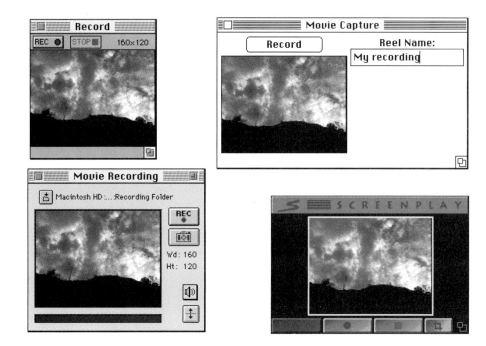

Figure 6.3 *Movie digitizing windows: VideoFusion/Radius's QuickFLIX!, Adobe's Premiere, Avid's VideoShop, and SuperMac/Radius ScreenPlay*

Now you know what you need, how to put it together, and what to look for in your software. So let's do it!

Once you have all of the equipment that you need, make a movie by following these steps. (If you don't have the equipment that you need, you should read through the steps anyway to see just how easy it would be if you did have the equipment!)

1. Make sure that you have all of the necessary hardware:

   • A video digitizer that's in your Mac—either you or someone else installed it, or you have an AV.

   • An audio digitizer that's in, or connected to, your Mac.

   • A Macintosh with a hard disk that has at least 20 megabytes of free space (that's just enough hard disk space to let you try this process out; ideally you want much more!).

   • A video source that's connected to the video and audio digitizers.

2. Make sure all of the necessary extensions are installed:

- QuickTime.
- Apple Multimedia Tuner.
- QuickTime Power Plug, if needed (see Chapter 1).
- Sound Manager, if needed (see Chapter 1).
- VDig, if needed (see "System Extensions" section in this chapter).
- Audio device driver, if needed (see "System Extensions" section in this chapter).

3. If QuickFLIX! isn't already installed on your hard drive, copy the QuickFLIX!™ 1.1.1 folder from the CD (in the FX Editors folder) to your hard drive.

   QuickFLIX! is good digitizing software—and by the way, the version on the QuickTime Guide CD is the full, commercial version!

4. Power up all equipment (restart your computer if the extensions were just installed).

5. Open QuickFLIX! and choose Show Record Window from the Record menu.

   A window appears. This is the window that you will use for recording.

6. Play your video.

   Make sure that you have a video image playing in your Record window (see figure 6.4).

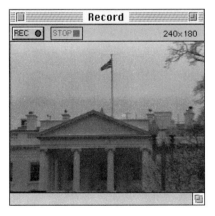

Figure 6.4   *Record window with video playing in it*

You're not capturing video yet. The video is just playing through on your Macintosh as if it were a TV.

If you don't see video, read ahead to the section "Video Settings" and check your source.

7. Start digitizing by clicking the Record button in the upper left of the Record window.

Now you're digitizing.

8. After a few seconds (definitely less than a minute), stop digitizing by clicking the Stop button, located next to the Record button (digitizing may stop on its own if you run out of memory or hard disk space).

A new movie-playing window titled Untitled-1 appears.

9. Save your movie: choose Save or Save As from the File menu, give the file a name, specify where you want it saved, and click on Save.

That's it. Now you have a movie! Odds are, however, that it didn't come out the way you'd like it—you probably got a low frame rate. If it didn't come out the way you'd like, continue reading to see what options you can set to get better results.

Tip

If your digitizing application starts to act strangely, or not at all, the Preferences file (stored in the Preferences folder in your System folder) may be damaged. Throw it out and try again.

Digitizing Options

No matter which piece of software you use for recording, there are various options for you to choose. In some cases, these options will help you make better movies by giving you better frame rates and better image or sound quality.

In this section we'll look at the options as they appear in QuickFLIX! and explain what they really mean. Note that they may not always be called the same thing in other programs as they are in QuickFLIX!, but the idea is the same. Note also that not all QuickTime movie recording software will have all of these options.

Standard Video Settings

In the Record menu, you'll see Video, which brings up a dialog box that is part of QuickTime's standard human interface. Figure 6.5 shows the Video dialog box. However, the settings shown in the figure may not precisely match the default settings you have. Most of the QuickTime recording applications use this dialog box, though it may be found under a different command and menu name.

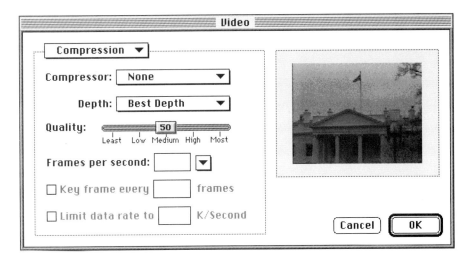

Figure 6.5   *Video dialog box showing compression options*

On the right side of the box is a window in which you can see your video playing; we recommend that you have your video playing before you open this dialog box.

The left side changes according to what you pick in the popup on the top left. You can set Compression, Image, and Source.

Compression

The Compression portion of the Video dialog box is where you'll set various options that determine to what degree your video will be squeezed down, both to take up less storage space and to have a small enough amount of data to play back on the machines on which you intend it to be played back. There are a number of options here; we'll fully explain them in Chapter 8.

What you should know now is that almost any compression made during digitizing results in lower frame rates, so unless you are using a hardware compression card, you should either set the compressor in this dialog box to None, or you should turn *post-compression* on. (We'll talk about post-compression in a following section; it's set in a different dialog box.) If you are using a hardware compression card, you'll want to choose the compressor that matches your card.

Also, in the lower half of the dialog box you can set the frames per second that you'd like your system to try to capture. If you don't specify anything, it will try to get the highest frame rate it possibly can. If you're getting *very* jerky results—that is, an effect where the video seems to start and stop—we recommend that you experiment with different numbers here until you find one low enough that the starting and stopping effect goes away. We've found that if you ask your system to do more than it can handle, it doesn't gracefully ignore the frames it can't capture; it instead lengthens the time that certain frames are on the screen.

Image

The sliders provided in the Image portion of the Video dialog box are very powerful for helping to correct poorly shot video. They are similar to the controls found on your television set: hue, saturation, brightness, contrast, sharpness, black level, and white level (see figure 6.6).

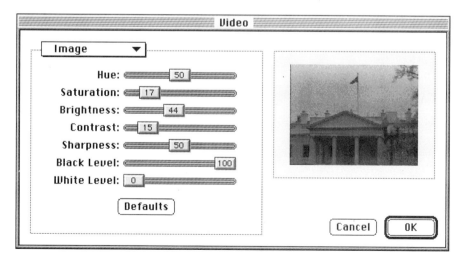

Figure 6.6   *Image options in the Video dialog box*

Depending on your digitizer, one or more of these settings may appear grayed out because either the software or hardware does not support it.

One thing that can really help to improve your QuickTime movies is to make sure your black and white levels are set so that blacks in your video really appear black and whites really appear white. To set these correctly for your particular system, you'll want to move the sliders back and forth while watching the video on the right. (Unfortunately, these settings are not available for the built-in digitizers in the Macintosh AVs.)

Source

In certain cases, you may have more than one video digitizer installed in your Macintosh. If so, you may need to tell your system which one to use (see figure 6.7).

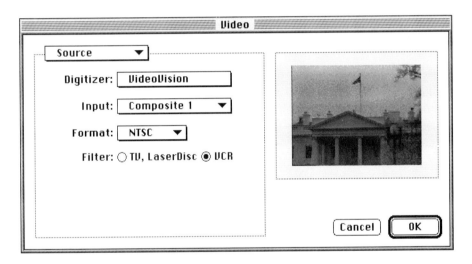

Figure 6.7   *Source options in the Video dialog box*

Remember that in most cases your software will be able to recognize your board only if you have a corresponding VDig in your System folder. If you forget the VDig, you won't see the board listed in this dialog box unless the digitizing software is specifically designed to work with the board. For AV users, the digitizer will be listed as "Built-in AV Digitizer;" as we mentioned earlier, no VDIG is necessary.

Also, if your board has more than one video-in port, as does the Radius VideoVision card, you'll need to specify which port you're using (see figure 6.8). If you're plugged into the S-video port and QuickTime is looking for video in the composite port, you won't be able to digitize your video.

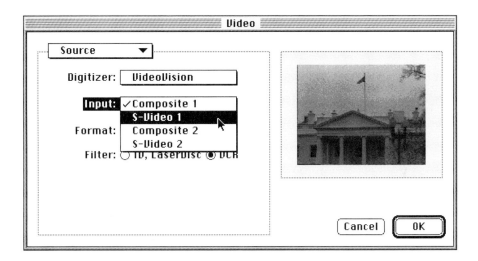

Figure 6.8   *Choosing the correct port when your digitizing card has more than one video-in port*

Post-Compression

In most applications, post-compression is either on or off. If post-compression is *off*, compression occurs *during* digitizing according to the compression settings in the Video Settings dialog box. If post-compression is *on*, compression occurs immediately *after* recording stops, again according to your compression settings. Typically, when post-compression is on, no compression occurs during digitizing.

Post-compression is not a good idea if you're using a hardware compression card, which is fully capable of doing compression while digitizing. For most other cases, post-compression is a good idea because you don't want your system trying to compress while it's capturing, but you would like the video compressed eventually. Turning post-compression on is basically a convenience—it saves you from having to take extra steps to set compression at some later point, usually when you save the clip.

In QuickFLIX!, post-compression options are available in the Record Preferences dialog box, which appears when you choose Record Preferences from the Record menu. In this dialog box, you can choose Off, None Codec, or YUV Codec for post-compression (see figure 6.9). These choices are slightly confusing. Choosing None Codec is equivalent to turning post-compression *on* in most other applications—that is, compression only occurs when recording stops. Choosing YUV Codec means that during capture the YUV compressor is used, and after capture the clip is recompressed according to the settings in the Video Settings dialog box (don't worry: we'll explain codecs in Chapter 8). Macintosh AV users are the only ones who want to use this YUV post-compression option (see the Read Me First file that comes with QuickFLIX! for more information).

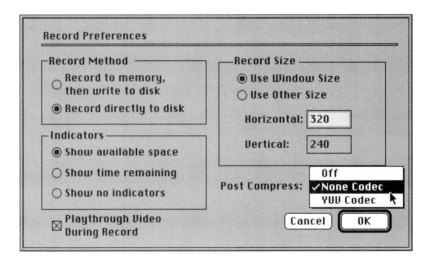

Figure 6.9   *Setting post-compression options in the Record Preferences dialog box*

Note

The Record Preferences dialog box is not a QuickTime standard. It will look different in different applications, and may or may not be used to set the same options that are in the QuickFLIX! Record Preferences dialog box. We'll cover the other options you see in the QuickFLIX! dialog box later in this chapter.

Video On/Off

Also in the Record menu, you'll find Turn Video Off. If you select this option, your Record window will fold up (see figure 6.10).

Figure 6.10   *Record window with video turned off*

When you record with the video turned off, only audio will be recorded. Why would you want to do that? It's what you do if you want to record a sound-only movie, perhaps so that you can merge it with some other video.

Playthrough Video During Record

In the Record Preferences dialog box in QuickFLIX!—the one in which you set post-compression—is a checkbox in the lower left corner which you can use to turn on or off whether you see the video on your screen as it is being recorded. (Other applications may or may not have such a choice, and it may or may not be located in a Record Preferences dialog box.)

Having video playthrough turned off can slightly improve digitizing performance since it relieves your system of having to show video on the screen while it's doing the work of trying to digitize. However, sometimes you need to see the video to know when to stop digitizing—you may find it too much of an inconvenience to not have video playthrough turned on during recording.

Standard Sound Settings

In the Record menu, you'll also see Sound Settings, which brings up the Sound dialog box. The sound dialog box is also part of QuickTime's standard human interface, so most QuickTime recording applications use it, though it may be accessed from a menu and command with different names than what QuickFLIX! uses.

As does the Video dialog box, the Sound dialog box has a left and right side. The right side doesn't change. It enables you to monitor and control the incoming audio. At the top of the right side is a popup that enables you to control whether the incoming audio is played back out of your speakers (see figure 6.11). It's usually a good idea to have this set to Off While Recording so that your computer won't be doing the work of playing the sound while it's trying to digitize. Consequently, using this setting may result in a slightly higher frame rate.

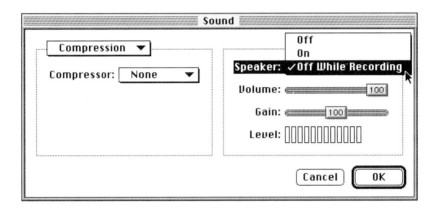

Figure 6.11   *Sound dialog box*

The left side changes depending on what's chosen in the popup in the upper-left side of the window: Compression, Sample, or Source.

Compression

Not only can you compress video, but you can also compress audio. However, in most cases, you should not choose to compress audio because it's relatively small to begin with and, if compressed, may sound awful. We'll discuss the settings in this portion of the Sound dialog box more fully in Chapter 8.

Sample

In the Sample portion of the Sound dialog box, you will often be given a choice of audio sampling rates. Usually rate choices will be approximately 11 kHz or 22 kHz, but the AV Macintoshes and a few high-quality audio boards will have choices of even higher sampling rates. If you are recording sophisticated audio, such as a concerto, you want the highest audio sampling rate you can possibly get. However, for most video clips that involve talking, 11 kHz is fine and will save you disk space and give you a movie with better playback performance. As for size, 16-bit will sound better than 8-bit, but the availability of 16-bit may be limited by your system. The same is true about using mono and stereo (see figure 6.12).

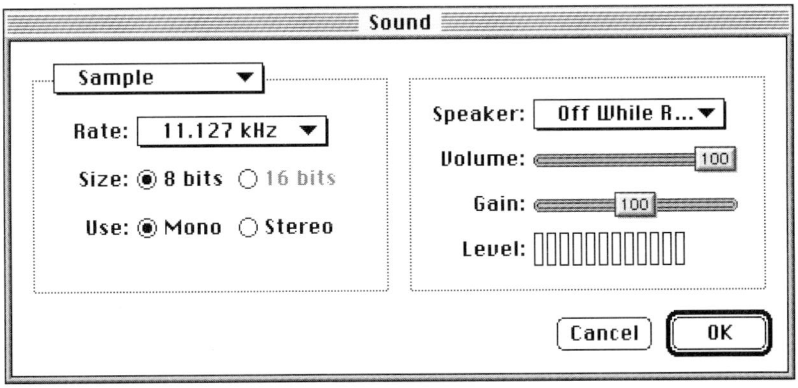

Figure 6.12   Sound Sample options in the Sound dialog box

Source

If, by some chance, you have more than one audio digitizer connected to your system or multiple input ports, you may have to choose the one that you want to use, in the same way that you may have to choose which video digitizer you want to use (see figure 6.13).

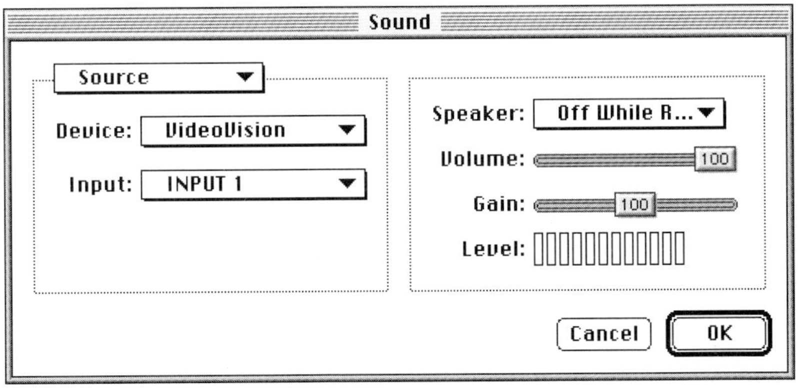

Figure 6.13   Sound Source options in the Sound dialog box

Sound On/Off

Just as there's a Turn Video Off choice, there's also a Turn Sound Off choice. Most of the time, you'll want to record audio at the same time as you record video. If your audio and video are tightly related (lips moving and words heard, for example), you should definitely record audio at the same time. However, if, for example, you have video with the sound of birds chirping in the background, you may not want to waste your computer's precious processing power recording the audio. Record only the video. You can record the audio separately and paste it in later using editing software. You'll be able to record a higher frame rate this way.

Record to Disk or Memory

In the Record Preferences dialog box, accessed by choosing the Record Preferences command in the Record menu, is an area labeled Record Method (see figure 6.14). This option determines where the data will be stored as you record; here you can choose to record to RAM first or directly to disk. For most Macintosh users, the amount of RAM in their Macintosh limits the amount of QuickTime data to a few seconds' worth. So, if you're like most Mac users, you need to record to hard disk if you want more than a few seconds' worth of video.

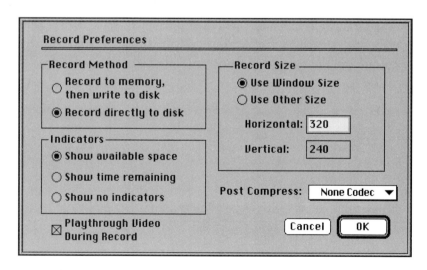

Figure 6.14   *QuickFLIX! Record Preferences dialog box*

On the other hand, your computer can write to RAM much more quickly than it can write to a hard disk. This means that you will be able to record more frames per second if you are writing to RAM. If you have lots of RAM, try using it! Keep in mind, however, that your system software and digitizing software can require close to 6 megabytes, so digitizing to RAM is impractical if you have only 8 megabytes of RAM. Getting more than a couple of seconds of digitized video into RAM requires at least 20 megabytes.

Tip

If you are getting very low frame rates, it may be because your hard disk is *fragmented*—it doesn't have any large contiguous blocks of space in which to store data, so it has to jump all over the place when digitizing. You should look into purchasing a disk optimizing/defragmenting program which can tell if the disk is fragmented, and if so, fix the problem.

Disk to Record On

With this option, you'll choose which hard disk you want the movie to be saved to. If you have more than one disk to choose from and you know that one is faster than the other, you should pick the one that has the fastest data transfer rate. You also want to make sure to pick a drive that has enough free space. You'll want approximately 1 megabyte of free space for each second of video that you wish to record. You don't need that much to permanently store the movie, but you'll probably need it during recording.

Tip

Don't bother recording to a RAM disk; you will do better just recording to RAM.

In QuickFLIX!, the disk to which you're recording is set in a dialog box obtained by choosing Preferences and then General in the File menu (see figure 6.15).

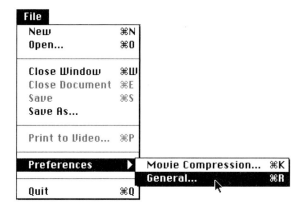

Figure 6.15   *Choosing General Preferences from the File menu*

In the bottom of the dialog box (see figure 6.16), you can choose a *scratch disk*, which is where your movie data will be stored temporarily as you record. If you don't save the movie file when you're finished, that data will be erased from the scratch disk. If you do save the movie, you can choose to put the file anywhere you'd like.

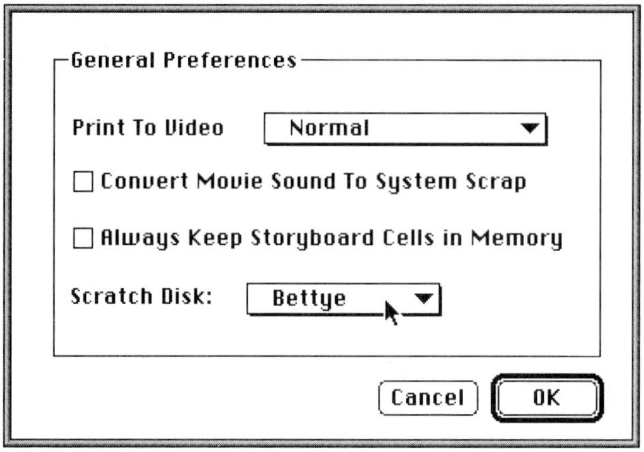

Figure 6.16   *General Preferences dialog box*

Crop Region

Do you have videotape in which action only takes place on the left side of the screen? Or the bottom? Or the upper right corner? You can make a more interesting QuickTime movie by just digitizing a portion of the screen if your software lets you crop the capture region. Not only will you capture the most interesting part, but because you are capturing less information, you may get more frames per second.

To set the crop region in QuickFLIX!, as well as in most other applications, you merely click and drag out a rectangle in your Record window (see figure 6.17). The area outside of your rectangle will be black, and video will be playing only within the rectangle (see figure 6.18). To return the recording area to the full window size, just double-click in the Record window.

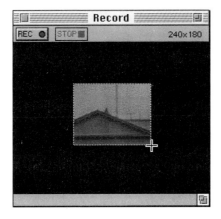

Figure 6.17   *Defining a crop region*

Figure 6.18   *Record window with crop region defined*

Window Size

Also in the Record Preferences dialog box (see figure 6.14) is an area labeled Record Size. Use this area to set the frame size of the movie you record. If you leave this set to the window size, the size of your Record window determines recorded frame size. You can change the size of the recording window either by dragging its size box, or by using the Record Window Size command in the Record menu.

Currently, most QuickTime movies are either 160 x 120, 240 x 180, or 320 x 240 pixels. These numbers provide proportional reductions of a full screen (640 x 480 pixels); in QuickFLIX!, as a matter of fact, you'll see that the three common options are labeled "1/4 size", "3/8 size", and "Half size". However, there's no law that says that a QuickTime movie has to be one of those sizes. Many digitizing applications will let you pick any size, but some may restrict you to these standard sizes.

Unless you have a hardware compression card (see next section), don't try to go larger than 320 x 240 pixels. In most cases, 240 x 180 is safest. The price you pay for a larger frame size is a smaller frame rate. Conversely, the smaller the frame size, the better the frame rate.

No matter what range of window size you choose, you'll get the best results if the pixel width and height are multiples of 4.

Miscellaneous Software Tips to Improve Digitizing

The basic rule you want to follow is to do everything you can to ensure that your computer is concentrating on the digitizing process. To maximize your computer's concentration, follow these tips:

- Turn off any unnecessary extensions—that is, anything but the QuickTime extensions, VDigs, and audio device drivers.

- Close all applications other than your recording application.

- Make sure Virtual Memory is off (check in the Memory control panel).

- Make sure AppleTalk is inactive by checking the Chooser. If you record using Adobe Premiere, you'll be asked if you want to turn off AppleTalk, and Premiere will do so if you respond affirmatively. Avid VideoShop will warn you to turn AppleTalk off.

Hardware to Improve Digitizing

When you've done all you can with a basic set of equipment, you may be ready to spend more money to improve the quality of the digital video movies you make.

Hardware Compression Cards

Cards that do hardware compression are required to digitize full-screen and full-motion movies. SuperMac/Radius's Digital Film is one digitizing board that has this capability; however, it's being discontinued. Radius and RasterOps both have compression *daughtercards* that plug into their standard digitizing cards: Radius's VideoVision Studio Upgrade plugs into the Radius VideoVision digitizing card, and RasterOps's MoviePak and MoviePak II plug into most of the RasterOps digitizers.

Then there are cards designed especially for the AV Macintosh. The AVs already have a basic video digitizer built in, but they also have an extra connector inside of them called the *DAV slot* (DAV stands for Digital Audio Video and is pronounced "dave"). You can attach a hardware compression card to a DAV slot, again giving you that full-motion, full-screen ability. The SuperMac Power Spigot AV and NuVideo EyeQ board are two cards that go in the DAV slot.

The Apple Video System card that goes in a 630 Mac has a DVA slot which is similar to a DAV slot in that it can take a hardware compression card, but the card that it takes isn't a DAV card.

Be aware, however, that the full-screen, full-motion movies you create with any of these cards will require the same or similar hardware to play back. You can, however, recompress them with one of QuickTime's software compressors if you need to distribute them to people without any specialized hardware.

Video Equipment

While any video camera, camcorder, or VCR will work in your digitizing station, you can definitely improve the quality of your movies, as well as the quality of your digitizing experience, with better video equipment.

Learn More

If you want in-depth coverage of video digitizing, read the book *How to Digitize Video* by Nels Johnson, published by John Wiley and Sons. Also read *QuickTime: Making Movies on your Mac* by Robert Hone, published by Prima Publishing, if you want to learn about how to shoot the best video for QuickTime movie making.

Video equipment can be divided into roughly three different levels:

- *Professional* is obviously the best and the most expensive. Professional formats include *Betacam SP* and 1-inch.

- *Consumer* is at the bottom of the rung and is what most of us use in our homes. Common consumer formats are VHS and 8mm.

- Prosumer (a combination of the other two words) falls between the other two in quality. S-Video formats fall into the prosumer category. Both Hi-8 and S-VHS are S-Video and are what many people are using for QuickTime.

In general, the better the video footage, the better looking your QuickTime movies will be, so go for the highest level possible. What's possible for you will primarily be limited by cost, but be aware that not all capture boards will take all inputs directly. Some of the older, less expensive boards have only RCA inputs (the standard plug for consumer-level equipment), and they don't have S-video inputs. And while S-Video equipment will have RCA outputs, you immediately lose the benefit of the S-Video if you use the RCA output.

Controllable Decks

Some video sources enable you to do what is called *controlled capture* or *step capture*. If a video source can move to any specific frame in the video, computer software that controls the video source can, in turn, go to any frame. If this is the case, the system can make as many passes over the material as needed for capturing every single frame. For example, with a controllable source, digitizing software might run a tape by once and grab every third frame, then rewind the tape and grab the next third frame, and so on. In this way it can capture every single frame to create a full-motion movie.

While laserdisc players, professional-level video decks, and some prosumer decks, such as the SONY CVD-1000, are controllable, most consumer-level camcorders and VCRs are not controllable.

One drawback to doing controlled capture like this is that going back and forth over your tape degrades the tape.

Video capture that's not controlled is called *real-time capture*. This means that your system will capture as many frames as it can as the video signal comes through. That's it: there's no second pass to grab what it missed the first time. If you are recording "live" or from a television source, you must, obviously, make a movie in real time.

Controllable decks offer a second benefit. If you have a controllable deck, you can, with the right software, log your videotape. With the log that you generate, you can later use your computer and deck to digitize all the clips at once without human intervention. This is called *batch digitizing*, and it provides tremendous time savings in comparison to digitizing each clip manually. Not only can you "set it and forget it," but you'll also have a record of precisely what you digitized in case you want to redo your digitizing quickly and easily. As far as software goes, Adobe Premiere and Avid VideoShop have logging and batch digitizing capabilities. So does a product called the Video ToolKit from Abbate Software.

Miscellaneous Hardware Tips for Digitizing

Here are some hardware tips that may improve your digitizing:

- Put a diskette in any floppy drive, a CD-ROM in any CD-ROM drive, and a cartridge in any removable cartridge drive. This prevents your system from wasting time checking empty drives to see if anything has been recently inserted.

- Make sure all cables—such as those connecting your video source or hard drive—are securely fastened. If they're not, you may get noise, either in the video or the audio.

- Make sure your videotape is in good shape. Don't use copies, don't use tapes longer than 60 minutes, don't reuse tapes, don't pause and rewind your tape a lot, don't use the first few minutes of a tape, but do "pack" your tape (that is, fast forward and rewind it before using it to get rid of any loose particles).

Storage Hardware

We mentioned earlier that the speed of your hard drive has an impact on your video capture. However, there are some specialized drive solutions that may considerably improve your frame rates.

A/V Hard Disks

If you're in the market for a new hard drive, look into *A/V drives*, which are designed for recording digital video. For one thing, they're relatively fast hard drives. They also don't do *thermal recalibration*, a process whereby the disk temporarily stops reading or writing in order to adapt itself to changes due to heat. Having one of these drives can improve your digital video recording experience—you should be able to noticeably increase your frame size and/or frame rate. And, they're not much more expensive than non-A/V hard drives of the same size.

Disk Arrays

If you have plenty of cash to burn, the next (big) step up is a *disk array*. The basic idea of a disk array is to take two (or more) disk drives, connect them together, and get your Mac to treat them as one. This way the computer can simultaneously write part of the information to one drive and part to the other and, in theory, double the speed at which you can write the data.

RAID (Redundant Array of Inexpensive Disks) is the standard for assembling disk arrays. There are actually six levels of RAID, but for digitizing purposes, RAID Level 0 is the one that matters because it provides faster performance; the other levels provide storage security benefits.

For best performance for a disk array, you'll want to get a SCSI card.

SCSI Cards

Adding a SCSI card to Macintosh will also increase hard disk performance. SCSI (Small Computer Systems Interface) is the standard that the Mac uses to interface with hard drives, scanners, CD-ROM drives, and other devices. Your Mac has a built-in SCSI interface, but you can add an additional SCSI card, which will have a faster implementation of the SCSI standard. With an add-in SCSI card, you may be able to bypass the need for a disk array.

In Search of Perfection?

Digitizing video is, in essence, a very simple procedure—plug a few things in, open digitizing software, start recording, stop recording, and save the file. Digitizing video *really well*, however, is another story. You just aren't going to get the kind of video you see on TV unless you spend lots of money to get all the very best equipment.

With or without expensive equipment, even getting decent results—as good as the clips we provide on the QuickTime CD-ROM guide—can be quite complicated. There are many interrelated variables. For example, you might have a fast hard drive, but you're running an extension that slows you down. Or, you could have a top-notch digitizer, one that even does hardware compression, but your hard drive isn't fast enough to keep up with that digitizer. You may have picked settings, such as a large frame size, that are too much for your system to handle. We could go on and on with all the factors to consider.

There is no simple, definitive answer to the question of how to get the best digital video movies. You'll need to experiment to see what gets the best results on your particular system with the particular video that you're digitizing.

Making QuickTime movies from sources other than video, however, is somewhat less tricky. In the next chapter we'll cover how to make movies from animations, still images, sound files, and more.

Chapter 7

Making Movies
without Video

*W*e devoted the preceding chapter to explaining how to create

QuickTime movies from video. While

that's the most talked about method of

movie creation, that's not the only way

to create a QuickTime movie.

There are all sorts of ways to create QuickTime movies that don't require a digitizer or a video source. As such, these ways are less expensive and usually less time-consuming than starting with videotape. Of course, these movies don't necessarily look like video, but they do provide dynamic ways to present information.

This chapter shows how you can make movies from sources other than video. We'll show you how to create movies of the four major track types: video, sound, text, and music. If you recall from Chapters 4 and 5, you know that these different tracks can be merged together using editing software.

Video Tracks without Video

Don't let the term *video track* confuse you. A video track doesn't have to be created from videotape, laserdisc, or any other video source. A video track, in the world of QuickTime, is a track that contains picture-based information. You can start with animations or even still images. We'll discuss both in this section.

Starting with an Animation

If you have any type of animation software, it's almost guaranteed that you have a way to make a QuickTime movie. Both two-dimensional (2-D) and three-dimensional (3-D) animation packages can be used.

Exporting Animations as QuickTime

Most of today's animation programs can export files in QuickTime format. This gives you several advantages. One advantage is that animators can now take advantage of the compression in QuickTime to create smaller files. Another advantage is that animations can be used in more places; when an animation is in QuickTime format, you can open it with any program that reads QuickTime files, including QuickTime editing software, enabling you to put together a large production in which you merge video and animation.

Here are a few examples of types of software that export files as QuickTime movies:

- **2-D Animation Programs**. One example, Macromedia Director, which we discussed earlier as a program that can import QuickTime movies into interactive presentations, also enables you to export your presentation as a QuickTime movie. To do this, you choose Export from the File menu; you'll be given a dialog box like the one shown in figure 7.1 in which you can choose QuickTime as the file type. Other animation programs, such as Cinemation, provide similar, though simpler, export-as-QuickTime options.

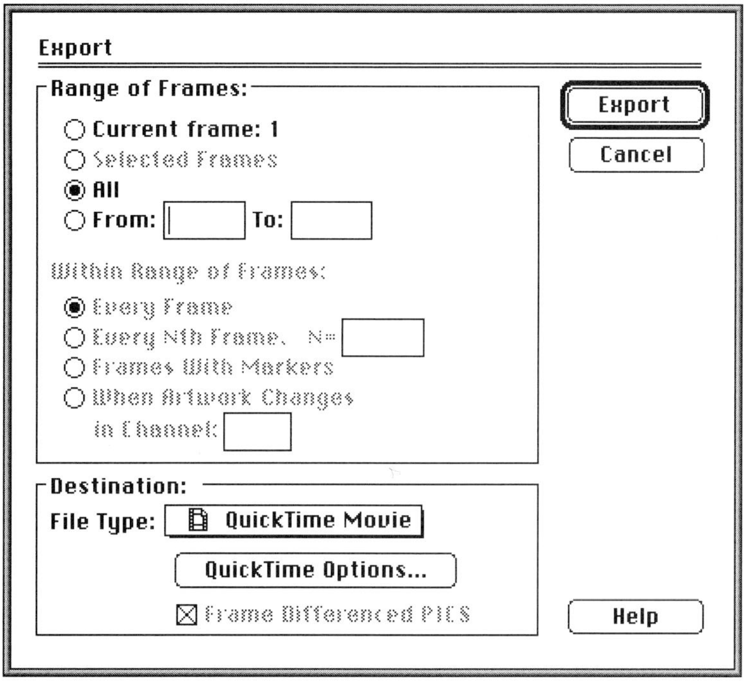

Export

Range of Frames:

○ **Current frame: 1**

○ Selected Frames

◉ **All**

○ **From:** [   ] **To:** [   ]

Within Range of Frames:

◉ Every Frame

○ Every Nth Frame,   N= [   ]

○ Frames With Markers

○ When Artwork Changes

    in Channel: [   ]

Destination:

File Type: [🗋 **QuickTime Movie**]

[**QuickTime Options...**]

☒ Frame Differenced PICS

[**Export**]

[**Cancel**]

[**Help**]

Figure 7.1   *Exporting as QuickTime in Macromedia Director*

- **3-D Modeling and Animation Software**. Specular Infini-D is a 3-D modeling, rendering, and animation program. With Infini-D, you create objects that appear to be 3-D. You can then move these objects over time by setting many frame locations, called *key frames*. Then the software builds the frames in between the key frames, creating an animation. Finally, the animation can be saved as a QuickTime movie. Other 3-D animation programs work in a similar way.

- **Painting Programs that Enable You to Put Together Sequences of Images**. Two children's painting programs, Broderbund's KidPix and Storm Software's Kid's Studio, both export slide shows as QuickTime movies (see figure 7.2). So does Painter, a high-end painting tool for adults. Many painting programs don't export as QuickTime movies because they're designed to let you work on only one image at a time. (See Chapter 8 to see how QuickTime is used on single still images.)

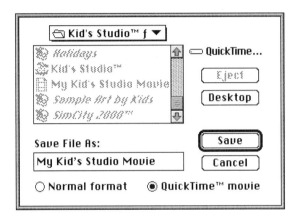

Figure 7.2   *Exporting as QuickTime in Storm Software's Kid's Studio*

- **Scientific Simulation Software**. Interactive Physics, from Knowledge Revolution, is a program for learning physics. With it you create interactive simulations where students can change values of variables and see how their changes affect the physics of the situation. You can export any of these simulations as a QuickTime movie, but when you do, you lose the ability to change the simulation.

- **Screen Recordings**. There are applications that let you record what happens on the screen and save the recording as a QuickTime movie. Such applications offer an excellent way to show someone how to do something on a Mac. Of course, because you have your screen recordings in QuickTime format, they can also be integrated with other types of QuickTime movies, such as video and audio. A currently available application for making QuickTime screen recordings is CameraMan from Motion Works International.

Note

SuperCard's scripting language, SuperTalk, includes commands for creating a QuickTime movie from the cards in a SuperCard project (of course, you'll lose any interactivity in the project if you choose these commands). The Open Movie command creates a new QuickTime file. The Record Movie command puts the current card into the movie as a new frame—you'd probably script a repeat loop so that you can go to and record multiple cards. And the Close Movie command closes the QuickTime movie file so that it can be played back in SuperCard or elsewhere.

Converting a PICS File to QuickTime

Even if an animation program can't save or export in QuickTime format, there's still a way to turn the animation created in that program into a QuickTime movie.

Chances are very, very good that any animation software will either save or export the animation as a file which has the *PICS* format (a PICS file is actually a sequence of *PICTs*; PICT is a standard format for storing still images).

On the Farm

With all of this talk about different file formats, you may be interested to know that the QuickTime movie file format is *MooV*. That's pronounced "MooooooooV."

When you have a PICS file, you can easily convert it into a QuickTime file. You do this using any application that plays QuickTime movie files. Let's try it now.

We've provided a PICS file on the CD. It's called "Glycine PICS" and is located in the Chapter 7 folder that's within the Media folder. If you have your own PICS file, or animation software that lets you create one, feel free to use yours rather than ours.

Credits

Glycine PICS was created with the freely distributable animation software MacMolecule 1.7, developed at the University of Arizona. It's available on many FTP sites and online services.

1. Open MoviePlayer.

2. Choose Import from the File menu (see figure 7.3).

Figure 7.3   *Choosing Import from the File menu*

An open dialog box will appear.

___

Tip

For most of the imports we discuss in this chapter, you can also choose Open from the File menu. It provides the same results as Import.

___

3. Locate the Glycine PICS file (in the Chapter 7 folder within the Media folder) on the CD and click on it.

   This dialog box normally has an Open button in its lower-right corner. However, if you click on the name of a PICS file, a Convert button replaces the Open button (see figure 7.4).

___

MPEG

Some MPEG movies can be converted to QuickTime using the application Sparkle. We'll talk about that in the next chapter.

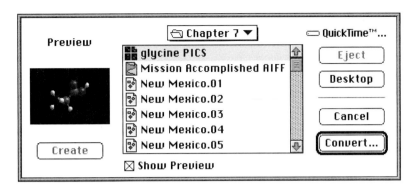

Figure 7.4 *Open dialog box when a PICS file has been selected*

4. Click on the Convert button.

   A Save dialog box will appear because you are going to be creating a new QuickTime movie. By default, it provides a name for the file—the original name followed by the word *movie*. This dialog box also has an Options button that enables access to the QuickTime compression settings (see figure 7.5). We won't look at that now; we'll assume that default settings are OK.

5. Navigate to a location on your hard disk where you'd like the file saved and click on Save.

   A progress indicator appears as the file is imported. Then you have a QuickTime movie without sound (see figure 7.6).

Warning!

With the current version of QuickTime, you cannot import PICS files with names that contain a period followed by a DOS-style file extension. For example, Glycine.PICS would be a problem. If an import fails or produces unexpected results, make sure the filename does not contain a period. This problem may also occur with other types of files such as MPEG and MIDI. However, some imports, such as PICT file imports, require the period (see next section).

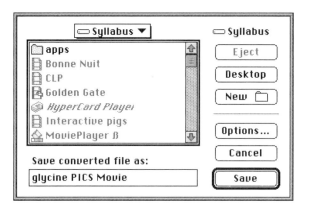

Figure 7.5   *Save dialog box with Options button*

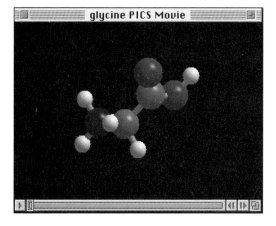

Figure 7.6   *Movie created by converting a PICS file*

Hyper about HyperCard?

HyperCard users who want to convert their HyperCard animations into QuickTime movies can use the freeware HyperCard stack StackToPICSFile (available on online services and BMUG's TV-ROM Too CD-ROM) to export the cards of a stack as a PICS file. The resulting PICS file can be converted to a QuickTime movie as we just described.

Starting with Still Images

Don't have animation software? Don't worry. You can start with still images. Photographic images are always nice, but any kind of graphics created in a paint or draw program will work, too.

A Series of PICTs

Put a collection of still images—photographs, painted, or drawn graphics—together so that they play one after another. Add a sound or a music track, and you have a pretty nice slide show.

If you aren't interested in showing these images at a fast frame rate, you have the freedom to create a nice small file or a full-screen presentation. Recall that the reason that QuickTime files usually fill only a portion of the screen and use up lots of disk space is because of the number of frames that usually need to be shown every second.

In Chapter 3, we had you use the Slide Show mode in the Present Movie function to play back a movie composed of a series of still images.

How do you create one of these movies? Well, in Chapter 4 you added text to a movie that already contained several other tracks. The same technique can be used to paste multiple still images into an empty movie, or perhaps into a movie that initially has only a sound or music track.

Pasting images in one-by-one is tedious, however. There's an easier way to do it. If you have a collection of still image files, you need to name them so that they have the same name followed by a period and then sequential numbers—Fred.1, Fred.2, Fred.3, Fred.4, Fred.5, Fred.6, for example. When named in this way, these files can be imported into a QuickTime movie in just a few steps.

On the CD that comes with this book, we've provided you with some still image files, which we've already named correctly so that you can convert them to a QuickTime movie. This type of conversion is one thing that MoviePlayer can't handle yet, so instead we'll use the unsupported application ConvertToMovie:

1. Open the application ConvertToMovie, which is in the Unsupported Stuff folder on the CD.

You immediately see an Open dialog box with an instruction to pick a file for conversion (see figure 7.7).

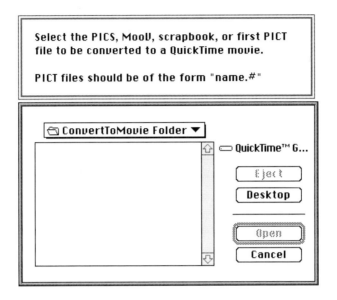

Select the PICS, MooU, scrapbook, or first PICT file to be converted to a QuickTime movie.

PICT files should be of the form "name.#"

ConvertToMovie Folder ▼

QuickTime™ G...

Eject

Desktop

Open

Cancel

Figure 7.7   ConvertToMovie when first opened

2. Navigate to the Chapter 7 folder that's within the Media folder.

   Notice that there is a group of sequentially numbered files.

3. Choose the first PICT file in the series, "New Mexico.01," and click on Open (make sure you don't get New Mexico.10 by mistake).

   Your instructions will tell you to pick the last PICT.

4. Scroll down and choose the last PICT file in the series, "New Mexico.10," and click on Open.

   Now a Compression Settings dialog box opens. We'll discuss this dialog box in detail in the next chapter.

5. Where it says "Frames per second," enter .5 and then click on OK (see figure 7.8).

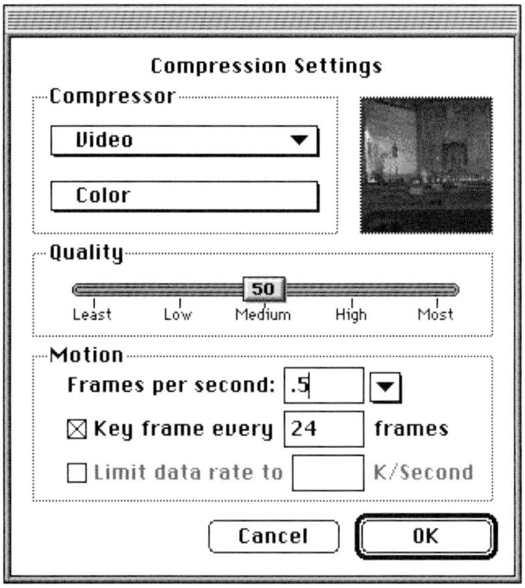

Figure 7.8   *Compression Settings dialog box*

Next you will see a Conversion Options dialog box (see figure 7.9). We'll leave these settings as they are.

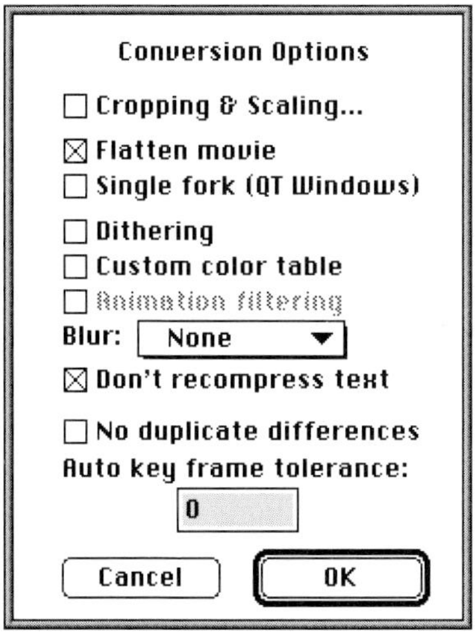

Figure 7.9   *Conversion Options dialog box*

6. Click on OK.

Finally, you're presented with a Save dialog box.

7. Navigate to a location on your hard disk where you'd like to save the file, change the name of the file if you wish, and click on Save.

A window appears in which each of the photographs is shown, one after the other, for a few seconds each. At the bottom is information telling you which frame is being shown of the total number (see figure 7.10).

Figure 7.10   *PICTs being converted into a movie*

8. When a dialog box appears asking what you want to do next, click on Quit ConvertToMoov.

9. Locate the file that you saved in Step 7, and double-click to open it.

It should open in MoviePlayer. You'll have a movie that contains 10 frames, one for each PICT file you imported. Each frame will remain on the screen for two seconds because you specified a frame rate of half a frame per second in Step 5.

Note

If you bought the QuickTime Starter Kit, you have the utility Movie Converter, which also provides the capability to turn numbered PICTs into a QuickTime movie, as well as do any of the other imports we discuss in this chapter.

By the way, you should know that creating a movie from PICTs works best if all of the images are the same orientation and size. If not, ConvertToMovie will use the dimensions of the first PICT in the series and crop all others to match it.

How do you get PICT files? Almost any graphics application—from Adobe Photoshop to ClarisWorks—can save in the PICT format. PICT files can also be found on many online services, such as America Online and e•World. You can also buy CD-ROMs filled with hundreds of photographic-quality PICT files or get your own photographic images stored on a Photo CD.

Kodak Photo CD

Heard about Photo CDs? If you have regular still image film (35mm or other formats), you can send it to Kodak (via your local camera store), and for around one dollar per picture, they'll return a CD-ROM, called a *Photo CD*, which has compressed digitized versions of your photographs. They'll also return your negatives and, for a few more dollars, standard color prints.

Foreign File Access   Apple Photo Access

If you have a Photo CD player, you can display these images on your TV. However, Macintosh users with a CD-ROM drive have the added advantage of being able to open and manipulate these images with their favorite graphics software. Photo CDs will work in almost all CD-ROM drives; you can call Kodak at 1-800-CD-KODAK (1-800-235-6325) and ask if your drive will work.

continues

All that's needed to display Photo CD images is QuickTime 1.5 or greater, the Foreign File Access extension, and the Apple Photo Access extension. The Foreign File Access extension is included with most CD-ROM drives. Currently, Photo Access is only available with the purchase of an Apple CD-ROM drive, but it will work with any drive. With these extensions installed, the Photo CD mounts on your desktop with color preview icons and a QuickTime movie called "Slide Show," which shows small-format versions of all of the images on the CD (see figure 7.11). The Photo CD files look and act just like regular PICT files. Each image comes in five different resolutions, ranging from 192 x 128 pixels to 3072 x 2048 pixels.

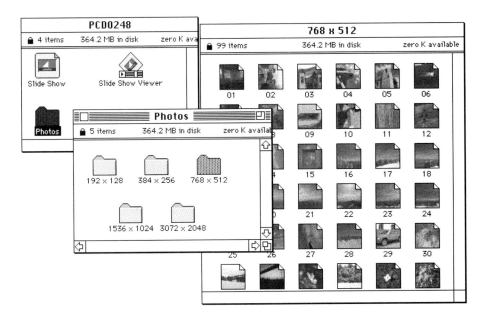

Figure 7.11   Photo CD mounted on your desktop

There are actually other ways to use Photo CDs on your Mac that don't make use of QuickTime, but they're less elegant, and besides, this is a book about QuickTime!

Dynamic Stills

Of course, you can use almost any of the editing packages discussed in Chapter 5 to build a movie based on still images. Any of these editors enable you to import a still image and specify how long you want it to remain on the screen.

Many editors also give you the ability to zoom in or out of still images or to pan across them; such effects are often used in documentary films to add motion to photographs.

Transitions, motion settings, and transparencies also make stills dynamic. On the CD, in the Chapter 7 folder in the Media folder, check out the movie "Elvis Baby," which was created in Premiere using three still images: "Elvis," "Elvis With a Heart," and "Pen in Hand." A clock wipe transition was used to go from Elvis to Elvis With a Heart while Premiere's motion settings and transparency abilities made Pen in Hand appear to draw the heart (see figure 7.12).

Figure 7.12   *QuickTime movie created by animating still images in Premiere*

More Credits

Junior Hansen, Jr., co-producer of BMUG's TV-ROM series of QuickTime CD-ROMs, is the creator of "Elvis Baby" and many other innovative QuickTime movies. She is a Bay area artist and Renaissance woman and can be reached at junior_hansen@bmug.org.

Morphing

The term *morphing* comes from the word *metamorphosis*, defined in the dictionary as "the transformation of something as by magic or sorcery." Most people have seen the Michael Jackson video for the song *Black & White*, where Michael Jackson changes from himself to an Asian woman and then to an African man and so on. Whether you call that magic or not, it's morphing!

So what does morphing have to do with QuickTime? There are programs for the Mac, such as Gryphon Software's Morph or Motion Works International's QuickMorph, that can create a QuickTime movie by morphing two still images.

To use these morphing programs, you take two still images and set points on one image that correspond to points on the other image. In figure 7.13, notice that the point on the right eye of the baby maps to the point on the right eye of the cat. Other points provide similar mappings—ears to ears, nose to nose, and so on. When you have defined these points, the software interpolates intermediate frames and creates a movie that starts with the first still image and ends with the second. To see an example of a morph movie, check out the Mike Morph Movie file that's in the Chapter 7 folder. It was created with Gryphon Software's Morph using two photos of the same man at different times.

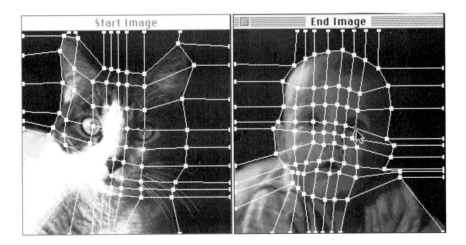

Figure 7.13   *Creating a morph from still images using QuickMorph*

QuickTime VR

QuickTime VR—the VR stands for *virtual reality*—enables a user to view a scene in 360 degrees. She can zoom in and out or look up and down or right and left. She can also change her point of view in the scene by jumping to other spots and looking around from there. It's also possible to have hot spots that enable the user to interact with an object, such as by clicking on it for more information or picking it up.

For an exciting example of what can be done with this new Apple technology, you'll want to get your hands on Star Trek: The Next Generation Interactive Technical Manual, a CD-ROM that lets you explore much of the Starship Enterprise. You can visit the Bridge, Sick Bay, and even Captain Picard's quarters. You can also pick up and examine certain objects and manipulate some of the computer control panels (see figure 7.14). It's a "must have" for trekkers!

Figure 7.14   Scenes from a QuickTime VR movie in Star Trek: The Next Generation Interactive Technical Manual—default view, view after panning to right, and zoomed-in view

We mention VR movies here because they're created by using QuickTime VR development tools to stitch still images together.

Unfortunately, VR is currently only available to selected developers, so, unless you're one of the lucky few, you won't be able to create your own VR movies just yet.

Text Track

In Chapter 4, we showed you how you can paste in text from a word processor into QuickTime movies. Just as with still images, you can use this technique to paste in text, one line after another. As you might guess, however, there's a faster way to do it.

Try this:

1. Open SimpleText, which is in the Utils folder on the CD.

   We're using SimpleText here because it's on the CD. You can use your own word processor or text editor, if you want to do so.

2. Type at least three lines of text, as in figure 7.15, making sure to put a return at the end of each line except for the last one.

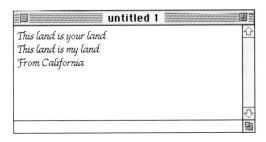

Figure 7.15   *Lines of text in SimpleText*

3. Save the file to your hard disk.

   If you're using your own word processor, you need to save the file in a text-only format.

4. Open MoviePlayer if it's not already open.

5. From the File menu, choose Import.

   The Open dialog box appears.

6. Locate the text file that you saved in Step 3 and click on it.

   The Open button turns into a Convert button.

7. Click on the Convert button.

   You'll see a Save dialog box.

8. Save the movie.

   You'll see a progress dialog box as the text is imported (see figure 7.16).

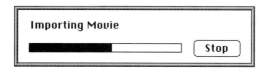

Figure 7.16   *Text file being imported as a movie*

When it's finished, you'll have a text track only movie, as in figure 7.17. Each line of text becomes a frame that appears for two seconds.

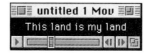

Figure 7.17   *Text track movie imported from a text document*

As you might expect, this text track movie can be merged with other QuickTime tracks.

Sound Track

Sound has been an integral part of the Macintosh since its beginnings, so it's not surprising that you can take pre-existing sound files and bring them into the world of QuickTime.

Importing AIFF Files

AIFF (Audio Interchange File Format) is a standard file format for storing sound on the Macintosh and other computers.

It's particularly easy to open AIFF files with QuickTime because no conversion actually happens—QuickTime just references the original sound file.

Try this:

1. Open MoviePlayer if it's not already open.

2. Choose Import from the File menu, and then go to the Chapter 7 folder within the Media folder on the CD and select the file "Mission Accomplished AIFF" (see figure 7.18).

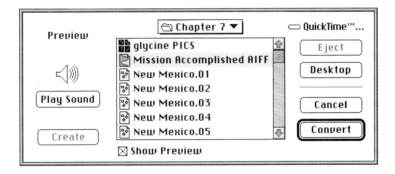

Figure 7.18   *Open dialog box when an AIFF file has been selected*

Notice that the Open button has been replaced by a Convert button. If you're really observant, you may notice that it's not a Convert… button—there are no ellipses because you're not going to see another dialog box. You are just going to open an untitled movie which references the AIFF file.

3. Click on the Convert button.

   You'll immediately see a sound-only QuickTime window.

4. Play the movie to hear the sound.

If you save this file "normally," the file will reference the original AIFF file. If you save it as a self-contained movie, the sound track is incorporated into the movie file.

Where do you get AIFF files to use in your movies? You can certainly record one yourself using software such as SoundEdit Pro. AIFF files can also be found on many online services, such as America Online and e•World. You can also check with BMUG or your local user group.

Note

System 7 sound files, such as your system beep files, can also be converted into QuickTime movies. Unlike AIFF files, they must be converted and saved as self-contained files, just like PICS files.

Audio CD Import

If you have a Macintosh with a built-in CD-ROM drive or an external AppleCD 300 series CD-ROM drive, you can use QuickTime (version 1.6.1 or later) to convert tracks of your favorite audio CD directly into QuickTime movies.

Feeling Left Out?

Even if you don't have an Apple CD-ROM drive, you may be able to do audio CD import. It's worth trying. If it doesn't work, the drive may actually be capable, but the system software that runs the drive may not support audio CD import; software from FWB called CD-ROM ToolKit *may* be able to provide the necessary software support—contact FWB at 415-474-8055. Be aware, however, that some CD-ROM drives—usually older ones—are just not capable of doing audio CD import.

Now let's import from an audio CD into a QuickTime movie:

1. Put your audio CD into your CD-ROM drive, as you would any CD-ROM.

   It should become visible on your desktop as Audio CD 1. If the audio CD does not appear, see the manuals that came with your drive to make sure that you've installed the software correctly.

2. Open MoviePlayer.

   MoviePlayer will need to be on your hard drive. You can use any QuickTime-savvy application to do this.

3. Choose Import from the File menu and use the standard file dialog box that you see to navigate your way to your audio CD.

4. Click on any of the files in the list (which will be named Track 1, Track 2, and so on).

   The Open button will change to a Convert button (see figure 7.19).

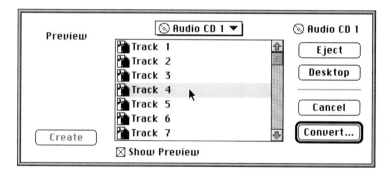

Figure 7.19   *Clicking on an audio CD track causes the Open button to become a Convert button*

5. Click on Convert.

   A Save dialog box with an Options button will appear.

6. Click on the Options button.

   You'll see the Audio CD Import Options dialog box (see figure 7.20).

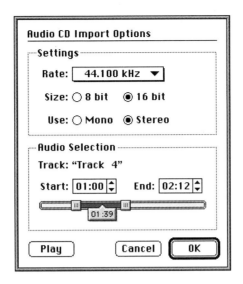

Figure 7.20   *Audio CD Import Options dialog box*

With this dialog box, you can configure various sound settings of the resulting QuickTime movie. In the lower part of the window, you will probably want to select only a portion of the track by specifying a start time and end time for the track. You can play the selection to be sure that you have the portion you want.

Note

Even if your Mac can't handle CD-quality sound—44 kHz, 16-bit stereo— you can still import the audio in this high quality format because you're really just copying digital data from the CD to your hard drive, not digitizing it.

7. Click on OK to return to the Save dialog box and save the file, renaming it if you wish, to your hard disk (you'll have to navigate there first).

A progress box appears as your CD audio track is converted to a QuickTime movie.

This audio-only movie can be opened in any QuickTime-savvy application.

Exporting QuickTime

This chapter is all about making QuickTime files from other types of files. A few of you, however, may be interested in the reverse process. Given a QuickTime movie, you can use MoviePlayer to convert it to a PICT still image file if it has a video track, an AIFF sound file if it has a sound track, or a text file if it has a text track. Do this by choosing Export from the File menu. You'll get a save dialog box that includes a popup menu to choose the format you'd like to save as (see figure 7.21). The choices you're given in this menu depend on what kinds of tracks you have in the movie. If you're saving as PICT or sound, you can click on an Options button to bring up a dialog box in which you choose compression options or sound options, respectively.

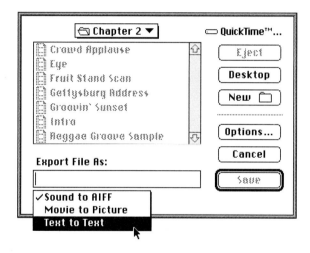

Figure 7.21   *Save dialog box when exporting a movie with video, sound, and text tracks*

An alternative to using the Export command is to copy and paste or drag and drop (if you have drag and drop) from the QuickTime movie to another application that can handle the type of data you're moving.

Music Track

You can convert a standard *General Musical Instrument Digital Interface* file (more commonly called a *General MIDI* file) into a QuickTime music file. Most of the commercial music software for sequencing and/or musical notation can export as General MIDI.

We have supplied a General MIDI file on the CD that comes with book. Let's make a QuickTime music track movie from that file:

1. Open the application MoviePlayer and choose Import from the File menu.

2. Navigate to the Chapter 7 folder in the Media folder on the CD and select the file "Space-bass part."

   Once again, the Open button changes to a Convert... button.

   ### Even More Credit

   The Space-bass part file is another Bruce Linde composition.

3. Click on the Convert button.

   You are presented with a Save dialog box. QuickTime has added the word *movie* after the original file name. There is also an Options button.

   ### Warning!

   Sometimes, if you convert a MIDI file, you'll end up with a text movie. This is due to a bug which occurs when the file contains a period, and can be remedied by changing the name of the file you are converting. For example, if you have a file called "CoolMusic.mid," rename it "CoolMusic mid" before trying to convert it.

4. Click on the Options button.

   A dialog box appears. Notice that this dialog box has the Standard Controller at the bottom (see figure 7.22).

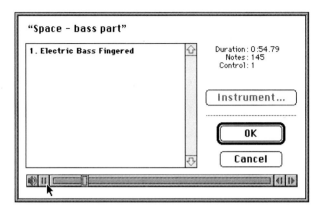

Figure 7.22   *Music Options dialog box*

5. Click on the play button to hear this musical piece.

   Above the Standard Controller is a list of the musical instruments in the piece. There is just one in this particular piece.

6. Click on the instrument in the list.

   The Instrument button becomes enabled.

7. Click on the Instrument button to get still another dialog box.

   This is the Standard Instrument Picker dialog box, which enables you to change the instruments just as you did in Chapter 4 when you edited music files (see figure 7.23).

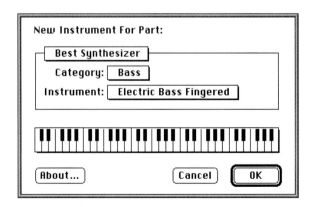

Figure 7.23   *Standard Instrument Picker dialog box*

8. Make any changes you'd like and click on OK. (Remember that instruments in italics are not available; if you choose one, another instrument will be substituted for it.)

9. Click on OK again to close the Music Options dialog box, and then save the file.

In the future, we'll probably see software for creating a QuickTime music file rather than converting from General MIDI as we just did.

Recording from a MIDI Device

Recording from a MIDI device is a fairly complex and expensive thing to do, and for most musicians, it is not very practical.

You connect your MIDI device—a keyboard, for example—to your Macintosh. You'll need a MIDI interface box to go between the Mac and the keyboard. This box will have MIDI In and MIDI Out and sometimes MIDI Thru ports; it will also have a serial cable connector, which you plug into the printer or modem port on your Mac.

After you have all of the hardware in place, you will need software: Apple's MIDI Manager and PatchBay (bundled together), and some type of MIDI or QuickTime music grabbing software. (For grabbing software you can use the shareware program called DeskTop TV 1.2, included on the QuickTime Guide CD as part of the Movie Trilogy). When you have the hardware and software in place, recording from a MIDI device is basically like recording from live video.

The problem is that when the file is recorded, you can't edit the notes. Most musicians don't play a piece straight through without a mistake.

Is This Really QuickTime?

Some people believe that movies created using these imports and conversions aren't really QuickTime. Our response: they certainly are.

Most QuickTime applications enable you do the same imports that we've shown you in this chapter. They're all a function of QuickTime, not MoviePlayer.

While video is what made QuickTime so popular in the first place, QuickTime was designed from the ground up to deal with all sorts of data types. It's multimedia in the true sense of the word.

In the future, you can expect to see more and more applications that save files in QuickTime format so that you can use them in your QuickTime productions without even having to do a conversion or import.

However you make your movies—whether exporting from other applications, importing into QuickTime applications, or digitizing video—understanding compression is instrumental to getting good results. Which leads us gracefully into the next chapter.

Chapter 8

Compression—
The Key to
QuickTime

W

e have mentioned compression here and there in previous chapters. Now we'll talk about why compression is so important to QuickTime, how QuickTime handles compression, how you interact with the compression in QuickTime, and what choices you need to make concerning compression. We will also talk about compressing photographic still images.

Why Compression is So Important

Compression is crucial to the video track, particularly if you want to see motion video. What you want to remember is that there is an incredible amount of information that has to be processed in order to record or show something resembling video. Just think: to get full-motion video (30 frames per second), you're asking the computer to show 30 images in one second. If we're talking about a full screen, each of those images is fairly complicated; a standard 13- or 14-inch monitor has over 300,000 pixels, each of which has to be assigned a color to give you an image. On a color system that shows millions of colors, it takes over 900 kilobytes to specify all of those pixels. (We explain these numbers in a moment.) To get 30 frames per second, you'd need close to 30 megabytes *for each second of video*. And that doesn't even include the audio!

To put this problem in perspective, a common size for Macintosh hard disks today is 80 megabytes. That's room for less than eight seconds of raw digital video. And imagine asking your computer to do *anything* with even a tenth of a hard disk's worth of information in one second. Would you expect, for example, your computer to be able to copy 30 megabytes of information in one second? It's too much information in its raw state to store and too much information to move onto your screen quickly enough to remotely resemble video. Even if you use only a portion of the screen, as in a QuickTime movie, it's *still* too much information.

How Big is That Image in the Window?

There are three "guns" inside a color monitor. One gun shoots red, another shoots green, and a third shoots blue. Using these three guns, the monitor has the ability to show all of the colors that a color TV can. Basically, each gun in the monitor can display 256 different shades. So, that gives you 256 x 256 x 256 = 16,777,216 colors (let's say 16 million colors). To specify one of these 16 million colors requires 24 bits of data per pixel: 8 bits to specify which red, plus 8 bits to specify which green, plus 8 bits to specify which blue.

Now, a standard Apple 13- or 14-inch monitor is 640 pixels across and 480 pixels down; this gives us 307,200 pixels. On a 24-bit color system, any one of these 307,200 pixels can be one of the 16 million colors. If you multiply the number of pixels by the number of bits to describe each pixel, you get 7,372,800 bits.

Because we're used to talking about computer storage in terms of bytes rather than bits, we now get to divide by 8 (there are 8 bits to a byte). That gives us 921,600 bytes per frame. If you lay it out equation-like it looks like this:

256 (reds) x 256 (greens) x 256 (blues) =16,777,216 (different colors)

And:

307,200 (pixels on 13" display) x 24 (bits per pixel) = 7,372,800 (bits to describe the whole screen)

Finally:

7,372,800 (bits to describe the whole screen) / 8 (bits per byte) = 921,600 (bytes to describe the whole screen)

Or approximately:

900 kilobytes to describe an entire screen image.

QuickTime and Compression

So what's a computer to do? Or rather, what's a software designer to do? Well, the basic idea is to cut down on the amount of data that has to be processed by and stored on the computer.

That's one of the things that the developers of QuickTime worked on. They worked on *compressing* the amount of information required to show something that looks like video. Essentially, they devised ways of cheating: although you may be seeing what looks like many megabytes of information per second, the data that's actually been stored is much less. They wrote programs, called *compressors*, that throw out nonessential data and also store the remaining data more efficiently. Complimentary programs, called *decompressors*, are required to read and play back the compressed data.

Audio Compression

Like video, the audio portion of your QuickTime movies can also be compressed. However, in most cases, you don't want to do this. As we've mentioned earlier, you are more sensitive to artifacts in sound than you are to artifacts in a moving image. When you compress audio, you lose fidelity and introduce artifacts that may make for an unpleasant or unbearable listening experience. You are also asking your computer to decompress audio and video at the same time—that's a tall order. With all of that said, there are still times that you will want to compress audio.

To compress audio, you access the different options in the Sound Settings dialog box, where there's a choice for setting compression (see figure 8.1). Here you'll see MACE (Macintosh Audio Compression and Expansion), an audio compression standard that's been available on the Mac for many years.

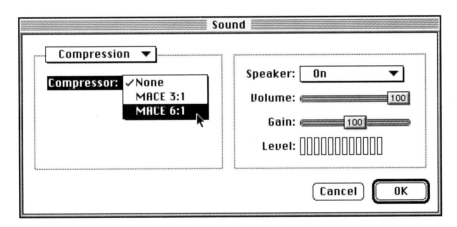

Figure 8.1   *Audio compression choices in the standard Sound Settings dialog box*

With QuickTime 2.0, Apple introduced IMA (Interactive Multimedia Association) compression, which has a 4:1 ratio. The quality of compressed audio from this compressor is very good compared to MACE. However, IMA was added to QuickTime 2.0 just before it shipped, and it doesn't show up in the standard Sound Settings dialog box. Look for it in the next version of QuickTime. Or, you can use the unsupported utility, Sound Converter, which is on the QuickTime Guide CD.

Lossless versus Lossy Algorithms

You may be familiar with general-purpose compression programs such as StuffIt or DiskDoubler. These programs know how to store data more efficiently. The difference between using a general-purpose compression program and using QuickTime compression is the difference between *lossless* and *lossy* algorithms.

Lossless means that what goes in is exactly what comes out. No information is lost. This is a very good technique to use to compress computer programs or word processing files because what you feed the compressor is the same before and after it is decompressed. If you have lost information, your program might not work, or your word processing document might have missing characters.

However, a lossless algorithm often does not provide sufficient compression when dealing with images.

The compression programs for QuickTime are almost all *lossy* algorithms. Lossy algorithms are those that actually throw away image data when you compress the file. However, these algorithms are designed in such a way that it is difficult to see the loss because crucial information is not lost.

Spatial and Temporal Compression

There are two basic ways that moving images can be compressed. These are called *spatial compression* and *temporal compression*.

When a compressor does spatial compression, it essentially throws out redundant data from individual frames. For example, if a large amount of the frame is blue sky, it doesn't save the information that Pixel 1 is blue, Pixel 2 is blue, and so on. Instead, it will just save the information that the top half of the frame is blue.

When a compressor does temporal compression, it throws out whatever data are repeated from one frame to the next. It saves a single frame in its entirety, but for subsequent frames, it saves only the parts of the picture that have changed. The first frame is called a *key frame*; the subsequent frames are referred to as *differenced frames*. Temporal compression works well when there is a large amount of information that stays the same from frame to frame. For instance, if the top half of the movie is a blue sky and that doesn't change for the entire length of the movie, then temporal compression can save a lot of space.

Codecs

When we talk about compression, we often refer to *compression ratios*. For example, a compression ratio of 3:1 (said "3 to 1") means that the original size was three times greater than the compressed size.

The compression ratios achieved in the first release of QuickTime were between 5:1 and 10:1. This amount of compression was good enough to get a 160 x 120 pixel movie playing almost full motion on a fast Macintosh. Of course, the developers of QuickTime knew that you wouldn't be completely happy with those results. So, knowing that the future would bring better methods of compression, they built QuickTime so that new compression programs could be added to your Macintosh system as easily as you can add new components to your stereo system.

These compression programs are called *codecs*, which stands for *compressor-decompressors*. Apple provides seven of these codecs within QuickTime. Other programmers can also write new codecs. Implementing a new codec doesn't require Apple having to write a whole new version of QuickTime. Instead, you just take that codec and put it into your System folder. When you make a movie with QuickTime, you just tell it to use this codec rather than a built-in one. When you play the movie, as long as the codec is in the System folder, QuickTime automatically knows to use that codec to decompress the movie.

And, as a matter of fact, within months of QuickTime's introduction, a new codec was announced that could give us movies with 320 x 240 pixels and 30 frames per second on a really fast Macintosh. It was developed jointly by Apple and SuperMac Technologies and could have been distributed as an external codec. But, Apple included it in version 1.5 of QuickTime, calling it *Compact Video*; it was renamed *Cinepak* in version 1.6.1.

Assume that the future will bring even better compression schemes. Everything about QuickTime will work the same way; it'll just be better.

Compression Choices You'll Make

When will you do compression on a movie? What software do you use? You'll find the ability to compress a movie in various types of software.

Digitizing software lets you compress at these different points in the process:

- **While digitizing**. You don't want to do this unless you are using a hardware compression card.
- **Immediately after digitizing**. This is post-compression, which we discussed in Chapter 6.
- **When you save your newly digitized file**.

Editing applications always provide a way to compress or recompress your creation when you save it as a QuickTime movie.

Note

When saving with VideoFusion and QuickFLIX! editors, you'll find your compression choices if you choose Save as Optimized.

Post-processing applications, such as ConvertToMovie (which we used in the preceding chapter) and MovieShop (which we'll discuss in the next chapter) also let you open a movie and recompress it.

You'll find that you need to make the same choices no matter where and when you're compressing. So let's dive into the details of compression in QuickTime.

In most applications, you'll see the same dialog box when you set your compression settings. That dialog box will look something like the one in figure 8.2.

To see and play with this dialog box yourself, open ConvertToMovie, which is in the Unsupported Stuff folder, and, when instructed, pick any movie file. The Standard Compression dialog box will appear.

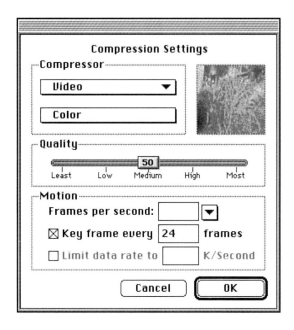

Figure 8.2   *Standard Compression dialog box*

Spatial Compression in the Standard Compression Dialog Box

The top portion of the Standard Compression dialog box has settings for spatial compression. We'll look at those first.

Image Sample

Start by looking in the upper-right corner. You'll see what's called the *image sample*, which shows you the effects of some of the choices you make in the dialog box. You can zoom in on the image by clicking on it while holding down the Option key. If the whole image doesn't fit, you can click and drag in the image sample to move the image around.

Compressor

The first choice you'll see is the choice for compressor (or codec). QuickTime has seven built-in compressors: Animation, Cinepak, Component Video, Graphics, None, Photo - JPEG, and Video (see figure 8.3).

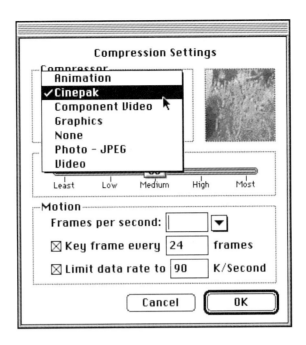

Figure 8.3   *Choosing a compressor in the Standard Compression dialog box*

If you're compressing digital video, you will normally choose one of the three compressors designed for compressing video: Video, Cinepak, or Component Video.

The *Video* compressor yields about 10:1 compression and was the first QuickTime video compressor. Although many people stopped using Video when Cinepak appeared, it's still useful, particularly when you need to compress quickly.

Apple Video Player

Apple Video Player, the software that comes with the Apple Video System for Macintosh 630s, doesn't provide a Standard Compression dialog box. Instead, in the Preferences window, you are given compression choices of None, Normal, and Most. None, of course, provides virtually no compression. If you choose Normal or Most, it uses the Apple Video codec with spatial quality settings of Most and Normal, respectively (the software never tells you this anywhere).

Cinepak achieves compression ratios double those of Apple Video, but it takes much longer to do the initial compression. Using the Cinepak compressor, a 30-second clip can easily take over an hour to compress, unless you are using a Power Mac—make sure you have something to keep you busy during this process!

Tip

If you're going to be doing much Cinepak compression, seriously consider getting a Power Mac, which will compress at least twice as fast as any other Macintosh. This efficiency is due to the QuickTime PowerPlug, which contains *native* versions of the QuickTime built-in compressors.

Both Video and Cinepak compressors decompress very rapidly; they need to decompress rapidly in order to show their complex images at a decent frame rate.

The third video compressor, *Component Video* (also called *Component - YUV* or just *YUV*), was released with QuickTime 1.6 and provides very high-quality images but very low compression ratios (2:1). The YUV compressor is useful with S-Video, such as S-VHS or Hi-8, when you need an intermediate storage format. That is, when you first digitize, use the YUV codec, which will give you great image quality movies to work with. Later, after doing all of your editing (applying multiple effects), you can recompress using a compressor that will give you much better compression.

The *Photo - JPEG* compressor is for high-resolution still images, such as digitized photos. *JPEG* stands for *Joint Photographic Expert Group*. It is a still image compression method used throughout the world on many different types of computers. It can be used for video, but unlike QuickTime's video compressors, it decompresses quite slowly. Its advantage is that it stores each frame like a high-quality photograph, providing very nice image quality, but better compression ratios than Component Video. For this reason, it's a good way to ship movies around when they're going to be further compressed. As a matter of fact, on the QuickTime Guide CD we provide a JPEG-compressed movie for you to further compress as part of your learning experience.

JPEG Hardware-Assisted Compression

In Chapter 6 we described hardware compression cards. Most of these cards use JPEG compression. Although JPEG is too slow a compression method to use when doing software-only compression, it works great with these hardware solutions. Most of the boards that do hardware compression use a specialized JPEG codec—often referred to as *Motion-JPEG*—for compression and decompression. When you go to choose a compressor, you'll see an extra JPEG compressor in the list.

If you use these hardware solutions to make your movies, remember that you must have the same hardware for full-screen, full-motion playback—the JPEG decompression algorithms won't work at all without the card.

A technique often used when producing many movies that need to play back on machines without compression hardware is to take the hardware JPEG-compressed movies, recompress them with the software JPEG codec that comes with QuickTime, and then copy the files to other machines for final compression to a video compressor like Cinepak. Why the intermediate step of compressing with software JPEG? JPEG compression is much faster than Cinepak compression, so it more quickly frees up your digitizing station, and lets you use any available Mac (or Macs) to do the final, lengthy compression to Cinepak.

The *Animation* compressor is primarily for computer-generated animations.

Apple's *Graphics* compressor is similar to the Animation one but only works in 256 colors. For a 256-color animation, Graphics is probably a better choice than Animation.

The final compressor is *None* (also referred to as *Raw*), which you'll use if you don't want any significant compression done on your movie, probably because you're going to apply compression at a later time. (You may recall that in Chapter 6 we recommended digitizing with the None compressor and then post-compressing with another compressor.)

Warning!

The digitizing application ScreenPlay (which you use only with SuperMac/Radius's Spigot line of digitizers) uses its own compression algorithm rather than one of the QuickTime built-in codecs. If you save the movie using the Save command from the File menu, you will save the file with SuperMac's compressor; any subsequent playback using any software other than ScreenPlay will require a special file that will do the decompressing (that is, it's not really a codec; it's just a "dec"). This is the file called "VideoSpigot extension" and comes with ScreenPlay. If, however, you use the Save As command, you'll be given a choice of the standard QuickTime compressors; using one of them will ensure that the movie can play back on any QuickTime-compatible Mac without that extra extension.

The seven built-in compressors are available to all programs that use QuickTime. You may see more than these, however. Remember that programmers can write additional codecs when new compression techniques are developed. If you've put such a codec in your System folder, it will appear in the list of compressors that you see (see figure 8.4).

One such codec is *Indeo*, developed by Intel. Like Cinepak, it can limit the data rate. However, it requires more horsepower for decent playback than does Cinepak. That is, Indeo really only works well on fast machines, whereas Cinepak works well on all Macs.

Keep in mind that you can use any compressor that appears in the list on your QuickTime movie, but the results will vary. If you're working with video, you probably want to stick with Apple's video compressors or some other compressor that is designed for video. Otherwise, you might not get something that looks like video. For example, JPEG is a compression method that was designed to work best with high-resolution still images. This means that if you compress with the Photo - JPEG compressor, you'll probably get a movie in which each individual frame has excellent quality, but the movie as a whole plays terribly because JPEG is not designed to decompress quickly enough to show frames in rapid succession. Instead, you'd get something that looks like one picture after another being flashed on the screen.

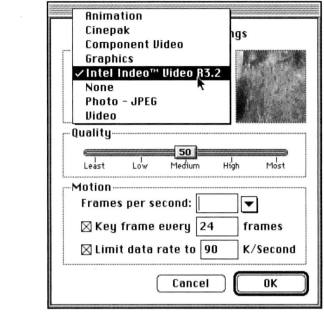

Indeo™ Video

Figure 8.4   *An additional codec and how it appears in the list of compressors*

MPEG

MPEG is an emerging standard for digital video. MPEG stands for the *Mo*tion *P*icture *E*xperts *G*roup. MPEG video has a very high compression ratio; you can fit 74 minutes of VHS-quality video and audio on a CD-ROM (compare this to current audio CDs which hold 74 minutes of only audio).

QuickTime 2.0 supports MPEG, but it doesn't actually compress or decompress MPEG-compressed movies. It has the capability to open and play MPEG-compressed files with the addition of an MPEG decoder (a card that does take care of decompression). In the future, Apple may include MPEG decoding hardware on the motherboard of its computers.

If you have an MPEG movie file and no MPEG hardware decompression board, you can use the shareware application Sparkle (included on the CD) to play the MPEG file. However, if you try to play anything but a small-framed MPEG movie (typically 160 x 120), performance will be terrible. Also, currently Sparkle won't play back MPEG files that contain audio.

Number of Colors

Immediately below the popup menu that enables you to pick a compressor, you'll typically see a popup that enables you to choose the number of colors of which the images in your movie are composed. This choice can range from black-and-white to millions of colors (this corresponds to *color depth*, which we talked about when we first showed you a QuickTime movie). The color depth choice you make will directly affect the image quality. If you look at the image sample, you will see the effects of your color choice, assuming your equipment can show the color choice you made.

Some compressors don't enable you to choose the number of colors. If you choose any of the Apple video compressors as your compressor, you'll see that you don't get a choice for number of colors; instead, the popup menu is stuck on *Color*. Though it doesn't say so, the Video compressor is really saving your image in thousands of colors, which provide a reasonable approximation to the color in a TV image. Cinepak and YUV save millions of colors, easily as many colors as could exist in a TV image.

Note that when you record, you can save information about more colors than your display can show. That is, even if 256 colors is the maximum color depth that you can set in your Monitors control panel, you can still record and compress a movie in thousands or millions of colors. You can't see all of those colors on your system, but if you take the movie to a system that can show thousands or millions of colors, those colors will be there, and the movie will look much more like normal video.

Of the other Apple compressors, only None and Animation give you the full range of number of colors to choose from. Graphics and Photo - JPEG give you only a choice of *Color* or *Grayscale*. Graphics automatically defaults to 256 colors. JPEG automatically defaults to millions.

Quality

Whenever you choose a compressor, you will be able to choose the quality of the image that you want after compression. You'll almost always make this choice in the same place where you choose a compressor. Typically, you'll set the quality with a slider, which has numerical values from 0 to 100 (see figure 8.5). You'll also see labels that say *Least, Low, Normal, High,* and *Most*. In applications that were developed before QuickTime 2.0, you may also see scales from 1 to 5 and 0 to 4, as well as numbers from 0 to 1024; in all cases, the highest number means the highest quality.

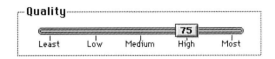

Figure 8.5 *Quality slider in the Standard Compression dialog box*

When you set quality, you directly affect the degree of compression—quality of image and degree of compression are inversely proportional. The higher you set the quality, the less compressed your movie will be. The lower the quality, the greater the degree of compression. Again, you should see the effects of your choice in the image sample in the upper right corner of the dialog box.

Temporal Compression in the Standard Compression Dialog Box

Finally, there are ways to set the way QuickTime does temporal compression. All of the QuickTime built-in compressors, except for JPEG, Component Video, and None, do temporal compression.

The options that are in this category are *frames per second*, *key frames*, and *data rate*. In the standard dialog box, they appear immediately below the Quality slider and are sometimes labeled *Motion* (see figure 8.6). Sometimes these options are located in other places in the software. Regardless of where they appear, they mean the same thing.

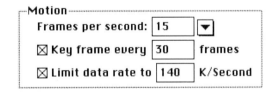

Figure 8.6 *Temporal settings portion of the Standard Compression dialog box*

Frames per Second

If you know that your movie is never going to play on anything but a slow machine, saving 30 frames per second, or even 20, is a bad idea. Remember that when

QuickTime plays on a slower computer, it drops out video frames in order to keep up. Why store all of that information that nobody is ever going to see? Also, your movies will perform better if no frame-dropping has to occur.

When you set the frames-per-second number, you're setting a maximum, not a minimum. Obviously, if you have a movie that's been recorded at 10 frames per second, asking it to be compressed at 15 frames per second isn't going to give you back frames that were lost in the digitizing process; instead it will simply duplicate existing frames.

Tip

For movies created by digitizing video, you'll get the best results if you set frame rates to be an even divisor of 30 (for example, 15 or 10 frames per second).

Key Frames

When QuickTime does temporal compression, it does what's called *frame differencing*. This is the process of figuring out what information has changed from a starting frame to subsequent frames. The starting frame is called a *key frame*. The key frame contains all of the information for a particular scene. Subsequent frames contain the information that changed.

You can specify here how often you want key frames to occur. If you don't have enough key frames, the quality of your movie will be very low because most frames are generated from others. Of course, more key frames also means a movie that is larger and won't be able to play as many frames per second. If you were doing a movie that was going to be played from a slow medium, such as CD-ROM, you would want key frames less often, resulting in a smaller movie with a lower data rate.

It's usually a good idea to set key frames to occur every second, or perhaps every other second. For example, a 15-frame-per-second movie should have a key frame every 15 frames or every 30 frames. Also, if QuickTime senses that more than 90 percent of the image data changes when it compresses, it will automatically insert a key frame.

Tip

If you hold down the Option key while the cursor is over the Quality Settings slider, the title of the box changes from Quality to Temporal, enabling you to set the degree of temporal compression that occurs between key frames. However, this will only work if the key frames option is turned on.

Data Rate

When you play a movie, a certain amount of data is available to be played every second. This amount is called the *data rate* of the movie. It is usually measured in kilobytes or megabytes per second. Recall from Chapter 4 that you can check the data rate of a movie using the Info dialog box in MoviePlayer.

Some computer configurations can handle higher data rates than others, so you may want to limit the data rate, depending on your target audience. For example, if you want a movie to play from single-speed CD-ROM drives, you need to limit the data rate to a maximum of about 130 k/sec. We'll talk more about CD-ROM data rates in the next chapter.

Currently, you can only set data rate if you are using the Cinepak compressor. If you choose any other compressor, the data rate option will be grayed out.

Compressor Summary

Table 8.1 provides a summary of compressors.

Table 8.1   Summary of Compressors

Compressor	Advantages	Disadvantages	Approx. Ratio
Video	Very fast compressing and decompressing of video. Good for testing clips. OK on hard disk playback.	Image quality is poor when compressing enough for CD-ROM playback.	10:1

continues

Table 8.1   Continued

Compressor	Advantages	Disadvantages	Approx. Ratio
YUV	A high quality compressor. Good for capture on AV Macs and as intermediate storage format.	Low compression ratios. Larger files.	2:1
Animation	Works best on computer generated animations with broad areas of flat color.	Doesn't work well when the scene has lots of color changes.	1.3:1
Graphics	Good for 8-bit graphics file. Usually better than the Animation compressor.	Slower to decompress than animation.	2.5:1
JPEG	Ideal for high-quality compressed still images. Also useful as intermediate storage format for movies.	Decompression is too slow to use for video-based movie playback.	5:1 to 50:1
Cinepak	Best compressor for video movies that require CD-ROM playback.	Very slow compressing.	25:1
None	Good for capture. Does almost no compression.	Big files.	2:1

QuickTime and Still Images

For many people, QuickTime opens the door to digital video. However, still image users also benefit from QuickTime's compression capabilities.

Those who work with large, high-quality still images will recognize the significance of this benefit immediately. Also, anyone who has tried to send images over phone lines or through networks can benefit from still image compression. The main problem with working with images is their file size.

Earlier in this chapter we pointed out that one frame of full-screen video could take up almost a megabyte. You might think that's not that big.

However, the resolution of your computer screen is only 72 dots per inch. If you're going to be printing the image, you want a high-resolution image, a minimum of 300 dots per inch. This requires almost 18 times the amount of information needed for an image that will only be shown on a computer screen.

In the past, you could have dealt with this problem by using utilities such as StuffIt or DiskDoubler. These utilities give you around 2:1 lossless compression. Using the Photo - JPEG compressor built into QuickTime, you can get anywhere from 8:1 to 100:1 lossy compression. This is quite a space savings while maintaining good quality at the same time!

Compressing Still Images

Many applications that work with photographic still images provide access to QuickTime's compression schemes.

If you use Apple PhotoFlash or Adobe Photoshop, you can do QuickTime compression if you save your file as a PICT file.

PhotoFlash allows you to choose from any of the standard QuickTime compressors. However, the Photo - JPEG compressor is designed for compressing photographic still images, so you'll want to choose it in most cases. A Quality Settings slider is also provided (see figure 8.7).

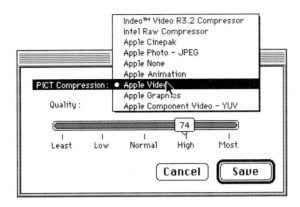

Figure 8.7 *PhotoFlash's Compression dialog box*

PhotoFlash

A demo version of Apple PhotoFlash is on the CD that comes with
this book.

Other applications, such as Photoshop, don't give you a choice of compressor—JPEG
is used automatically. You choose quality by clicking a radio button rather than
moving the slider (see figure 8.8).

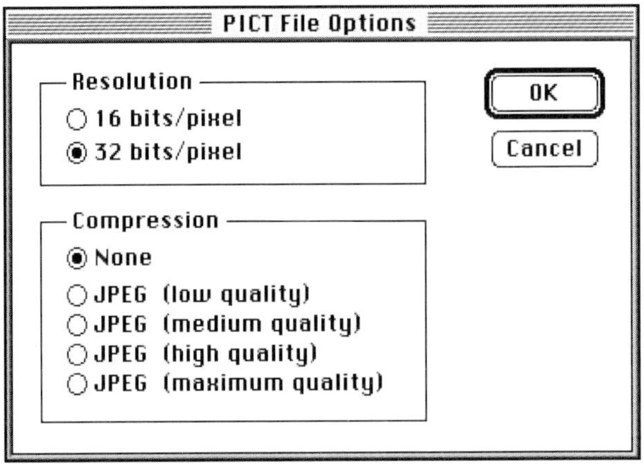

Figure 8.8 *Setting compression in Photoshop*

Opening QuickTime Compressed Images

If you have an application that can open a PICT image, you don't need anything but the QuickTime extension to view an image compressed with QuickTime. Opening a QuickTime-compressed PICT file requires the same steps as opening a normal PICT file, but it may take a little longer for the image to open because it first must be decompressed.

Learning More about Compression

The best way to learn about compression in QuickTime is to experiment. It's fun and educational to take a single movie and compress it in a variety of ways so that you can see just what the differences between the various settings mean. Change the compressor, color depth, quality settings, temporal settings, and key frames. In the Chapter 8 folder within the Media folder is a file called "Fabulous Fish," which is JPEG compressed. It's a good file to experiment with.

Some of the same experiments can be done with still images.

Waiting for QuickTime to do compression can be quite tedious. However, as you're learning, you should try at least a few different settings for any movie or still image you create to see what works best for that particular file.

Remember also that QuickTime is extensible. You can add new and better compressors as they're developed.

Ultimately, some of your decisions about compression will be dependent on how you're planning to distribute your movies. In the next chapter we talk about all sorts of distribution issues.

Chapter 9

Distributing Movies—Sharing Your Work

W

hen you've made your own movies and edited them to your satisfaction, you need to think about how to distribute them to other people. After all, you don't want to keep these masterpieces to yourself, do you?

Sometimes you can fit a movie on a floppy disk—if it has only a music track and text track, for example—but that's not usually possible. Removable media is also a possibility, but it can be expensive and requires drives that your audience may not have.

In this chapter, we explore the variety of ways that people are sharing their QuickTime movie productions—CD-ROM, networks, videotape, and more.

Digital Distribution

We'll first cover those methods of distribution that maintain the digital format of your movie files—that is, methods that will require your audience to have a computer.

CD-ROM

In many cases, it makes sense to consider distributing your QuickTime movies on CD-ROM. The advantages of using CD-ROM are that a single disc can hold over 600 megabytes of data, it is compact, and it is relatively inexpensive to produce if you produce enough copies. The disadvantages are that CD-ROM is a very slow medium, and it is a read-only medium. Also, your audience must have CD-ROM drives in order to play the movies. However, the speed of CD-ROM drives is increasing, and prices are dropping so these two problems aren't really significant barriers to using CDs any more.

Costs

What are the costs of producing a CD-ROM? You may have heard people saying that each CD-ROM costs one dollar to make. Well, there are more costs than that involved. You must pay a fee of about $1,000 for *mastering*. Mastering, simply put, is the process that the factory uses to format the data to make a *master*.

The master is then used to produce the hundreds or thousands of single CDs, each of which costs in the range of $1.10–$1.60 per disc depending on the quantity you have made. (See table 9.1 for an example of how much a CD may cost to produce.) Most of the mastering houses give you two colors on the *label*—the image on the disc—for "free;" they will charge you for more color and special inks. Each standard *jewel case* (the plastic box that the CD comes in) costs about 35 cents; other types of packaging are about the same or more. Then you may have the costs of packaging and printing the *liner notes* (the paper inserts that come with a CD). You also need to factor in the amount of time you can give the mastering house to produce the CD. Some factories can turn a disc around in one day, but you will pay a premium for faster processing!

Table 9.1   Sample Costs to Make 1000 Discs

Item	Cost
Mastering (7-day turnaround):	$1,000.00
Cost per disc (@1.17 each):	1,170.00
Jewel Case (@.35 each):	350.00
Liner notes (4 pages/4 colors, .63 each):	630.00
Total (x 1000) =	$3,150.00

There are devices, known as *CD-ROM writers, one-off machines,* or *CD-ROM recorders,* that *burn* single copies of CD-ROMs, which then serve as test discs. It's a very good idea to make test CDs (more than one!) before spending thousands of dollars mass producing them. CD-ROM writers are becoming very popular and are dropping in price—you can now buy one for a few thousand dollars.

Processing Movies for CD-ROM

If you do want to distribute your QuickTime movies on CD-ROM and you expect that they'll be played directly from the CD-ROM drive (rather than being copied first to a hard disk), you'll need to make sure that the data rate—the amount of data that has to be processed by your computer to put those images on the screen—is low enough. Cinepak is the only compressor that can get low enough data rates for CD—around 140 kbps for single speed CD-ROM playback, and 280 kbps for double-speed playback—and still have the movies look OK. Just about any application that enables you to compress movies, such as any QuickTime editing package, gives you access to Cinepak's internal data rate setting capabilities (you'll see that data rate setting field at the bottom of the Compression dialog box).

Note

Before QuickTime 2.0, you needed to stick with 90 to 100 kbps data rates for single-speed CD-ROM playback. QuickTime 2.0, however, is so much more efficient that you can bring those numbers up by almost 50 percent. However, you must make sure that QT 2.0 is running on the computers that you expect to use to play back movies with these higher data rates.

Unfortunately, just picking a data rate is usually not enough. To have the best playing movies you possibly can have, you want to *post-process* the movies, optimizing them for CD playback.

Currently, one of the best applications for post-processing movies is Apple's MovieShop, another unsupported application. When you use it, you choose various settings, including data rate, compressor, key frame spacing, and audio sampling rate; and then MovieShop carefully analyzes your movie and recompresses it in an optimal fashion, showing you its progress as it goes (see figure 9.1). It also properly interleaves the audio and video. Advanced users can switch to Expert level and use the Methods and Data Rate dialog box to control which specific techniques MovieShop uses in its optimizing (see figure 9.2). MovieShop is on the CD that comes with this book, but it is completely unsupported. Even though it is one of the most important tools for CD-ROM developers, it will probably not be updated in the future because its author, George Cossey, had to move on to other projects.

Apple now recommends using the application ConvertToMovie, which we introduced in previous chapters, for post-processing movies for CD-ROM playback because it is more up-to-date. Like MovieShop, it also optimally recompresses and reduces the data rate, as well as provides cropping, scaling, flattening, and single-forking functions. In addition, it will build a custom color table and filter, and will dither your images (see figure 9.3). It further differs from MovieShop—negatively—in that it doesn't give you anywhere near the control over the optimizing process as does MoviePlayer, and it doesn't batch-process movies. So, if you want that control or if you are processing a lot of movies, you will have to use MovieShop. ConvertToMovie is also on the CD that comes with this book, but remember that it is completely unsupported.

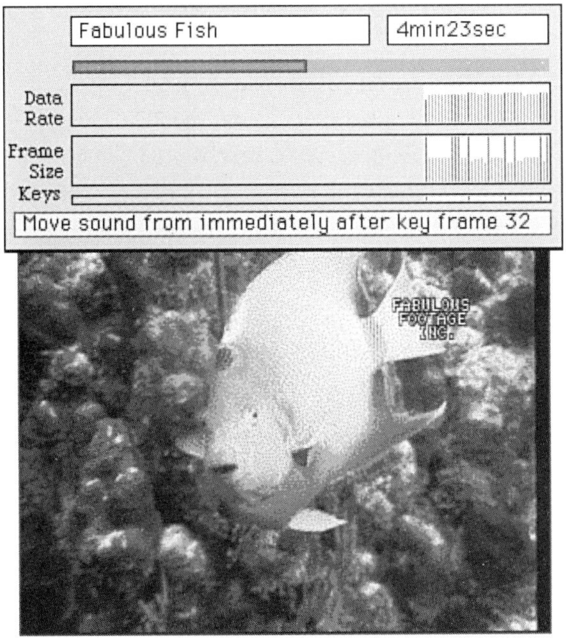

Figure 9.1   *MovieShop working to compress a movie in Novice level*

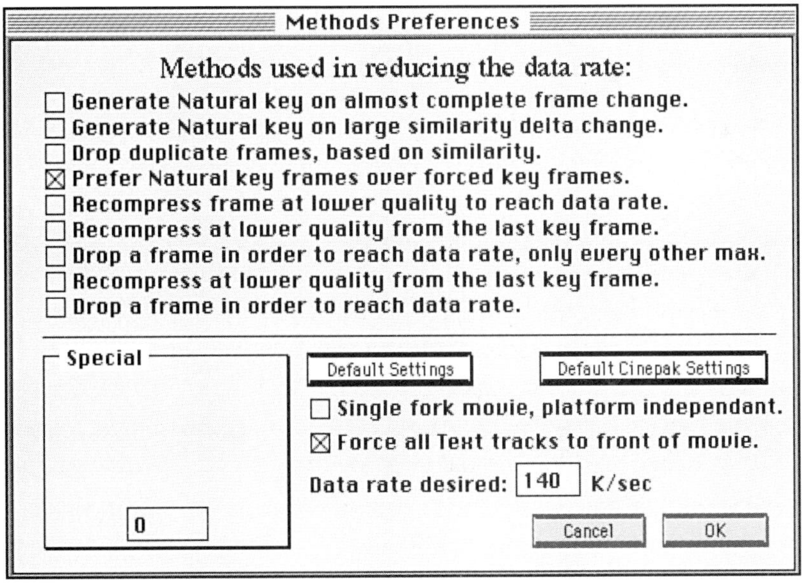

Figure 9.2   *MovieShop Methods and Data Rate dialog box in Expert level*

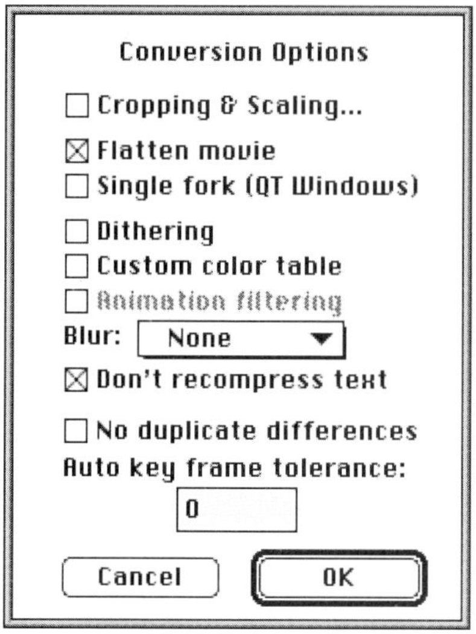

```
┌──────────────────────────────────────┐
│  ╔════════════════════════════════╗  │
│  ║      Conversion Options         ║  │
│  ║  ☐ Cropping & Scaling...        ║  │
│  ║  ☒ Flatten movie                ║  │
│  ║  ☐ Single fork (QT Windows)     ║  │
│  ║  ☐ Dithering                    ║  │
│  ║  ☐ Custom color table           ║  │
│  ║  ☐ Animation filtering          ║  │
│  ║  Blur: [  None          ▼ ]     ║  │
│  ║  ☒ Don't recompress text        ║  │
│  ║  ☐ No duplicate differences     ║  │
│  ║  Auto key frame tolerance:      ║  │
│  ║       [ 0            ]           ║  │
│  ║                                  ║  │
│  ║   ( Cancel )   (( OK ))          ║  │
│  ╚════════════════════════════════╝  │
└──────────────────────────────────────┘
```

Figure 9.3   *ConvertToMovie's Conversion Options dialog box*

QuickTime for Windows

Not only can you play QuickTime movies with a variety of Macintosh applications, you can also play the same movies on Microsoft Windows computers!

Basic Features

With QuickTime for Windows, you can play the movies on a Windows computer that you created on a Macintosh; you can even incorporate them into multimedia presentations you create on a Windows computer. QuickTime for Windows 2.0 has most of the same capabilities as QuickTime for the Macintosh. It can handle multiple-tracked movies, including text and music, custom color tables, and MPEG playback. It can't be used for compression or editing, however.

Note

Minimum system requirements for QuickTime for Windows are a 386SX at 20 MHz or better, at least 4 megabytes of RAM, an 80-megabyte hard disk, a minimum of a VGA display card, a sound card (if you want to play movies with sound), Windows 3.1, and DOS 5.0.

Why would you want to play your Macintosh movies on a Windows computer? Let's say you work in an office with both Windows and Macintosh computers, and you want to distribute a digital video movie. You would need only to create that movie once to play it back on both computers—a minor savings in time and effort. Or, if your goal is to produce a multimedia CD-ROM, you won't have to create two sets of movies—a major savings in time and effort. Also, many people think that QuickTime for Windows is the best available standard for displaying digital video on a Windows machine.

QuickTime for Windows can be licensed from Apple, so you can distribute it with your movies. It also comes with certain Windows applications that use QuickTime for Windows, such as Macromedia Authorware and Action, and Apple Media Tool.

With QuickTime for Windows, you get an application called Movie Player, which is very similar to the MoviePlayer you know and love. Open a movie file, and you'll see a familiar sight (see figure 9.4).

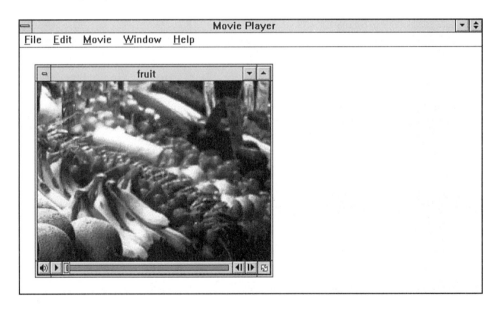

Figure 9.4 *A QuickTime movie on a Windows computer*

Notice that the controller looks just like the one with which you've already played. Anyone who knows how to play a Macintosh QuickTime movie also knows how to play a Windows QuickTime movie.

Moving a Movie to Windows

The process for moving your Macintosh QuickTime movie to a Windows computer is simple. In order to make a movie that can be played on a Windows machine, your movie file must have three important characteristics:

- The file must be a *self-contained* movie file—that is, it must have no dependencies. Another term for this kind of movie file is *flattened*.

- The file must be *single-forked*. The Macintosh keeps a file's data stored in two places, a data fork and a resource fork. A Windows computer stores data in only the data fork. So, the Macintosh file's resource data fork must be moved into its data fork. The process of making a single-fork file is sometimes wrongly referred to as *flattening*. The term *flattening* really only means making a self-contained file, but because people often do both processes at the same time, the term has become misused.

- The file must be named with DOS "8 dot 3" file naming conventions and with an extension of "MOV" (for example, "ABCDEFGH.MOV").

In Chapter 3, we explained saving movies as self-contained files. You did this using the Save dialog box in MoviePlayer. In that same dialog box is a checkbox labeled "Playable on non-Apple computers" (see figure 9.5). If you check this checkbox, the file will be saved as a single-fork file.

If you save the file with these options, you can continue to play this movie on your Macintosh. You can even edit it, but if you want to move the edited version to a Windows computer, you'll have to repeat the process to make the file single-forked.

Note

Software other than MoviePlayer can be used to save a movie so that it's playable on non-Apple computers. Two examples are Adobe Premiere, which uses the term "flattened movie," and Avid VideoShop, which uses the term "cross-platform movie." On the CD that comes with this book is an unsupported application called SingleForkFlattener that will also create a flattened, single-fork file.

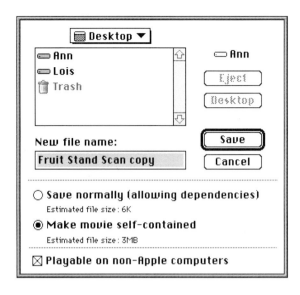

Figure 9.5   *Save dialog box from MoviePlayer 2.0*

When you have a flattened, single-forked, appropriately named movie, you're ready to move it to your Windows computer. There are a number of ways to move files from the Macintosh to a Windows/DOS computer. If your movie file will fit on a floppy disk, you can transfer it that way, as long as you have a high density floppy drive and software to enable your Macintosh to read from and write to Windows/DOS formatted disks. Of course, QuickTime files provide special challenges because they tend to be too large to fit on a floppy disk. Other solutions are to move the files over a modem or network or to use larger capacity removable media, such as SyQuest cartridges or magneto optical disks. Any of these other solutions will require additional hardware and/or software.

Network Playback

Can you play QuickTime movies over a local area network? With a fast network—one using Ethernet, for example—you can have one user play a small-framed, relatively low frame rate movie over the network. However, don't try to have more than one user look at the same movie because performance will be unacceptable.

If you really need reasonable performance of QuickTime movies over a network or want multiple users to be able to view the same movie at the same time, you'll want to look into specialized video network servers, which can set you back upwards of $20,000. One example is Starlight Network's system.

QuickTime Movies on the Internet

For the most part, QuickTime movies on the Internet means QuickTime movies on the World-Wide Web. The Web is a bunch of machines, connected on the Internet, with the ability to show formatted text and pictures in a point-and-click interface (see figure 9.6 for an example). You will need to be connected to the Internet to use the Web.

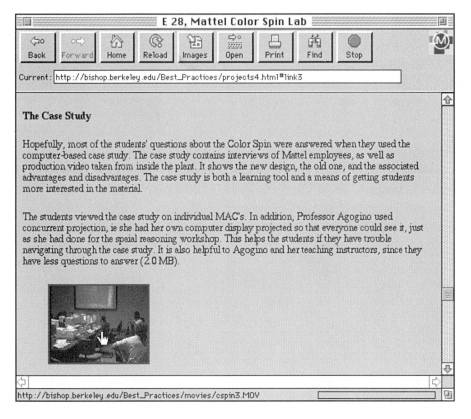

Figure 9.6   *A Web page containing a QuickTime movie*

Viewing Movies on the Internet

There are various browser programs, such as MacWeb, NetScape, and Mosaic, which are used to access the Web. If you need information on these browser programs or on the World-Wide Web in general, check out *Internet Start Kit for Macintosh, 2nd Edition*, by Adam Engst (Hayden Books, 1994).

When you see a movie on a Web page, you can click on it to have it downloaded to your computer.

Movies on the Web may not be QuickTime movies, however. Often movies on the Internet are in the MPEG format because most of the computers on the Net are UNIX-based, and there is no QuickTime for UNIX. Also, all of the MPEG viewing and creation software for UNIX is basically free, so that makes it the standard. To view these MPEG files on the Macintosh, you will need to use a program called Sparkle, which we've included on the CD that comes with this book.

Putting Movies on the Internet

If you want to create your own page(s) that other people on the Internet can access, you'll need to learn how to set up a Web *server*. If you want more information on setting up Web servers, check out the Web server at http://info.cern.ch/hypertext/WWW/TheProject.html.

To put QuickTime movies on your Web page(s), you make them single forked and flattened, as you would for QuickTime for Windows. Any Macintosh or PC user with QuickTime or QuickTime for Windows will be able to download and play your QuickTime movies. UNIX users can use a product called XAnim, which will play QuickTime movies (without sound).

An alternative is to convert your QuickTime movies to MPEG before putting them on the Net. You can use Sparkle to do this as well (see figure 9.7). You'll find that the file size of your MPEG files are smaller than the QuickTime originals. However, unless you use only small-framed movies (160 x 120), the movies will not perform as well. You also can't create an MPEG file with audio from a QuickTime movie—at least not yet.

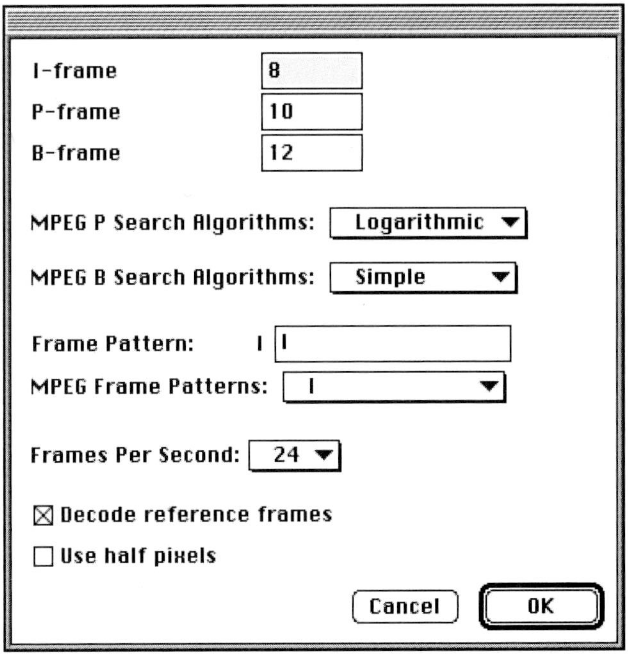

Figure 9.7   *Sparkle's Save As MPEG dialog box*

Warning!

Movies on the Internet is a rapidly changing and growing area. Expect the information in this section to soon be outdated.

Nondigital Distribution

Sometimes you want to convert your movies to a format that's accessible to those without computers: old-fashioned videotape or even more old-fashioned paper.

Outputting to Videotape

What if you create a QuickTime movie that you want to distribute to people who don't have computers that can play QuickTime movies? Outputting to videotape may be the solution. For example, training videos can be inexpensively produced by shooting videotape, digitizing it, using QuickTime editing tools on it, and then outputting it to videotape.

One option for getting what's on your screen to videotape is to point your video camera right at the screen and record that way. However, if you do this, you'll find on your videotape a white line rolling down your screen again and again. This line is caused by the frequency difference between your monitor and video camera, and it can sometimes be temporarily remedied by software that changes the timing of your monitor's refresh rate. Unfortunately, this adjustment is not permanent and needs constant oversight, making this a poor solution.

A better solution is to use an *encoder*, a device that converts the digital signal on your monitor to a video signal that can be recorded to videotape. You can use one to record to videotape anything that shows on your monitor, not just QuickTime movies. The process is essentially the reverse of creating a QuickTime movie from video. That is, you connect cables from your Macintosh to your VCR via the encoder box. You set your VCR to record and send the signal that would normally go to your monitor to the encoder, so that what you would normally see on your monitor gets recorded to videotape.

One feature that you may want to look for in an encoder is *convolution*, which eliminates a problem that occurs when you make a recording of a Macintosh application in use. Without convolution, all of the one-pixel lines, such as window borders, will flicker on the videotape, giving a headache to anyone who watches it for any length of time. The encoders in Radius' VideoVision board and in the Macintosh AVs have convolution. If all that you're recording is digital video, however, convolution isn't needed.

Encoders range in price from a few hundred dollars to a few thousand dollars. However, in a few cases, you won't need to purchase one. The Macintosh AV computers have built-in encoders. Certain QuickTime digitizing boards, such as Radius' VideoVision, also have built-in encoders, so you can use them for going out to videotape, as well as digitizing from videotape.

Keep in mind that you can only record to video what you can see on your monitor. If you want full-screen video on tape, you'll need to be using a hardware compression/decompression card (see Chapter 6). Alternatively, you might be able to get away with using a Print-to-Video function (see Chapter 3) to double the size of a quarter-screen clip.

Paper Output

"Can you print it?" is a question that we've heard often. While you may wonder why anyone would want to print a QuickTime movie, we finally found a couple of fun little utilities that might just provide a reason. These programs can be used to turn a movie into a flipbook, a little book consisting of each frame of a movie printed on a separate page, which can be held by the stapled side and flipped so the movie comes to life. One such program is S.H. Pierce's FlipBook. Another program is FlipBookMaker, which we include on the QuickTime Guide CD.

You can do more than just print a movie, however; you can use a movie to produce art that might get printed. The Image Hose is a new tool in Fractal Design Painter 3.0 (see figure 9.8). With this tool, you can use a QuickTime movie as your paintbrush. You basically hose down your canvas with the QuickTime movie changing over time. You can have the images come out and be randomly placed on the canvas, or they can be snapped to a grid. After you make this masterpiece, you can print it.

Figure 9.8   *Image Hose*

Legal Issues

If you plan to distribute a QuickTime movie to a larger audience than just your family and friends, you'll need to make sure that you are not distributing content that belongs to someone other than yourself.

Copyright law is the first thing to know about if you want to avoid legal hassles. Almost all television programming and video that you buy is copyrighted. It's perfectly legal for you to make a QuickTime movie from TV as long as it's only for personal use. Educators have a little leeway; under the Fair Use provisions of U.S. copyright law, they can show limited amounts of copyrighted works for limited amounts of time in their own classrooms. But don't plan on distributing someone else's work, even if it's only a few seconds of that work. The same goes for audio recordings.

If you're shooting your own video or photographs, you should also be concerned about the unauthorized use of a person's image. Though it's tempting to use material recorded in a public place, it may not be legal. If you do tape a person who isn't a close friend or relative, get a *model release form*, a document that a subject signs saying that it is OK to use his likeness in your production (see example in figure 9.9).

If you are distributing QuickTime movies and you want to play it safe, contact a lawyer before distributing any QuickTime movies to which someone else might have a legal claim. It's better and cheaper to consult a lawyer up front than to have to pay for legal services when you are sued. At the very least, read up on this area. A recently published book that might help is *The Multimedia Law Handbook*, by Diane Brinson and Mark F. Radcliffe.

I, _____, do hereby give BMUG Inc. the right to use
my video image for the TV-ROM, a CD-ROM collection of digital video clips. I
understand that the digital video clips in this collection may be used, without
further permission from me, in any form, including composite or distorted
representations, for advertising, trade or any other lawful purposes. I am of full
age. I have read this release and am fully familiar with its contents.

Witness: _____   Signed: _____

Address:_____   Address: _____

                                   Date: _____, 19___

Figure 9.9   *TV-ROM release form*

Get Your Movies Out There!

We've discussed a few different ways for you to share your work. Whether you want
to publish a CD-ROM that'll sell millions or just send a diskette to your parents (or
kids!), we hope that you'll create work that you want to show people.

Of course, it's OK, too, if you do it just for yourself.

The important thing to remember is that QuickTime is a tool for all of us. From
computer novices to big-time multimedia producers, there's something in QuickTime
for everyone.

Other QuickTime Software that's on the CD

*T*he software described in this appendix are utilities that people who are making lots of movies need whether they know it or not. We've handpicked the ones that are most useful, while skipping those that don't provide unique capabilities and those that we know to be particularly "buggy."

Unsupported Utilities from Apple

In the Unsupported Stuff folder on the CD, you'll find a number of useful tools. However, *unsupported* means that you cannot call anyone to get help. Also, you use these at your own risk. In other words, they may not have been thoroughly tested, and they may crash! They may also corrupt your data files—use them only on *copies* of files that you care about.

ConvertToMovie

This utility has many uses. We described two important functions—importing PICT files and recompression of movies—in Chapters 7 through 9. You can also use ConvertToMovie to build a custom color table, filter, scale, crop, flatten, single-fork, and dither movies. Refer to Chapters 7 through 9 in this book and the Read Me file that's with the program for instructions on use.

ComboWalker

ComboWalker is another utility with multiple uses, and it can be used for batch processing. When we have movies that will be pressed to CD, we open ComboWalker and choose Movie Walker from the Action menu. The dialog box that then appears (see figure A.1) is used for many tasks, including adding custom color icons and setting the creator of the movies to TVOD, which ensures that the movie will open with MoviePlayer when clicked.

Refer to the Read Me file that comes with the program for instructions on how to use it.

MakeMovieColorTable

MakeMovieColorTable creates a custom color table for a movie and adds it to that movie file. This table can make the movie look better when played in 256 colors (see Chapter 4 for more information on custom color tables).

As with ConvertToMovie; when you first open MakeMovieColorTable, you're provided with an Open dialog box in which you choose the movie you'd like to process. A simple dialog box appears, which we set as in figure A.2.

There's a Read Me for this program, too.

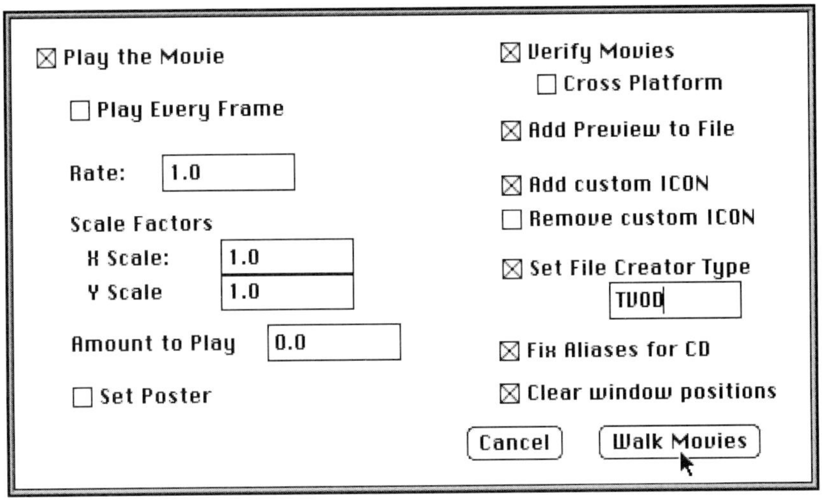

Figure A.1 *ComboWalker dialog box chosen by selecting Movie Walker from the Action menu*

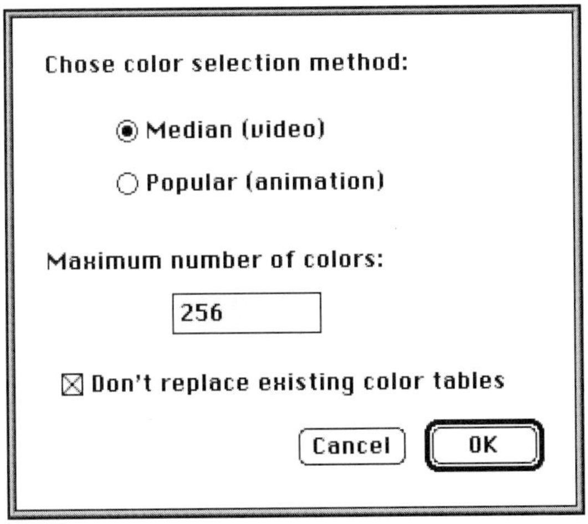

Figure A.2 *MakeMovieColorTable dialog box*

Note

You may think you can just use ResEdit to add a clut resource to a QuickTime movie, but we'll save you some time and let you know that it won't work. If you have a clut resource, the easiest way to add it is with MoviePlayer (see Chapter 4).

Dumpster

Dumpster is a utility that's not for the average QuickTime moviemaker. Hackers will love it, however. It enables you to view and edit "moov" resources. This is very handy when you need to find out specific information about a movie or change some movie settings. If you don't know about the internal workings of QuickTime, the information provided will be quite cryptic (see figure A.3). The Read Me file for this one won't help you either.

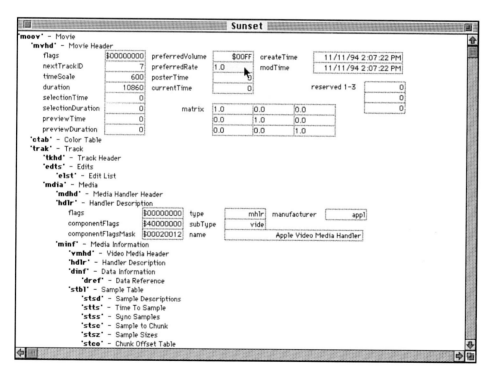

Figure A.3   *Movie settings shown using Dumpster*

MovieShop™

MovieShop™ is the application, discussed in Chapter 9, that most CD-ROM developers turn to for post-processing their QuickTime movies to ensure they play smoothly from the CD. The version we provide, 1.2.1+, is the most current version.

This utility has a novice and an expert level. We recommend that you start with the novice level.

Refer to Chapter 9 for some basic information on MovieShop. Unfortunately, there's no documentation available for the current version; we provide documentation for an older version which you'll still find useful.

MovieAnalyzer™

MovieAnalyzer™ is another amazing tool created by George Cossey, the programmer who created MovieShop (at one point MovieAnalyzer was part of MovieShop). This application carefully examines your movies, checking things like the data rate of every frame and looking for wasted or poorly laid-out data in your movies. It reports back with a coded text list of potential problems and graphs (see figure A.4). It'll warn you if the movie will have problems playing from CD. If one of your movies is playing poorly, this program will probably tell you why.

Text Movie Converter

This is the tool you use to "burn" your text track, as described in Chapter 4.

When you pick a movie with a text track, a Save dialog box appears in which you have a few options, including a button that will take you to a standard compression dialog box in which you set compression for the text (see figure A.5). Simple documentation is provided that will briefly explain each of the options.

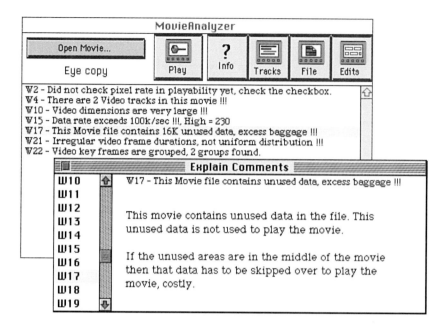

Figure A.4   *MovieAnalyzer comments*

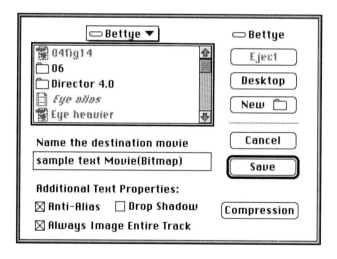

Figure A.5   *Save dialog box in Text Movie Converter*

SoundConverter

SoundConverter, written by Kip Olson, is currently the only way to access the IMA 4:1 compression that's available in QuickTime 2.0 (see Chapter 8 for information on sound compression). You'll need QuickTime 2.0, System 7.0 or later, and Sound Manager 3.0 installed. SoundConverter lets you open and compress AIFF and sound files, as well as QuickTime movies extracted from audio CDs. It won't be able to open ordinary QuickTime movies, however. When you open a file, you're provided a fairly simple dialog box (see figure A.6). After you compress a sound file with SoundConverter, you can import it in MoviePlayer or another QuickTime editor to use as part of a QuickTime movie.

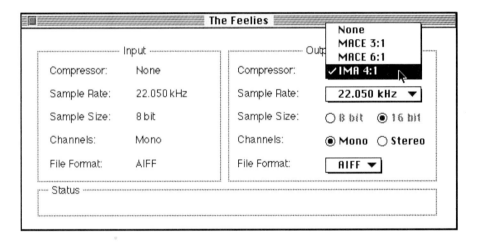

Figure A.6   *SoundConverter dialog box*

SingleForkFlattener

This program does more than its name implies. It doesn't just single-fork and flatten movies. It also creates movies which open up faster from CD. It lays out the movie resource at the beginning of the file instead of at the end, which removes 2 seeks when opening the file, and it rechunks the file after flattening it. Both of these features improve performance when playing from a CD.

This progam has no interface. You can drag and drop a folder full of movies onto the application's icon; the application will then single fork and flatten all the movies in that folder. You can also simply open the software and choose a single file to single fork and flatten. Though it's worked fine for us, we've heard stories of the program corrupting movie files, so be sure to only use it on a copy of your file.

Music Configuration

This is a small application that works in conjunction with Apple's MIDI Manager software. The Music Configuration program enables you to channel the music data from a QuickTime music movie out to an external synthesizer. If you have a MIDI interface box and a MIDI keyboard connected through the modem port, you open Music Configuration 2.0 and, under the MIDI Synthesizers, click on the Modem radio button to indicate the port you'll be sending the music data through. When you play your QuickTime music movie, the external synthesizer is used rather than the built-in Macintosh software synthesizer.

There is no documentation for this application but it's fairly straightforward.

AddTimeCode

This utility allows you to add a time code track, and enter time code information into your movie. Having time code information attached to a movie is incredibly helpful if you ever need to redigitize that particular clip. It's also great if you've digitized one long segment and plan to cut it into smaller pieces. The time code information remains with each clip, accurately representing the actual location of that particular clip on the original video. Time code is mostly useful for people capturing 30 frame per second movies using hardware compression cards and controllable video sources.

To use it, double-click to open it. You'll be presented with a standard open dialog box in which you choose a movie file. Then you get a dialog box in which you name the tape and set other parameters of the time code.

XCMDs

Last, but definitely not least, is a collection of four HyperCard stacks containing XCMDs from Ken Doyle at Apple. These stacks make it possible for a HyperTalk scripter to do just about anything with a QuickTime movie from within HyperCard. QTMovie, contained in "QTMovie Stack," is for playing your movies back with maximum control—it's a more powerful and complicated alternative to the Movie XCMD that comes with HyperCard, which we discuss in Chapter 3. "Editing Stack" contains QTEditMovie, which enables you to edit QuickTime movies, including track editing. "Movie Making Stack" contains QTRecordMovie, which enables you to digitize video movies; it also enables you to capture time-lapse movies. "QTPict Stack" contains QTPict, which enables you to display and compress PICT files. In the folder with the stacks is one file that provides documentation for all four stacks.

Shareware and Freeware

We've put both shareware and freeware in the Shareware folder on the CD. In this section, we've indicated which programs are shareware and which are freeware.

Shareware is something that's very special to the Macintosh community. Lots of very talented programmers have created very cool tools and put them out in the world for you to use. In return, they ask you to pay a small fee—usually $25 or less. If people don't pay their shareware fees, shareware authors can't continue creating innovative shareware.

The price of the QuickTime Guide does not cover shareware fees! If, after trying any shareware, you want to continue using the program, pay the fee! Instructions for how and where to send your shareware fees are found in text files that you'll find in the folder containing the shareware program itself.

Anything that's labeled freeware is completely free.

There are Read Me files for most of the programs that will explain how to use these applications, pay any fees, and get upgrades.

Easy Play 2.0

Easy Play 2.0 is shareware.

This is your basic movie playing application with two unique differences: it can create catalogs, and it is scriptable.

You can make a catalog of all of the movies on your hard drive, a CD-ROM, or even an FTP site (for an example of a catalogued FTP site, open the file "MACSYS QuickTime Lib 93-02-20," which is in the Easy Play folder).

Easy Play can also receive Apple events and is thus scriptable. You can read about its support for Apple events in the file "EasyPlay 2.0 Apple Events."

No documentation, other than the Apple Events file, is available, but the program is relatively straightforward.

FlipBookMaker 1.1

FlipBookMaker 1.1 is shareware.

This enables you to print your QuickTime movies as flipbooks, as described in Chapter 9. For simple instructions on how to use it, choose About FlipBookMaker from the Apple menu when the application is open.

MovieInfo v2.2

MovieInfo v2.2 is shareware.

This simple program provides data about any movie. It doesn't provide as much information as MovieAnalyzer, but it provides slightly more than what you'd find in MoviePlayer's Info window.

MovieTrilogy Folder

MovieTrilogy is shareware.

MovieTrilogy is a set of five programs—yes, five—that have functions that overlap each other and other applications on this CD, but most have something unique to offer:

- *DesktopTV 1.2.0* is a video monitoring and recording program. It's similar to other recording applications, except that you have to choose New Movie from the File menu first, and you tell the software to start and stop recording by choosing from the File menu, rather than by clicking a button. This program can also be used to record a QuickTime music movie with MIDI hardware and additional software (Apple's MIDI Manager). You can also use it to put video as your desktop pattern. The documentation says that this program is only for Macintosh AV computers, but we were able to use it to record a digital video movie on a Centris 650.

- *QuickMovie 1.0b2* is a player and simple editor with much the same functionality as MoviePlayer 2.0.

- *ScreenMovie 1.1.0* is a screen recording application like those discussed in Chapter 7.

- *DeskTopText 1.1.1* is a program for creating a text track movie. While MoviePlayer lets you do this, too, DeskTopText lets you set various properties, including text color, justification, location on the screen, drop shadowing, and scrolling options.

- *DeskTopMovie 1.1.1* is another player and editor, but somewhat different from QuickMovie. It doesn't use the Standard Controller; instead, all movie control functions are accessed from menus. It has more functions than MoviePlayer. It enables you to record sound and add it to your movie without leaving the application. If you have Apple's Speech Manager installed, it will speak the text in a text track. It also enables you to have one movie play through another by specifying a color to be transparent.

Documentation is light and is scattered through various files that come with these applications. The shareware fee for all five programs is only $30, but beware that some features don't always work as they should; the author, Paul C.H. Ho, is constantly upgrading and changing the programs. He puts updated version on FTP sites at sumex-aim.stanford.edu and their mirrors (check ftp://sumex-aim.stanford.edu/info-mac/grf/util/ and ftp://sumex-aim.stanford.edu/info-mac/cmp/).

Sparkle 2.2

Sparkle 2.2 is freeware.

This is the software MPEG player and converter that we refer to in Chapter 9. We consider it an amazing bit of programming. If you're surfing the Internet, you may already have a copy, but we've provided current versions—one a Power PC version—just in case. Extensive documentation comes with this program. Read it.

Theater Maker

Theater Maker is shareware.

This program enables you to create a standalone movie (there's information about this program in Chapter 5). Read the file "Theater Maker Read Me" for instructions.

About BMUG

BMUG is a membership-based, nonprofit organization dedicated to helping users of graphical interface computers. It represents the interests of over 12,000 Macintosh users in more than 50 countries.

BMUG offers something for everyone. Here are a few of the reasons that more than 12,000 people belong to BMUG:

- *The BMUG Newsletter*. Published twice a year, each Newsletter contains 400 pages of reviews, reference material, and commentary (and no advertising!).

- **Planet BMUG and BMUG Boston, the BMUG BBSes**. These are our FirstClass graphical interface electronic bulletin board services. Use your modem to exchange messages with BMUG members around the world, send mail via the Internet, and download software from BMUG's vast software library.

- **The Helpline**. Access to our technical Helpline is available to members during business hours by phone, fax, or in person.
- **The Software Library**. One of the largest and most up-to-date collections of Publicly Distributable software anywhere. It is sold on disks and CD-ROM or can be downloaded from the BBSes.
- **Publications and CD-ROMs**. BMUG publishes CD-ROMs of Shareware and books on scripting, resource editing, software programs, and more.
- **The Meetings**. BMUG holds weekly main meetings in Berkeley, monthly general meetings in San Francisco and San Jose, and special interest group meetings virtually every night of the week. See interesting product demos, meet other computer users, and hear the latest industry rumors.

Contacting BMUG

There are many ways to contact BMUG.

By Phone

Announcement Line	(510) 549-2684 x8
Business Office	(510) 549-2684
Fax	(510) 849-9026
Planet BMUG (BBS)	(510) 849-2684
BMUG Boston (BBS)	(617) 356-6336
BMUG (product orders only)	(800) 776-2684

By Mail

BMUG Inc.
1442A Walnut Street, #62
Berkeley, CA USA 94709-1496

Our Office Location

BMUG Inc.

2055 Center Street, cross street Shattuck Avenue,

in downtown Berkeley, California

The BMUG Philosophy

BMUG started as a small users group in 1984, shortly after the introduction of the Macintosh. As a nonprofit corporation, BMUG strives to give the plain, unbiased truths about product performance and the industry in general. We don't sell advertising in our newsletters and make it quite clear that we will not exchange good reviews for product donations. BMUG is neither affiliated with, nor receives monetary support from, Apple Computer or any other for-profit entity.

Our goal is clearly stated in our motto:

"We're in the business of giving away information."

BMUG Memberships

BMUG is member supported. Membership privileges include semi-annual issues of the famous BMUG *Newsletter*, technical assistance, and access to Planet BMUG or BMUG Boston.

Join BMUG today and find out why *MicroTimes* lists BMUG among the 100 most important influences on the computer industry and said, "BMUG is what every user group dreams of becoming."

California Business magazine rates BMUG in the top 100 of California's hottest digital information providers.

To join, select one of the following membership packages for individuals:

- **Six Month Membership—**$28

  One issue of *The BMUG Newsletter*

  Access to The BMUG Helpline for one person for six months

  A six month account on a BMUG BBS (60 min/day)

- **Contributing Membership**—$45

  Two issues of *The BMUG Newsletter*

  Access to The BMUG Helpline for one person

  An account on a BMUG BBS (60 min/day)

- **Sustaining Membership**—$70

  Two issues of *The BMUG Newsletter*

  Access to The BMUG Helpline for one person

  An account on a BMUG BBS (90 min/day)

  Access to online magazines when available (such as BoardWatch, NewsBytes, USA Today)

- **Hero Membership**—$100

  First-class mailing of two issues of *The BMUG Newsletter*

  Access to The BMUG Helpline for one person

  An account on a BMUG BBS (90 min/day)

  Access to online magazines when available (such as BoardWatch, NewsBytes, USA Today)

  Acknowledgment in *The BMUG Newsletter*

- **Satellite Club Membership**—$250

  First-class mailing of two issues of *The BMUG Newsletter*

  Access to The BMUG Helpline for one person

  An account on a BMUG BBS (120 min/day)

  Access to online magazines when available (such as BoardWatch, NewsBytes, USA Today)

  Two of each BMUG product released during the year of your membership (except PD library floppy disks)

  Acknowledgment in *The BMUG Newsletter*

The BMUG Newsletter

BMUG newsletters are published twice a year. Each is approximately 400 pages long, contains no advertising, and is written and edited by BMUG members, volunteers, and staff. We encourage you to contribute your efforts as well. Remember, the only way to receive the current newsletter is to be a BMUG member!

The newsletter includes software and hardware reviews, "how-to" guides, commentaries on the computer industry, and Choice Products—BMUG's respected product recommendations.

Each newsletter comes with a disk of the latest and greatest Shareware and Freeware, as well as a program to help you access our electronic Bulletin Board Service.

BMUG Online: Planet BMUG and BMUG Boston BBSes

Got a modem? That's about all you'll need to get online with BMUG on our electronic Bulletin Board Systems (BBSes). Members can request a free account on either of our FirstClass, graphical user interface BBSes. We support baud rates from 300 to 14,440 on all 17 lines in Berkeley and all 11 lines in Boston. Nearly 6,000 members log on and discuss every subject under the sun, and many of the conferences are directly gatewayed between the two BMUG BBSes. We exchange mail with the Internet via UUCP mail. Much of the most current Shareware and Freeware is available.

BMUG is also on many of the commercial forums across the nation. You can reach BMUG at the following electronic addresses:

Internet:	bmuginfo@bmug.org
America Online:	BMUG or BMUG1
e•World:	BMUG1
AppleLink:	UG0001
The WELL:	bmug

Meetings

All BMUG meetings are open to the public. You do not have to be a member
to attend. We welcome new and old Macintosh users alike. Call BMUG at
(510) 549-2684 and press 8 for current meeting information and location.

Main Meetings

BMUG holds weekly Macintosh meetings on the University of California Berkeley
campus. Approximately 100 members and nonmembers gather to discuss the latest
industry gossip, ask technical questions, and watch vendors demonstrate new and
soon-to-be-released software and hardware. The meetings are free of charge and
open to the public, and there is a raffle at the end of each one.

BMUG West

Each month BMUG holds a Macintosh meeting at the Exploratorium's McBean
Theater in San Francisco from 6:00 p.m. to 9:00 p.m. on the last Monday of the
month. Although they have the same format as our main meetings, including the
raffle, they are smaller and more intimate.

BMUG South

BMUG also holds a monthly meeting in San Jose every third Monday at the Santa
Clara County United Way office at 1922 The Alameda, unless otherwise noted. The
meeting starts at 6:30 p.m.

Special Interest Groups (SIGs)

BMUG has meetings almost every week night, and some on weekends as well, on
specific fields of interest. All SIGs meet in our offices in Berkeley, unless otherwise
noted, and are free of charge and open to the public. Call the BMUG Announcement
Line for dates, times, and location.

Technical Assistance

One big advantage of BMUG membership is access to first-class technical assistance.

The Helpline

BMUG's Helpline for members is the only place where you can get technical help on virtually any subject pertaining to the Macintosh. If all lines are busy, leave a message, and we'll attempt to return your call within two business days. If you haven't heard from us within that time, please place your call again. The best time to call the Helpline is on Wednesday from 1:00 p.m. to 5:00 p.m. We also return calls on Saturdays from 1:00 p.m. to 5:00 p.m., so please leave a weekend telephone number where you can be reached. BMUG also accepts your technical questions via fax and on Planet BMUG or BMUG Boston!

Emergency Data Recovery

Broken hard drive, crashed floppy?? If you're a member, we'll do our best to recover your data, free of charge. Appointments are usually made on Wednesdays and Saturdays from 1:00 p.m. to 5:00 p.m.

BMUG Software Library

BMUG has one of the largest collections of Freeware and Shareware software in the world. The library contains over four hundred 800k disks organized into categories such as Utilities, Fonts, Games, Education, and so on. Disks are available to both members and nonmembers at $4 each, to cover our costs. Specially priced disk packs are also available. BMUG carefully and painstakingly checks everything we sell for viruses.

BMUG strongly encourages users to support Shareware authors and their efforts by sending in Shareware fees.

BMUG Publications

The Tao of AppleScript, BMUG's Guide to Macintosh Scripting, Second Edition

This book, new as of August 1994, takes you on a journey of discovering Apple's revolutionary new scripting language, AppleScript. With *The Tao of AppleScript* and the included software, you can control your Mac as never before. The disk includes AppleScript, QuickTime, StuffIt Lite, and scripting utilities written specifically for the book!

Zen and The Art of Resource Editing, Third Edition

This book contains a series of articles to help you navigate through the cryptic world of ResEdit. The newest edition is 240 pages and includes System 7 tips. The book comes with a disk containing the current version of ResEdit and templates.

ToonWare—A Humor Interface

This collection of the humorous and the absurd is a sure bet for any computer enthusiast. It has 96 pages of comic art, the perfect gift for anyone with a sense of humor and a Mac.

BMUG CD-ROMs

BMUG's TV-ROM™ Too with Update ROM

The successor of the original TV-ROM, this disc was created with the very latest QuickTime technology. With over 500 megs of QuickTime movies, 100 musical clips, and over 200 photographic color images, this CD-ROM has captured the imagination of Mac users around the globe. Copyright light, these clips can be used in any presentation without payment or paperwork! It comes with BMUG's TV-ROM Too Update ROM described next.

BMUG's TV-ROM Too Update ROM

In August 1994, BMUG released the TV-ROM Too Update, an updated CD-ROM for owners of BMUG's TV-ROM Too and/or those curious about the new features of QuickTime 2.0. The $20 disc contains the brand new version of QuickTime and a sampling of movies, including favorites redigitized from BMUG's TV-ROM Too and enhanced additions and new renditions that take advantage of QuickTime's newest tricks.

A BMUG-developed HyperCard stack serves as a guide to viewing, learning, and experimenting with the movies on the CD-ROM. Simple and familiar navigational tools allow the user to be a mouse potato or have a truly interactive learning experience. Each movie's card contains vital information, such as frame rates, file size and duration, as well as the ability to play the movie in a variety of ways. This hands-on experience will give any user a better understanding of some of the new capabilities of QuickTime.

The BMUG PD-ROM™

In addition to our entire library of Shareware and Freeware, the PD-ROM contains stuff available only from BMUG (such as *Newsletter* back issues). With over 600 megs of fonts, games, and other programs, it's the best source of Publicly Distributable software and is all System 7.5 compatible and 32-bit clean.

The BMUG ResEdit Collection, CD-ROM

From the authors of *Zen and The Art of Resource Editing* comes a collection of cool and exciting things! This CD includes the latest version of ResEdit, new editors, thousands of icons, patterns, resources, utilities, QuickTime, and Frontier Runtime.

The BMUG Font ROM, version B

With nearly 1000 fonts, this disc is the place to get any Shareware or Freeware font you would ever want. Over 120 megs of TrueType fonts, Type 1 PostScript fonts, and Adobe screen fonts up to number 289 are available. The contents are entirely Finder accessible.

The BMUG Games ROM, version 2

Mastered new as of July 1994, The BMUG Games ROM contains 170 megabytes of Publicly Distributable Freeware and Shareware games. This disc is a superset of the games found on the popular BMUG PD-ROM. It also includes lots of new stuff.

All files come with online documentation to explain their use and any applicable Shareware fees. You can read them in Saint Edit format, TeachText, or any application capable of reading text files. The BMUG Games ROM is completely Finder accessible and organized by type, such as card games, space games, and so on.

Other BMUG Products

The BMUG Tie-Dyed T-Shirt

This t-shirt has become legendary. It's the fashion statement of BMUG. The front has "BMUG" in large letters, and the back says "The BMUG T-shirt. Tie-Dyed in Berkeley by Deadheads."

Tote Bag

Our 100% cotton, all-purpose tote bag has been tested across the globe by BMUG staff and volunteers with great results.

The Official BMUG Mug

Finally, a B-MUG! We've been talking about it for years, but somehow we never got to it. Well, it's finally here! With our infamous tie-dye design, this ceramic beauty is just the thing to make a BMUG statement everyday!

BMUG Distributes New Products!

Power Macintosh Programming Starter Kit

by Tom Thompson
Published by Hayden Books
Retail price: $39.95   BMUG price: $30

Learn how to program powerful applications for the new Power Macs. This book provides a tour of the Power Macintosh environment, from fundamental concepts to an extensive overview of the Power Macintosh run-time architecture. This great new book also provides in-depth information on the Power PC processor family, resources, and file I/O (with error detection examples); expert techniques for controlling file sharing, fat trap patching, and making applications that run on both Power PC and 680 x 0 Macintosh computers; and source code for practical utility applications.

Internet Starter Kit for Macintosh, Second Edition

> by Adam Engst
>
> Published by Hayden Books
>
> Retail price: $29.95   BMUG price: $22

Other books just tell you about the Internet. This book takes you there!

This new edition includes an automatic installer for getting connected easily, more information on the World-Wide Web, special coverage of PPP connections and troubleshooting, and access to a special FTP site containing over 50 megs of essential Internet software.

You also get two weeks of free trial connect time and a 25 percent discount on flat rate with full Internet access from Northwest Nexus (requires a long distance call outside of the Puget Sound/Seattle area).

The software that comes with this book includes MacTCP 2.0.4, MacPPP 2.0.1, InterSLIP 1.0.1, Anarchie 1.2.0, Eudora 1.4.3, MacWAIS 1.29, MacWeb 0.98a, and TurboGopher 1.0.8b4—the software alone is worth the price of the book!

Internet Explorer Kit for Macintosh

> by Adam Engst and William Dickson
>
> Published by Hayden Books
>
> Retail price: $29.95   BMUG price: $22

So you're connected to the Internet and ready to hit the road. Where are you going to go? What are you going to do? This book is the ultimate road trip with two world-class Internet experts.

Relax, sit back, and let Adam Engst and Bill Dickson take you along on their Internet journeys. They won't just tell you about life on the Internet—they'll show you. In a conversational format, the authors wander in and out of Internet social groups and special interest discussions, and share all of the customs and jokes online. You'll learn how to browse the Internet's vast byways to find the specific information you need.

Internet Explorer Kit comes with a disk of useful software as well. You'll get Anarchie 1.1.3, Finger 1.3.7, MacWAIS 1.28, Mac Weather 1.1.1, and TurboGopher 1.0.8b4. This is the companion volume to the best-selling *Internet Starter Kit*.

The Online User's Encyclopedia, Bulletin Boards and Beyond

> by Bernard Aboba
>
> Published by Addison Wesley
>
> Retail price: $32.95   BMUG price: $26

This is truly *the* telecommunications encyclopedia! This practical guide to global computer networks is essential reading if you're looking to get the most out of your modem.

The Online User's Encyclopedia includes an abundance of useful material never before collected into one book: details on how to access the Internet using a graphical user interface; a complete guide to TCP/IP software for the IBM PC and Macintosh; a guide to modems, cables, and accessories; tips for saving money on your phone bill; chapters on file transfer, conversion, and compression for the Mac, IBM PC, and UNIX machines; guides to graphical bulletin board software; chapters on the FidoNet, RIME, ILink, and One Net Member networks; and histories of the networks as told by their creators.

Also, you get hundreds of useful listings of communications products and bulletin board systems and dozens of Internet resources. Whether you're a newcomer, a computer professional, or a hobbyist, *The Online User's Encyclopedia* has something for you.

Approaching Home Automation, A Guide to Using X-10 Technology

by Bill Berner and Craig Elliot

Published by Approaching, Inc.

Retail price: $19.99   BMUG price: $15

Simplify your life by controlling lights, appliances, and even your thermostat from one location inside your house; turning house lights on from your car when you return home; and controlling your home remotely from any touch-tone telephone. Feel secure by making your house look lived in, even when you're away.

Why X-10 Technology? You don't need an engineering degree to figure it out. You can build a system for as little as $30 and expand the system over time. You don't need to install special wiring—just plug the components into an electrical outlet and go! If you're into gadgets, computers, or electronics, this stuff's for you. It's a blast!

Why *Approaching Home Automation*? It covers the basics so that a new user can get up to speed quickly without any guesswork. It also covers advanced topics for the knowledgeable user. Diagrams, tables, illustrations, a complete glossary, and a detailed index help you find the information you need.

Remembery Chips—An Electronic Book for Children

by Cathy Rudolph

Published by Wayward Fluffy Publications

Retail price: $15   BMUG price: $12

This new interactive electronic book is not only a delightful tale of a child's imagination and creativity, but it also answers the question "What's a computer?" A charming original story with beautiful color illustrations, spoken phrases, personalization, and more, *Remembery Chips* is the perfect electronic book for parents to share with their young ones (ages 2-8). By Cathy Faye Rudolph, Mac writer and BMAG (BMUGs electronic MAGazine) Editor-in-Chief.

Index

Symbols

2-D animation software, 234-235
3-D animation software, 235

A

A/V hard disks, 230-231
Adams, Mark, 136
adapters, 206-209
Add command (Edit menu), 99-101
Adobe
  After Effects software, 134-137, 162-167
  Photoshop software, 128
  Premiere 4.0 software, 135-137, 148-156, 183-190
After Effects software (Aldus/Adobe), 134-137
  special effects, 162-167

AIFF (Audio Interchange File Format)
  files, importing, 252-253
Aldus After Effects software, 134-137, 162-167
aliases, playing movies upon startup, 54
Animation compressors, 271
  comparison summary, 278
animations, creating video tracks with, 234-240
Apple Computer
  Apple Media Tool software, 62
  Apple Multimedia Tuner X.X, 4
  Apple Video Player, compression, 269
  MoviePlayer, *see* MoviePlayer
  unsupported software, 300-307
applications, *see* software
Approaching Home Automation, A Guide to Using X-10 Technology, 323
Astound software (Gold Disk), 62
attenuation, 209

audio, 16-17
    compression, 220, 264
    muting/resetting, 39
    overdriving, 41
    recording, enabling/disabling, 222
    sampling rates, 220-221
    special effects control, 133-134
        Premiere, 154
        VideoFusion and QuickFLIX!, 162
        VideoShop, 145
    volume, controlling, 28-30, 39
audio CDs, importing for creating sound
    tracks, 253-256
audio digitizers, 198-199
    plugging in, 205
    selecting, 221
Authorware Professional software
    (Macromedia), 62
automatically playing movies upon
    startup, 54-55
Avid's VideoShop 2.0.3 software, 16,
    135-148, 167-176

B

Badge icon, 34
BBSs (Bulletin Board Systems), BMUG,
    315
beginning of movies, jumping to, 38
blank screens, setting amount of time for,
    59
BMUG
    BBSs (Bulletin Board Systems), 315
    CD-ROMs, 318-320
    contacting, 312-313
    features, 311-312
    meetings, 316
    membership, 313-314
        newsletters, 315
        philosophy, 313
        products, 320
        publications, 318
            distributed by BMUG, 320-323
        technical assistance, 317
Broderbund's KidPix software, 236
burnt text, 106
buttons
    Pause (Standard Controller), 26-27
    Play (Standard Controller), 26-27
    Size box, 31-33
    Step (Standard Controller), 28
    Volume Control (Standard Controller),
        28-30
    Zoom box, 32-33

C

cables, 206-209
CameraMan software (Motion Works
    International), 236
cameras (video), QuickCam (Connectix),
    197
capturing video, controlled, 229-230
CD accompanying this book
    ComboWalker, 300
    ConvertToMovie, 241-245, 300
    DeskTopMovie 1.1.1, 309
    DeskTopText 1.1.1, 309
    DesktopTV 1.2.0, 308-309
    Dumpster, 302
    Easy Play 2.0, 307-308
    FlipBookMaker 1.1, 308
    freeware, 307-310
    HyperCard stacks containing XCMDs,
        306-307
    MakeMovieColorTable, 300-302

MovieAnalyzer, 303
MovieInfo v2.2, 308
MovieShop, 303
MovieTrilogy, 308-309
Music Configuration, 306
Premiere 4.0 software (Adobe), 135-137,
   148-156, 183-190
QuickFLIX! (VideoFusion/Radius),
   135-137, 156-162, 176-183
QuickMovie 1.0b2, 309
ScreenMovie 1.1.0, 309
shareware, 307-310
SimpleText software (Utils folder),
   250-251
SingleForkFlattener, 305-306
SoundConverter, 305
Sparkle 2.2, 310
Text Movie Converter, 303-304
Theater Maker, 310
Unsupported Stuff folder, 300-307
VideoShop 2.0.3 (Avid), 135-148,
   167-176
CD-ROM
   BMUG, 318-320
   distributing movies, 284-288
   Kodak Photo CDs, 245-246
   Star Trek: The Next Generation
      Interactive Technical Manual, 249
CDs (audio), importing for creating sound
   tracks, 253-256
Choose Language command (Movie
   menu), 111-112, 115
Cinemation software (Vividus), 62, 235
Cinepak compressors, 270
   comparison summary, 278
clearing selections, 79

clips, combining
   Premiere 4.0 software (Adobe), 184-185
   QuickFLIX! software (VideoFusion/
      Radius), 178-179, 182
   VideoShop 2.0.3 software (Avid),
      169-170
codecs (compressor-decompressors), 266
   selecting, 268-273
color depth, 12
color tables, custom, 117-118
colors
   optimizing playback performance, 50-51
   selecting number of for spatial
      compression, 274
   Standard Controller, changing, 24
combining
   clips
      Premiere 4.0 software (Adobe),
         184-185
      QuickFLIX! software (VideoFusion/
         Radius), 178-179, 182
      VideoShop 2.0.3 software (Avid),
         169-170
   tracks, 98-106
ComboWalker software, 300
commands
   Edit menu
      Add, 99-101
      Copy, 79
      Delete Tracks, 108-109
      Enable Tracks, 109-111
      Extract Tracks, 107
      Find, 60-61
      Paste, 80
      Replace, 101
   File menu
      Export, 256
      Get Info, 5
      Import, 238-239, 252-255, 257-259

New, 80
Open, 93-94, 238
Present Movie, 57-59
Quit, 9, 84
Save, 83-84, 91
Movie menu
  Choose Language, 111-112, 115
  Get Info, 88-90, 96, 113-124
  Loop, 40-41
  Loop Back and Forth, 40
Print to Video, 56
compatibility, QuickTime, 2
Component Video (YUV) compressors, 270
  comparison summary, 278
compositing movies, 130-131
  Premiere, 152
  VideoFusion and QuickFLIX!, 159
  VideoShop, 142
Composition window (After Effects), 163
compression, 11
  audio, 220, 264
  codecs (compressor-decompressors), 266
  determining when to compress, 267
  importance of, 262-263
  lossless versus lossy algorithms, 265
  spatial, 265, 268-275
  still images, 279-281
  temporal, 265, 275-277
  video, 214-215
    post-compression, 217-218
compression cards, 215, 227-228
compressors, 263
  comparison summary, 277-278
  selecting, 268-273
configuring tracks, 42-47
Connectix's QuickCam video camera, 197
connectors, 206-209

Construction window (Premiere), 148-149
control panels, Sound, 4, 29
controllable decks, 229-230
converting
  General MIDI files to music tracks, 257-259
  PICS files to QuickTime, 237-240
ConvertToMovie software, 241-245, 300
convolution, 295
Copy command (Edit menu), 79
copying portions of movies, 78-80
copyright law for distributing movies, 297
Cossey, George, 303
creating
  dynamic previews, 96-97
  movies, 80-81
cropping
  frames, 132
  setting crop regions, 225-226
"Crowd Applause" movie file, 42

D

data rate of movies, 277
data recovery, BMUG, 317
decompressors, 263
Delete Tracks command (Edit menu), 108-109
deleting tracks, 108-109
dependent files, 86-92
desk accessories, Scrapbook, 90
DeskTopMovie 1.1.1 shareware, 309
DeskTopText 1.1.1 shareware, 309
DesktopTV 1.2.0 shareware, 308-309

device drivers
  audio, 205
  VDigs (Video Digitizers), 204
dialog boxes
  Get Info, 96
  Info, 118-124
  Open, 93-94
  Present Movie, 57-59
  Save, 83-84
  Sound Settings, 219-221
    audio compression, 264
  Standard Compression, 267
    spatial compression, 268-275
    temporal compression, 275-277
  Standard Instrument Picker, 116-117
  Video Settings, 214-217
digitizers
  audio, 198-199
    selecting, 221
  video, 195-198
digitizing video
  audio
    compression, 220
    enabling/disabling recording, 222
    sampling rates, 220-221
  audio digitizers, selecting, 221
  compression, 267-278
  crop regions, selecting, 225-226
  frame sizes, setting, 226
  hardware
    compression cards, 227-228
    controllable decks, 229-230
    requirements, 194-203
    setting up, 205-209
    storage hardware, 230-231
    video equipment, 228-229
  post-compression, 217-218

software
  optimizing digitization, 227
  requirements, 203-205
  using, 210-213
  storage, selecting, 222-224
video
  compression, 214-215
  disabling recording, 219
  improving images, 215-216
  playthrough during recording, 219
  video digitizers, selecting, 216-217
Director software (Macromedia), 234-235
  scripting QuickTime, 71-73
disabling
  audio recording, 222
  tracks, 109-111
  video recording, 219
disk arrays, 231
disk space
  optimizing for storage, 105
  versus memory, 48-49
dissolve (fade) transitions, 127
distributing movies
  legalities, 297-298
  on CD-ROM, 284-288
  on Internet, 292-294
  on LANs, 291-292
  playing on Windows computers,
    288-291
dithering, 50
doubling movie sizes, 38
Doyle, Ken, 64-65, 306
Drag and Drop, 79-80
Dumpster software, 302
dynamic
  previews, 94
    creating, 96-97
  still images, 247

E

Easy Play 2.0 shareware, 33, 307-308
Edit Decision Lists (EDLs), 156
Edit menu commands
  Add, 99-101
  Copy, 79
  Delete Tracks, 108-109
  Enable Tracks, 109-111
  Extract Tracks, 107
  Find, 60-61
  Paste, 80
  Replace, 101
editing
  audio integration, 16-17
  determining if possible, 84-85
  frames (rotoscoping), 128
  QuikFLIX!, 16
  text in text tracks, 105-106
  VideoShop, 16
EDLs (Edit Decision Lists), 156
Effect Controls window (After Effects),
  164-165
"Elvis Baby" movie file, 247
emboss filters, 129
Enable Tracks command (Edit menu),
  109-111
enabling
  audio recording, 222
  tracks, 109-111
encoders, 295
end of movies, jumping to, 38
exiting MoviePlayer, 84
Export command (File menu), 256
exporting
  animations as QuickTime, 234-237
  QuickTime files, 256

extensions, 5-8
  Apple Multimedia Tuner X.X, 4
  installing, 3
  Musical Instruments 2.0, 3
  Power Plug 2.0, 4
  QuickTime Musical Instruments, 117
  Sound Control Panel 8.0.1, 4
  Sound Manager 3.0, 4
    optimizing playback performance, 51
  video digitization, 204-205, 212
Extract Tracks command (Edit menu), 107
extracting tracks, 107
"Eye" movie file, 42-43

F

fade (dissolve) transitions, 127
file formats, MooV, 237
File menu commands
  Export, 256
  Get Info, 5
  Import, 238-239, 252-255, 257-259
  New, 80
  Open, 93-94, 238
  Present Movie, 57-59
  Quit, 9, 84
  Save, 83-84, 91
files
  AIFF (Audio Interchange File Format),
    importing, 252-253
  compression, 11
  dependent, 86-92
  General MIDI, converting to music
    tracks, 257-259
  PICS, converting to QuickTime, 237-240

PICT
  compression, 279-281
  creating video tracks with, 241-246
  QuickTime, exporting, 256
  reference, 89
  sizes, viewing, 86-88
filters, 129-130
  Premiere 4.0 software (Adobe), 150,
    188-189
  QuickFLIX! software (VideoFusion/
    Radius), 159, 180-181
  VideoFusion software (VideoFusion/
    Radius), 159
  VideoShop 2.0.3 software (Avid), 140,
    142, 173
Find command (Edit menu), 60-61
flattening movies, 92
FlipBookMaker 1.1 shareware, 308
Fractal Design Painter software, 128, 236
fragmented hard disks, 223
frame differencing, 276-277
frame rates
  setting, 215
  standard, 10
frames
  cropping, 132
  editing (rotoscoping), 128
  key, 276-277
  playing all, 38
  sizes
    resizing, 132
    setting, 226
  stepping through, 28, 39
  Theater Maker, 136
frames per second, setting, 275-276
freeware
  BMUG software library, 317
  on CD accompanying this book, 307-310
"Fruit Stand Scan" movie file, 24-26

G

General MIDI files, converting to music
  tracks, 257-259
Get Info command
  File menu, 5
  Movie menu, 88-90, 96, 113-124
"Gettysburg Address" movie file, 43
"Glycine PICS" movie file, 237
Gold Disk Astound software, 62
graphics
  compression, 279-281
  creating video tracks with, 241-246
Graphics compressors, 271
  comparison summary, 278
"Groovin' Sunset" movie file, 45-46
Gryphon Software's Morph software, 248

H

halving movie sizes, 38
Hansen, Junior, Jr., 247
hard disks
  A/V, 230-231
  fragmented, 223
  memory versus hard disk space, 48-49
  minimum megabytes, 194
  optimizing playback performance, 48-49
  recording to, 222-224
  SCSI cards, 231
hardware
  A/V hard disks, 230-231
  compression cards, 215, 227-228
  controllable decks, 229-230
  disk arrays, 231
  fragmented hard disks, 223
  making movies, 15-16

SCSI cards, 231
video digitization
  requirements, 194-203
  setting up, 205-209
video equipment, 228-229
help (BMUG), technical assistance, 317
hiding Standard Controller, 34
Hone, Robert, 228
hot spots, 166
How to Digitize Video, 228
HyperCard
  scripting QuickTime, 64-69
  stacks
    containing XCMDs, 306-307
    StackToPICSFile, 240
HyperStudio software (Roger Wagner
  Publishing), 62

I

icons
  Badge, 34
  Micons (VideoShop), 138
IMA (Interactive Multimedia Association)
  compression, 264
image samples, spatial compression, 268
Import command (File menu), 238-239,
  252-259
importing
  AIFF (Audio Interchange File Format)
    files, 252-253
  audio CDs for creating sound tracks,
    253-256
  text documents for creating text tracks,
    250-251
Indeo codec (Intel), 272
Infini-D software (Specular), 235

installing software, 9
  Premiere 4.0 (Adobe), 184
  QuickFLIX! (VideoFusion/Radius),
    176-177
  QuickTime, 3-8
  VideoShop 2.0.3 (Avid), 167-168
instruments, changing on music tracks,
  115-117
Intel Indeo codec, 272
interactive
  movies, 166-167
  presentations
    including QuickTime in, 62-63
    scripting QuickTime, 63-73
Interactive Media's Special Delivery
  software, 62
Interactive Multimedia Association (IMA)
  compression, 264
Interactive Physics (Knowledge
  Revolution), 236
Internet, distributing movies, 292-294
Internet Explorer Kit for Macintosh,
  321-322
Internet Starter Kit for Macintosh, Second
  Edition, 321
"Intro" movie file, 36-37
Iris transitions, 127

J

jog shuttle (Standard Controller), 37-38
Johnson, Nels, 228
JPEG compressors, 270-272
  comparison summary, 278
jumping to beginning/end of movies, 38

K

key frames, 276-277
keyboard shortcuts
  audio overdrive (Shift+Volume
    Slider), 41
  Copy (⌘+C), 77
  Cut (⌘+X), 77
  double/halve frame size (Option+Size
    box), 38
  increase/decrease volume (Up/Down
    Arrow), 39
  jump to beginning/end of movie
    (Option+Step button), 38
  mute/reset audio (Option+Volume
    Control button), 39
  Paste (⌘+V), 77
  play all frames (Option+Play
    button), 38
  playing and pausing, 39-40
  Quit (⌘+Q), 84
  scratching slider (Ctrl+Step button),
    37-38
  select
    Shift+Slider, 78
    Shift+Step button, 81
  step through frames (Left/Right
    Arrow), 39
KidPix software (Broderbund), 236
Kid's Studio (Storm Software), 236
Knowledge Revolution's Interactive
  Physics software, 236
Kodak Photo CDs, 245-246

L

LANs, distributing movies, 291-292
legalities of distributing movies, 297-298
libraries, BMUG, 317
Linde, Bruce, 257
Lingo scripting language, 70-72
Loop Back and Forth command (Movie
  menu), 40
Loop command (Movie menu), 40-41
looping movies, 40-41
lossless versus lossy algorithms, 265

M

MACE (Macintosh Audio Compression
  and Expansion), 264
Macintoshes
  movie-making capabilities, 199-203
  QuickTime, 2
  video digitization requirements, 194
Macromedia
  Authorware Professional software, 62
  Director software, 71-73, 234-235
MakeMovieColorTable software, 300-302
membership, BMUG, 313-314
memory
  versus hard disk space, 48-49
  Virtual, 49
Micons (VideoShop), 138
Microsoft PowerPoint software, 62
MIDI (Musical Instrument Digital
  Interface)
  devices, recording from, 259
  General files, converting to music tracks,
    257-259
modes, Slide Show, 58-59

modifying QuickTime, 17-20
MooV file format, 237
Morph software (Gryphon Software), 248
morphing still images, 248
motion (special effects on movies),
    131-132
    Premiere, 152
    VideoFusion and QuickFLIX!, 161-162
    VideoShop, 144
Motion Works International
    CameraMan software, 236
    MovieClick software, 166-167
    QuickMorph software, 248
movie files
    "Crowd Applause", 42
    "Elvis Baby", 247
    "Eye", 42-43
    "Fruit Stand Scan", 24-26
    "Gettysburg Address", 43
    "Glycine PICS", 237
    "Groovin' Sunset", 45-46
    "Intro", 36-37
    "Reggae Groove Sample", 44-45
    "Tom's Summary with Text", 60
Movie menu commands
    Choose Language, 111-112, 115
    Get Info, 88-90, 96, 113-124
    Loop, 40-41
    Loop Back and Forth, 40
Movie XCMD, 64-67
movie-in-a-movie composite effects, 130
    Premiere, 152
MovieAnalyzer software, 303
MovieClick software (Motion Works
    International), 166-167
MovieInfo v2.2 shareware, 308

MoviePlayer (Apple Computer), 8-9
    alternate tracks, 111-115
    converting
        General MIDI files to music tracks,
            257-259
        PICS files to QuickTime, 238-240
    editing movies, 76-85
    exiting, 84
    exporting QuickTime files, 256
    importing
        AIFF files, 252-253
        audio CDs for creating sound tracks,
            254-255
    Info window, 118-124
    information about movies, obtaining,
        88-90
    interactive presentations, 57-59
    previews, 93-98
    Standard Controller, 24-33, 36-41
    text track searching, 59-61
movies
    audio, 16-17
    creating, 80-81
        by digitizing video, see digitizing video
        hardware for, 15-16
    current viewing point, changing, 27-28
    distributing
        legalities, 297-298
        on CD-ROM, 284-288
        on Internet, 292-294
        on LANs, 291-292
        playing on Windows computers,
            288-291
    editing, determining if possible, 84-85
    flattening, 92
    information about, obtaining, 88-90,
        118-124
    interactive, 166-167
    jumping to beginning/end, 38

Macintosh capabilities for creating,
   199-203
optimizing storage space, 105
outputting
   to paper, 296
   to videotape, 294-295
pausing, 26-27
   shortcuts, 39-40
playing, 26-27
   all frames, 38
   by single frames, 28, 39
   improving performance, 48-52
   looping, 40-41
   presenting with nothing else around,
      55-59
   shortcuts, 39-40
   upon startup, 54-55
reference, 92
resizing, 31-33
   halving/doubling, 38
saving, 83-85
   in QuickFLIX! software (VideoFusion/
      Radius), 183
   in VideoShop, 145-146, 175-176
   normal versus self-contained, 86-92
   Premiere 4.0 software (Adobe), 189
selecting, 78-83
self-playing (standalone), 92
speed, adjusting, 37-38
viewing, 2, 8-9
   see also tracks
MovieShop software, 303
MovieTrilogy shareware, 308-309
MPEG (Motion Picture Experts Group)
   standard, 273
Music Configuration software, 306

music tracks, 43-45
   adding to movies, 102
   creating by converting General MIDI
      files to, 257-259
   instruments, changing, 115-117
Musical Instruments 2.0, 3
muting audio, 39

N

networks, distributing movies, 291-292
New command (File menu), 80
newsletters, BMUG, 315
None (Raw) compressors, 271
   comparison summary, 278

O

O'Connor, Michael, 33
Olson, Kip, 305
online services, BMUG forums, 315
*The Online User's Encyclopedia, Bulletin
   Boards and Beyond*, 322
Open command (File menu), 93-94, 238
opening
   Premiere 4.0 software (Adobe), 184
   QuickFLIX! software (VideoFusion/
      Radius), 176-177
   VideoShop 2.0.3 software (Avid),
      167-168
optimizing storage space, 105
outputting movies
   to paper, 296
   to videotape, 294-295
overdriving audio, 41

P

Painter software, 236
palindroming, 40
paper, outputting movies to, 296
Passport Producer Pro software (Passport Design), 62
Paste command (Edit menu), 80
Pause button (Standard Controller), 26-27
pausing movies, 26-27
  shortcuts, 39-40
Photo - JPEG compressors, 270, 272
Photo CDs (Kodak), 245-246
photographs
  compression, 279-281
  creating video tracks with, 241-246
  legalities, 297
Photoshop software (Adobe), 128
PICS files, converting to QuickTime, 237-240
PICT files
  compression, 279-281
  creating video tracks with, 241-246
Play bar (Standard Controller), 27-28
Play button (Standard Controller), 26-27
Player window (VideoFusion and QuickFLIX!), 156-157
playing movies, 8-9, 26-27
  all frames, 38
  by single frames, 28, 39
  improving performance, 48-52
  looping, 40-41
  presenting with nothing else around, 55-59
  shortcuts, 39-40
  upon startup, 54-55
playthrough during video recording, 219
Popcorn shareware, 33

post-compression, 217-218
posters, 94
  changing, 95
Power Macintosh Programming Starter Kit, 320-321
Power Plug 2.0, 4
PowerBooks, optimizing playback performance, 49
PowerPoint software (Microsoft), 62
Premiere 4.0 software (Adobe), 135-137
  combining clips, 184-185
  installing, 184
  opening, 184
  saving movies, 189
  special effects, 148-156
    filters, 188-189
    titling movies, 189
    transitions, 186-188
Present Movie command (File menu), 57-59
presentations, interactive
  including QuickTime in, 62-63
  scripting QuickTime, 63-73
previews
  dynamic, 94
    creating, 96-97
  posters, 94
    changing, 95
  types, 97-98
  viewing, 93-94
Print to Video command, 56
printing, outputting movies to paper, 296
programs, *see* software
Project windows
  After Effects, 163
  Premiere, 148-149
publications
  BMUG, 318
  distributed by BMUG, 320-323

Q

QTMovie Stack, 64
QTMovie XCMD, 64-67
QuickCam video camera (Connectix), 197
QuickFLIX! software (VideoFusion/
   Radius), 16, 210-213
   audio
      enabling/disabling recording, 222
      settings, 219-221
   combining clips, 178-179, 182
   crop regions, selecting, 225-226
   frame sizes, setting, 226
   installing, 176-177
   opening, 176-177
   post-compression, 217-218
   saving movies, 183
   special effects, 135-137, 156-162
      filters, 180-181
      titling movies, 181
      transitions, 179-180
   storage, selecting, 222-224
   video
      optimizing digitization, 227
      playthrough during recording, 219
      settings, 214-217
      turning off recording, 219
QuickMorph software (Motion Works
   International), 248
QuickMovie 1.0b2 shareware, 309
QuickTime, 1
   advantages, 13-18
   capabilities, 18-20
   compatibility, 2
   installing, 3-8
   limitations, 10-13
   modifying, 17-20
QuickTime files, exporting, 256

QuickTime for Windows, 288-291
QuickTime Musical Instruments
   extension, 117
QuickTime VR, 249-250
*QuickTime: Making Movies on your
   Mac*, 228
Quit command (File menu), 9, 84

R

Radius, 198
   QuickFLIX!, *see* QuickFLIX!
   VideoFusion software, 134-137, 156-162
RAID (Redundant Array of Inexpensive
   Disks), 231
RAM (random access memory)
   minimum megabytes, 194
   recording to, 222-223
Ram Doubler, optimizing playback
   performance, 49
Raw (None) compressors, 271
   comparison summary, 278
recording
   from MIDI devices, 259
   movies
      selecting crop regions, 225-226
      selecting storage, 222-224
      setting frame sizes, 226
recovering data, BMUG, 317
reference files, 89
reference movies, 92
"Reggae Groove Sample" movie file, 44-45
*Remembery Chips—An Electronic Book
   for Children*, 323
repeating movies continuously, 40-41
Replace command (Edit menu), 101

resizing
    frames, 132
        VideoShop, 143
    movies, 31-33
        halving/doubling, 38
        presenting with nothing else
            around, 58
Roger Wagner Publishing's HyperStudio
    software, 62
Rosenthol, Leonard, 33
rotoscoping frames, 128

S

sampling rates, 220-221
Save command (File menu), 83-84, 91
saving movies, 83-85
    normal versus self-contained, 86-92
    with Premiere 4.0 software (Adobe), 189
    with QuickFLIX! software (VideoFusion/
        Radius), 183
    with VideoShop, 145-146, 175-176
scaling, time, 134
scientific simulation software, 236
Scrapbook desk accessory, 90
scratching slider (Standard Controller),
    37-38
screen-recording software, 236
ScreenMovie 1.1.0 shareware, 309
ScreenPlay software, compression, 272
screens, setting amount of time for
    blank, 59
scripting languages
    HyperTalk, 64, 67-69
    Lingo, 71-72
    SuperTalk, 69-70, 237

scripting QuickTime for interactive
    presentations, 63
    HyperCard, 64-69
    Macromedia Director, 71-73
    SuperCard, 69-70
SCSI (Small Computer Systems Interface)
    cards, 231
searching text tracks, 59-61
selecting movies
    fine tuning, 81-83
    portions of, 78-80
self-playing (standalone) movies, 92
Sequencer window (VideoShop), 139
shareware
    BMUG software library, 317
    Easy Play, 33
    on CD accompanying this book, 307-310
    Popcorn, 33
    Theater Maker, 136-137
SimpleText software, 33, 250-251
SingleForkFlattener software, 305-306
Size box, 31-33
sizes of files, viewing, 86-88
Slide Show mode, presenting movie with
    nothing else around, 58-59
Slider (Standard Controller), 27-28
sliders
    adjusting video images, 215-216
    scratching slider (Standard Controller),
        37-38
    Slider and Play bar (Standard
        Controller), 27-28
    Volume Slider (Standard Controller),
        28-30
software
    2-D animation, 234-235
    3-D animation, 235
    After Effects (Aldus/Adobe), 134-137,
        162-167

Apple Media Tool (Apple Computer), 62
Astound (Gold Disk), 62
Authorware Professional
   (Macromedia), 62
CameraMan (Motion Works
   International), 236
Cinemation (Vividus), 62, 235
codecs
   (compressor-decompressors), 266
ComboWalker, 300
ConvertToMovie, 241-245, 300
DeskTopMovie 1.1.1 shareware, 309
DeskTopText 1.1.1 shareware, 309
DesktopTV 1.2.0 shareware, 308-309
Director (Macromedia), 71-73, 234-235
Dumpster, 302
Easy Play 2.0 shareware, 33, 307-308
FlipBookMaker 1.1 shareware, 308
HyperCard, 64-69
HyperStudio (Roger Wagner
   Publishing), 62
Infini-D (Specular), 235
installing, 3-9
Interactive Physics (Knowledge
   Revolution), 236
KidPix (Broderbund), 236
Kid's Studio (Storm Software), 236
MakeMovieColorTable, 300-302
Morph (Gryphon Software), 248
MovieAnalyzer, 303
MovieClick (Motion Works
   International), 166-167
MovieInfo v2.2 shareware, 308
MoviePlayer (Apple Computer), see
   MoviePlayer
MovieShop, 303
MovieTrilogy shareware, 308-309
Music Configuration, 306
Painter (Fractal Design), 128, 236

painting, 236
Passport Producer Pro (Passport
   Design), 62
Photoshop (Adobe), 128
Popcorn shareware, 33
PowerPoint (Microsoft), 62
Premiere 4.0 (Adobe), 135-137, 148-156,
   183-190
QuickFLIX! (VideoFusion/Radius), 16,
   135-137, 156-162, 176-183, 210-213
QuickMorph (Motion Works
   International), 248
QuickMovie 1.0b2 shareware, 309
scientific simulation, 236
screen-recording, 236
ScreenMovie 1.1.0 shareware, 309
ScreenPlay, 272
SimpleText, 33, 250-251
SingleForkFlattener, 305-306
SoundConverter, 305
Sparkle 2.2 freeware, 310
Special Delivery (Interactive Media), 62
SuperCard, 69-70
Text Movie Converter, 303-304
Theater Maker shareware, 136-137, 310
unsupported (Apple), 300-307
using Standard Controller, 33-36
video digitization requirements, 203-204
VideoFusion (VideoFusion/Radius),
   134-137, 156-162
VideoShop 2.0.3 (Avid), 16, 135-148,
   167-176
see also extensions
software libraries, BMUG, 317
Sound Control Panel 8.0.1, 4, 29
Sound Manager 3.0 system extension, 4
   optimizing playback performance, 51
sound, see audio

Sound Settings dialog box, 219-221
  audio compression, 264
sound tracks, 42
  creating
    by importing audio CDs, 253-256
    with AIFF (Audio Interchange File
      Format) files, 252-253
SoundConverter software, 305
Sparkle 2.2 freeware, 310
spatial compression, 265
  colors, selecting number of, 274
  compressors, selecting, 268-273
  image samples, 268
  quality, selecting, 274-275
Special Delivery software (Interactive
  Media), 62
special effects
  audio control, 133-134
  compositing, 130-131
  cropping, 132
  filters, 129-130
    Premiere 4.0 software (Adobe),
      188-189
    QuickFLIX! software (VideoFusion/
      Radius), 180-181
    VideoShop 2.0.3 software (Avid), 173
  motion, 131-132
  resizing, 132
  software
    After Effects (Aldus/Adobe), 162-167
    common features, 134-137
    Premiere 4.0 (Adobe), 148-156
    QuickFLIX! (VideoFusion/Radius),
      156-162
    VideoFusion (VideoFusion/Radius),
      156-162
    VideoShop 2.0.3 (Avid), 138-148
  time scaling, 134
  titling movies, 132-133

Premiere 4.0 software (Adobe), 189
  QuickFLIX! software (VideoFusion/
    Radius), 181
  VideoShop 2.0.3 software (Avid),
    173-175
transitions, 126-128
  Premiere 4.0 software (Adobe),
    186-188
  QuickFLIX! software (VideoFusion/
    Radius), 179-180
  VideoShop 2.0.3 software (Avid),
    170-172
Specular's Infini-D software, 235
speed of movies
  adjusting, 37-38
  time scaling, 134
StackToPICSFile HyperCard stack, 240
standalone (self-playing) movies, 92
Standard Compression dialog box, 267
  spatial compression, 268-275
  temporal compression, 275-277
Standard Controller, 23
  applications using, 33-36
  color, changing, 24
  components, 33
  hiding, 34
  keyboard shortcuts, 38-39
  Play/Pause buttons, 26-27
  scratching slider, 37-38
  Slider, 27-28
  Step buttons, 28
  Volume Control button, 28-30
Standard Instrument Picker dialog box,
  116-117
Star Trek: The Next Generation
  Interactive Technical Manual, 249
startup, playing movies upon, 54-55
Step buttons (Standard Controller), 28
stepping through frames, 28, 39

still images
  compression, 279-281
  creating video tracks with, 241-250
Storm Software's Kid's Studio
  software, 236
Storyboard window (VideoFusion and
  QuickFLIX!), 156-157
SuperCard
  creating QuickTime movies, 237
  scripting QuickTime, 69-70
SuperMac, *see* Radius

T

tables, custom color, 117-118
*The Tao of AppleScript, BMUG's Guide to
  Macintosh Scripting*, Second
  Edition, 318
technical assistance, BMUG, 317
temporal compression, 265, 275-277
text
  burnt, 106
  editing in text tracks, 105-106
  titling movies, 132-133
    Premiere 4.0 software (Adobe),
      154, 189
    QuickFLIX! software (VideoFusion/
      Radius), 162, 181
    VideoFusion software (VideoFusion/
      Radius), 162
    VideoShop 2.0.3 software (Avid),
      144-145, 173-175
Text Movie Converter software, 303-304
text tracks, 43
  adding to movies, 103-106
  creating by importing text from text
    documents, 250-251
  searching, 59-61

Theater Maker shareware, 136-137, 310
time scaling, 134
Time Layout window (After Effects),
  164-165
Time View window (VideoFusion and
  QuickFLIX!), 156-157
timecode tracks, 47
titling movies, 132-133
  Premiere 4.0 software (Adobe), 154, 189
  QuickFLIX! software (VideoFusion/
    Radius), 162, 181
  VideoFusion software (VideoFusion/
    Radius), 162
  VideoShop 2.0.3 software (Avid),
    144-145, 173-175
"Tom's Summary with Text" movie file, 60
ToonWare—A Humor Interface, 318
tracks
  combining, 98-106
  configurations, 42-47
  deleting, 108-109
  enabling/disabling, 109-111
  extracting, 107
  information about, obtaining, 118-124
  music
    changing instruments, 115-117
    creating by converting General MIDI
      files, 257-259
  sound
    creating by importing audio CDs,
      253-256
    creating with AIFF (Audio Interchange
      File Format) files, 252-253
  text
    adding to movies, 103-106
    creating by importing from text
      documents, 250-251
    searching, 59-61

transcript, 147-148
video
  creating with animations, 234-240
  creating with still images, 241-250
transcript tracks, 147-148
transitions, 126-128
  Premiere 4.0 software (Adobe), 149, 186-188
  QuickFLIX! software (VideoFusion/ Radius), 158, 179-180
  VideoFusion software (VideoFusion/ Radius), 158
  VideoShop 2.0.3 software (Avid), 140, 142, 170-172
transparencies, 130-131
  Premiere, 150
  VideoShop, 143

U

Unsupported Stuff folder (accompanying CD), 300-307
  ConvertToMovie software, 241-245
Utils folder (accompanying CD), SimpleText software, 250-251

V

VCR Controls window (After Effects), 163
VDigs (Video Digitizers), 204
video
  compressing, 214-215
  digitizing, see digitizing video
  equipment, 228-229
  images, improving, 215-216
  playing movies by single frames, 28
recording
  turning off, 219
  video playthrough during, 219
sources, video digitization requirements, 195
Video compressors, 269-270
  comparison summary, 277
video digitizers, 195-198
  plugging in, 205
  selecting, 216-217
Video Digitizers (VDigs), 204
Video Settings dialog box, 214-217
video tracks, 42-43
  adding to movies, 99-101
  creating
    with animations, 234-240
    with still images, 241-250
VideoFusion Inc., see Radius
VideoFusion software (VideoFusion/ Radius), 134-137
  special effects, 156-162
VideoShop 2.0.3 software (Avid), 16, 135-137
  combining clips, 169-170
  installing, 167-168
  opening, 167-168
  saving movies, 175-176
  special effects, 138-148
    filters, 173
    titling movies, 173-175
    transitions, 170-172
videotape, outputting movies to, 294-295
viewing
  file sizes, 86-88
  movies, 2, 8-9
    changing current viewing point, 27-28
  previews, 93-94
Virtual Memory, optimizing playback performance, 49

virtual reality, creating video tracks from still images, 249-250

Vividus' Cinemation software, 62, 235

volume, controlling, 28-30, 39

Volume Control button (Standard Controller), 28-30

Volume Controller (Standard Controller), 28-30

W

wave filters, 130

Windows, playing movies, 288-291

windows

  Composition (After Effects), 163

  Construction (Premiere), 148-149

  Effect Controls (After Effects), 164-165

  Player (VideoFusion and QuickFLIX!), 156-157

  Project

    After Effects, 163

    Premiere, 148-149

  Sequencer (VideoShop), 139

  Storyboard (VideoFusion and QuickFLIX!), 156-157

  Time Layout (After Effects), 164-165

  Time View (VideoFusion and QuickFLIX!), 156-157

  VCR Controls (After Effects), 163

WPA Multimedia Collection, 77

WWW (World-Wide Web), distributing movies, 292-294

X–Z

XCMDs

  HyperCard stacks containing, 306-307

  scripting with, 64-67

YUV (Component Video)

  compressors, 270

  comparison summary, 278

Zen and The Art of Resource Editing, Third Edition, 318

Zoom box, 32-33

License
Information

VideoShop 2.0.3

Software End-User Limited License Agreement and Limited Warranty

Avid VideoShop 2.0.3

Limited Use License:

Avid Desktop Software, Inc. ("Avid", "Licenser") grants you, the end user ("Licensee"), as the party taking a license, the right to use the Avid VideoShop software ("the Software") on a single computer unit at a single location. You must obtain a supplementary license from Avid before using the Software in connection with systems or multiple central processing units. Please contact Avid at the address indicated in this license for further information.

Limited Warranty and Disclaimer of Liability:

Avid warrants that the Avid VideoShop documentation ("the Documentation") and the media on which the Software is furnished will be free from defects in materials and workmanship under normal use for a period of one (1) year from the date of the original purchase. If a defect appears during the warranty period, return the diskette or Documentation pages to the place you obtained them, with a photocopy of your original diskette label and your receipt, and you will receive a free replacement, or at Avid's option, a refund of your purchase price. EXCEPT AS TO THE MEDIA, THE SOFTWARE IS LICENSED "AS IS" WITHOUT WARRANTY OF ANY KIND, EITHER EXPRESSED OR IMPLIED. IN NO EVENT SHALL AVID BE RESPONSIBLE FOR ANY INDIRECT, SPECIAL, INCIDENTAL, CONSEQUENTIAL OR SIMILAR DAMAGES OR LOST DATA OR PROFITS TO YOU OR ANY OTHER PERSON OR ENTITY REGARDLESS OF THE LEGAL THEORY, EVEN IF AVID TECHNOLOGY, INC. HAS BEEN ADVISED OF THE POSSIBILITY OF SUCH DAMAGE. SOME STATES DO NOT ALLOW THE LIMITATION OR EXCLUSION OF LIABILITY FOR INCIDENTAL OR CONSEQUENTIAL DAMAGES SO THE ABOVE LIMITATION OR EXCLUSION MAY NOT APPLY TO YOU. LICENSER'S LIABILITY TO YOU OR ANY RELATED THIRD PARTY FOR ACTUAL DAMAGES FOR ANY CAUSE WHATSOEVER WILL BE LIMITED TO THE AMOUNT THAT YOU PAID AVID TECHNOLOGY, INC. FOR THE SOFTWARE.

Title:

This License is not a sale of the Software or any copy. Avid retains title and owner-
ship of the Software and all copies, regardless of the form or media on or in which
the original or any copy may exist.

Update Policy:

In order to be able to obtain updates of the Software, you must register the software
with Avid (see Read Me file for contact information). However, Avid is under no
obligation to make any updates available to you. Avid will make reasonable efforts to
notify registered users about future updates and the procedures to obtain such
updates. All updates provided to you shall be deemed part of the Software and the
use of such updates shall be governed by this License.

Restrictions on Copying:

You are hereby licensed to make one copy of the VideoShop software in machine-
readable form solely for backup purposes provided that you include the Avid copyright notice on the backup copy. You may not copy, nor encourage or allow copying
of, the Software or Documentation.

Restrictions on Transfers:

You may transfer the Avid VideoShop Software into the memory of a single computer, but you may not electronically transfer the Software from one computer to
another. You may not modify, reverse engineer, decompile, create other works from,
or disassemble the Software. You may not copy, modify, adapt or create other works
based upon the Documentation. You may not transfer, convert, rent, sub-license, or
otherwise distribute the Software or Documentation, or any rights in them, to any
person or entity.

Term:

This License is effective until terminated. You may terminate the License at any time
by returning the Software and all Documentation to Avid and by removing the
Software from the memory of any computer into which the Software has been
transferred. This License shall terminate automatically if you fail to comply with any
term or condition. Upon termination, you must return to Licenser, at your own
expense, the Software and Documentation and any copies whether or not the copy
was authorized hereunder.

Government End Users:

For the Department of Defense: Use, duplication or disclosure by the Government is subject to restrictions as set forth in subparagraph (c)(1)(ii) of the Rights in Technical Data and Computer Software clause at DFARS 252.227-7013. The Contractor/ Manufacturer is:

Avid Desktop Software, Inc.
One Park West
Tewksbury, MA 01876

For Civilian Agencies of the United States Government: Use, reproduction or disclosure is subject to restrictions set forth in subparagraphs (a) through (d) of the Commercial Computer Software-Restricted Rights clause at 52.227-19 and the limitations set forth in Avid's standard commercial License agreement for the Software. This Software was developed at private expense, is existing computing software and no part of it was developed with government funds, and is a trade secret of Avid. The Software is proprietary data, all rights of which are reserved under the copyright laws of the United States.

If this Software was acquired under a GSA Schedule: Use, duplication or disclosure shall be in accordance with the applicable GSA Schedule contract. The Government has agreed to refrain from changing or removing any insignia or lettering from the Software or the Documentation that is provided, and from producing copies of manuals or media (except for backup purposes and in accordance with the terms of this License.)

General:

You must register the software to be eligible for customer support and service. Should you have any questions concerning this License Agreement, please write to:

Avid Desktop Software, Inc.
Corporate Counsel
One Park West
Tewksbury, MA 01876

Choice of Law:

This Agreement will be governed by the laws in force in the Commonwealth of Massachusetts, excluding the application of its conflicts of law rules.

Apple Disclaimer and Warranty Regarding HyperCard, Installer, System AVID'S LICENSER, APPLE COMPUTER, INC. ("APPLE"), MAKES NO WARRANTIES, EXPRESSED OR IMPLIED, INCLUDING WITHOUT LIMITATION THE IMPLIED WARRANTIES OF MERCHANTABILITY AND FITNESS FOR A PARTICULAR PURPOSE, REGARDING THE SOFTWARE. APPLE DOES NOT WARRANT, GUARANTEE OR MAKE ANY REPRESENTATIONS REGARDING THE USE OR THE RESULTS OF THE USE OF THE SOFTWARE IN TERMS OF ITS CORRECTNESS, ACCURACY, RELIABILITY, CURRENTNESS, OR OTHERWISE. THE ENTIRE RISK AS TO THE RESULTS AND PERFORMANCE OF THE SOFTWARE IS ASSUMED BY YOU. THE EXCLUSION OF IMPLIED WARRANTIES IS NOT PERMITTED BY SOME STATES. THE ABOVE EXCLUSION MAY NOT APPLY TO YOU. IN NO EVENT WILL APPLE, AND THEIR DIRECTORS, OFFICERS, EMPLOYEES, OR AGENTS, COLLECTIVELY APPLE, BE LIABLE TO YOU FOR ANY CONSEQUENTIAL, INCIDENTAL, OR INDIRECT DAMAGES INCLUDING DAMAGES FOR LOSS OF BUSINESS PROFITS, BUSINESS INTERRUPTION, LOSS OF BUSINESS INFORMATION, AND THE LIKE, ARISING OUT OF THE USE OR INABILITY TO USE THE SOFTWARE EVEN IF APPLE HAS BEEN ADVISED OF THE POSSIBILITY OF SUCH DAMAGES. BECAUSE SOME STATES DO NOT ALLOW THE EXCLUSION OR LIMITATION OF LIABILITY FOR CONSEQUENTIAL OR INCIDENTAL DAMAGES, THE ABOVE LIMITATIONS MAY NOT APPLY TO YOU. APPLE'S LIABILITY TO YOU FOR ACTUAL DAMAGES FROM ANY CAUSE WHATSOEVER, AND REGARDLESS OF THE FORM OF ACTION (WHETHER IN CONTRACT, TORT (INCLUDING NEGLIGENCE), PRODUCT LIABILITY OR OTHERWISE, WILL BE LIMITED TO $50.

First edition: November 1991

Avid Desktop Software, Inc.
One Park West
Tewksbury, MA 01876
(508) 640-6789

QuickFLIX!

By breaking the seal on the disc envelope, you accept all of the terms and conditions of this license agreement. If you do not agree with the terms and conditions of this agreement, return the book and CD unopened to the place of purchase for a full refund.

Legal use of this program:

The computer program that is enclosed, QuickFLIX!™, is licensed, not sold, to you subject to the terms and conditions of this agreement. You own the disc on which the QuickFLIX! software is recorded, but the software itself remains the property of VideoFusion Incorporated.

You may use the software on a single central processor, but you may not rent, loan, lease, or use this software on a multi-user system without first obtaining a supplementary license from Radius Incorporated. You may make one copy of this software in machine-readable form solely for purposes of backup. This software is protected by United States copyright law. You must reproduce the QuickFLIX! copyright notice on each copy along with any other legal notices which may appear. This software contains trade secrets. You may not reduce this software to any form perceivable by humans. You may transfer your rights to this QuickFLIX! software to a third party provided you furnish Radius Incorporated with written notice and the third party reads and accepts the terms and conditions of this license agreement.

Terms of this agreement:

This license is effective until terminated. Radius Incorporated has the right to terminate this agreement immediately if you do not comply with any of its terms. If terminated, you must agree to destroy this original and all copies of the QuickFLIX! software and documentation. This agreement will be governed by the laws of the state of California excluding application of its conflicts of law rules.

Warranty:

This product carries a limited warranty effective for ninety (90) days from the date of delivery as verified by your purchase receipt. Radius Incorporated warrants that this software will perform for you substantially in the manner detailed in the program documentation during this period. If it does not, return this software and all documentation along with your sales receipt to the place of purchase to claim your warranty rights. Radius Incorporated has the right, at its option and cost, to provide corrections for such errors, replace the software, or refund the purchase price. Radius Incorporated makes no warranties, expressed or implied, for merchantability or fitness of purpose. Radius Incorporated does not warrant the performance or results that you obtain using this software or documentation, and Radius Incorporated is not liable for any indirect or consequential damages resulting from the use of this software. Radius Incorporated's liability, in aggregate, for all warranties hereunder shall not exceed the payment received by Radius Incorporated under this agreement. This warranty gives you specific rights. You may have other rights, which vary from state-to-state.

Restrictions on government end-users:

Use, duplication, or disclosure by the government is subject to the restrictions detailed in subparagraph (c)(1)(ii) of the Rights in Technical Data and Computer Software Clause at DFARS 252-227-7013. Use, duplication, or disclosure by civilian agencies is subject to subparagraphs (a) through (d) of the Commercial Computer Software Restricted Rights Clause, 52-227-19.

Acceptance of this agreement:

READ THIS AGREEMENT CAREFULLY BEFORE OPENING THE DISC PACKAGE. BY BREAKING THE SEAL, YOU AGREE TO BE BOUND BY ITS TERMS AND CONDITIONS. If you do not agree, please return the book and disc package, unopened, to your place of purchase. Once you have agreed to this license, you must register with Radius Incorporated to be eligible for user support and service (to do so, write to the address or call the phone number listed below).

215 Moffett Park Drive
Sunnyvale, CA 94089-1374
(408) 541-6100

What's on the QuickTime Guide CD

The CD-ROM that comes with this book contains all the software you'll need to get started with QuickTime, Apple's revolutionary technology for putting digital video on your desktop. As a matter of fact, it contains *all* the software many QuickTime users will *ever* need—software to play movies, make movies, edit movies, and even optimize them for CD-ROM playback. The CD has over 600 MB of files including:

- **Crucial System Extensions.** We provide the latest version of QuickTime (2.0), which supports music/MIDI movies, text movies, and MPEG, as well as digitized video. Associated extensions for making the most of QuickTime—the QuickTime PowerPlug, QuickTime Musical Instruments, Apple Multimedia Tuner, and Sound Manager 3.0—are included as well.

- **Special Effects Editors.** You get complete and full working versions of VideoFusion's QuickFLIX! and Avid's VideoShop! Plus, there are demo versions of Adobe Premiere 4.0 and VideoFusion's VideoFusion 1.6.

- **Hard-to-find, not commercially-released utilities from Apple's QuickTime team.** We include MoviePlayer 2.0, an application written by the same people who wrote QuickTime; it does things no other QuickTime editing package can do! There are also the most current versions of all sorts of utilities for optimizing your movies.

- **The best QuickTime shareware and freeware.** There's FlipBookMaker for printing your QuickTime movies as flip books; Sparkle, the Internet standard MPEG movie player and maker; and others. Also, check out the MovieTrilogy in five parts; it does things you can't do in any other applications.

- **Cool movies for hands-on exercises and your viewing pleasure.** You can play with movies from some of the best collections available—including those from WPA/MPI, Fabulous Footage, BMUG's TV-ROM series, Bullfrog Films, and the International QuickTime Film Festival. Plus, check out the Making of Myst movie which gives you a behind-the-scenes look at the making of one of the most popular games ever.